AT HOME ABROAD

Mark Twain in Australasia

AT HOME

Sketch of Mark Twain at the
City Hall, Dunedin. *A Sketch
from the Stalls* by W. Hodgkins

(Field-Hodgkins Collection
Alexander Turnbull Library,
Wellington, New Zealand)

Miriam Jones Shillingsburg

ABROAD
Mark Twain in Australasia

UNIVERSITY PRESS OF MISSISSIPPI
Jackson

Publication of this book was made possible by a grant from
Mississippi State University

The paper is this book meets the guidelines for permanence
and durability of the Committee on Production Guidelines for
Book Longevity of the Council on Library Resources.

Library of Congress Cataloging-in-Publication Data

Shillingsburg, Miriam Jones.
   At home abroad : Mark Twain in Australasia / Miriam
Jones Shillingsburg.
     p.   cm.
   Bibliography: p.
   Includes index.
   ISBN 0-87805-349-2 (alk. paper)
   1. Twain, Mark, 1835–1910—Journeys—Australia. 2.
Twain, Mark, 1835–1910—Journeys—New Zealand. 3. Au-
thors, American—19th century—Biography. 4. Australia—
Description and travel—1851–1900. 6. New Zealand—
Description and travel—1840–1950. I. Title.
S1334.S55 1988
818'.403—dc19
[B]   87–36892
                                                         CIP

CONTENTS

PREFACE

Mark Twain, along with his wife Olivia and daughter Clara Clemens, spent the last fifteen weeks of 1895 lecturing in Australia and New Zealand, collectively called Australasia. While it would be difficult to say whether this second leg of his last full-length lecture season was the most successful of a lifetime of successful, if intermittent, lecturing, it is tempting to do so. And while the study of Australasian cultural history is not yet complete enough to allow comparison between Twain's reception and that accorded to other literary visitors, it is certainly safe to say that his visit was welcomed in every colony and by all classes of people. It was an event long hoped for by the colonists, long remembered by both the Clemenses and the colonists, and commemorated in Twain's last travel book, *Following the Equator* or, as it was known around the world, *More Tramps Abroad*.[1]

The social significance of Twain's visit is indicated by the welcome he received from the highest classes of society. The family was entertained for meals by Sir Henry Parkes, probably the most important colonial politician in New South Wales, and twice by the commander of the Australian Naval Station. They attended a ball at Government House, Sydney. Sir Edmund Barton and the Honorable Alfred Deakin, the future first two prime ministers of a federated Australia, met Twain several times at supper clubs and called on him privately in his hotel when he was ill. Well-known business and professional men in Sydney, Melbourne, Hobart, Auckland, and smaller places took the family sightseeing. Mrs. and Miss Clemens were guests at "ladies'" entertainments, such as teas and art exhibitions, and were in the company of the vice-regal party at horse races and a concert. In every colony where Twain spoke, the lieutenant governor and his entourage attended a performance; most of the premiers are also known to have attended; and Twain called on the governor general of New Zealand at his home.

---

1. *Following the Equator* (Hartford: American Publishing Company, 1897); *More Tramps Abroad* (London: Chatto and Windus, 1897).

The official seriousness of Twain's pilgrimage to Australasia is indicated not only by the private engagements with important people but by the public welcomes in virtually every town he visited. Sometimes these ceremonies took place at the railway station, but more often they were at the Town Hall. In the smaller towns the mayor and city officials (as well as the press corps) gave short speeches and expected a humorous response from Twain. In the cities various American officials and former Americans who had positions within the colonial administration augmented the welcoming party. Twain was also entertained by several men's clubs, being made an honorary member of some of them: Sydney's Athenaeum Club, Melbourne's Institute of Journalists and Yorick Club, the Adelaide Club, Christchurch's Canterbury Club and Savage Club, the Wellington Club, and that city's Modesty Club (possibly a fanciful name Twain gave to the small supper party attended mostly by prominent Maoris).

The artistic importance of the lecturing season is seen from the number of writers and artists who met the humorist. Twain was besieged by journalists, many anonymous, but some of whom are known: Herbert Low, David Syme, J. L. Dow, S. V. Winter. Louis Becke, whose book on Hawaii Twain admired, playwright J. le Gay Brereton, and poet and story writer Henry Lawson definitely made the effort to see Twain. Brereton told about taking Lawson, then attached to the *Bulletin* and a good friend of Herbert Low, to one of the performances at Protestant Hall in Sydney. Although they came late to the crowded auditorium, Lawson made an usher put a chair up front just a few feet from the stage because he was hard of hearing. Brereton recalled that the poet cheered so enthusiastically that Twain's shock of white hair vibrated when Lawson kicked the nearby planking.[2] Twain also spent time in Cronulla at *Bulletin* editor J. F. Archibald's seaside cottage and may have gone fishing there.[3] And in Melbourne novelist Rolf Boldrewood was reported to have tried in vain to get Twain to go for a walk with him.

The humorous import of his arrival is easily demonstrated by the number of local comic writers and artists who found in Twain an inspi-

---

2. William E. FitzHenry, unpublished history of the *Bulletin*, National Library of Australia, Canberra. I am especially grateful to the late Barry Andrews for drawing my attention to this manuscript.

3. Ibid.

ration for their own work. Most of the former remain anonymous or pseudonymous, but they were numerous and ubiquitous. From Bendigo to Dunedin, from Napier to Adelaide, Twain's visit freed dozens of repressed jokesters. Cartoonists are more readily identified: Livingston Hopkins, Tom Durkin, and W. M. Hodgkins have left signed drawings to commemorate Twain's visit and the Australasian response to it. Apparently he was "sent up" not only in the magazines but also in a revue referred to as "Tudor and Friedman's latest tip-topical absurdity" (*Melbourne Punch*, 26 Sept., 1895, p. 203). Herr Friedman was a well-known singing teacher.

But the popular appreciation of Twain as the foremost humorist in the English language—although less detailed in the evidence—was, if possible, even more overwhelming than the cordiality among the more articulate and glamorous classes already cited. For fifty performances the buildings were "packed" and "crammed" to overflowing. Often there was standing room only, and at many shows people sat, sweltering, not only in the orchestra but actually on the stage. The only empty seats occurred in the more expensive sections, except for one night when the prices proved to be too high for the drought-ridden countrymen to afford. While the ex-premier might get his name in the paper as having been seen at one of the "At Homes," the scores of clergymen, journalists, and lawyers who attended usually were not named. And of the lower classes—who attended in their myriads—virtually none can be identified. Yet they all laughed spontaneously, uproariously, and classlessly. Some of the "larrikins" shouted from the balconies allusions to Twain's books; one "in the gravest manner possible, advised him to 'have his hair cut'" (*Herald* [Melbourne], 27 Sept., 1895), others sang "For He's a Jolly Good Fellow"; and the oldsters started up a clack with their walking sticks when Twain was a little late appearing onstage.

A study of Twain's tour of Australasia tells us both about the Australasians and about Twain. He wrote very few letters during the tour, his notebooks are still in manuscript in California, and his resulting travel book—the last he ever wrote—has been practically ignored by critics. Still, scholars have given the tour some attention: the itinerary, the texts of some of Twain's lectures, and excerpts from reviews and interviews have been accessible for a quarter of a century; the outlines have been known since 1912. The scholars who have gone before me have worked mainly with Twain's own scrapbooks and with the colonial newspapers in the British Library; their sifting and sorting, extracting and quoting, identifying and listing, collecting and republishing the written residue of the trip made this present study feasible. Although I have had access to more information about the tour than any one of them (perhaps than all of them), it would have been impossible even to have collected it without such rudimentary tools as a chronology to guide me and a checklist to prod me.

When I began this work I believed that only the Victorian country towns, which were almost completely overlooked, would yield much new information. It was not until I began turning the pages of the old *Bulletin* magazine—and a handsome journal it was in 1895—that I began to see the enormously interesting context of Twain's visit. The correction of minor errors (some of which Twain himself had made in his notebooks), the discovery of several previously unknown or unlocated interviews and speeches, and most of all the recognition that the pictorial material was either overlooked or not understood convinced me that a modest book could provide a repository of materials that might be useful both to admirers of Twain and to Australasian scholars as they continue to discover and interpret their own literary heritage.

It was somewhat surprising to me to discover how familiar Australasians were with American literature, how popular it was, and how willing they were to make their own critical judgments about it. The reaction to Twain's unfortunate comment made in Sydney about Bret Harte's having "no heart, except his name" is a case in point. In their reviewing and their interviewing, Australasians revealed themselves willing to stretch the cultural bonds of English taste, even if they were not yet ready to break the political ones. It has been continuously fascinating to see a native literature and appropriate criticism emerging from a somewhat nervous and self-conscious Australian adolescence. For example, the journalists repeatedly asked Twain whether they were more like the Britons or the Americans, what his "impressions" were of their country, and what he thought of some of their writers. Although Twain was not always cordial to newspapermen, in Australia and New Zealand he welcomed their attention. In interviews and in his notebook he wondered at and praised the quality of journals in both countries. Such intelligent and well written journalism evoked intelligent and felicitous commentary from Twain. And at least some Australasians were quite satisfied when he said he thought they were more like their American cousins than their mutual ancestor. As the tour progressed, the title of his performances seemed more and more appropriate: "Mark Twain 'At Home.'"

The two versions of Twain's book about the world tour are sufficiently different to require care in making critical comments. Some years ago, for example, a New Zealand journalist wrote that he "marvelled" that the Union Company "did not take some action" against Twain's "criticism" of his voyage from Christchurch to Wellington.[4] But the journalist was citing *Following the Equator*—most likely in the Harper's authorized edition—not *More Tramps Abroad*, which would have circulated in New Zealand and in which the passage he quoted does not appear. I have used the Chatto and Windus *More Tramps Abroad* mainly for two reasons.

First, it was the book known and reviewed in Australasia, and the allusion in the title to his other travel books, *Innocents Abroad* and *A Tramp Abroad*, seems unmistakable. Furthermore, examination of the reception of his lectures reveals the interesting paradox of Twain's being truly "At Home" abroad.

Second, my decision to use the English edition as my source was determined by the text itself: Chatto and Windus used the manuscript (rather than a typescript) as copy; the typesetters exercised "commendable fidelity" to that text; Chatto was considerate and careful in editing, and his book is longer than the American one; and Twain read the proofs. In contrast, the American editor was "so unscrupulous in the textual changes he took it upon himself to make, that there is every reason to adopt *More Tramps Abroad* as the authentic and authorized text of this work, and *Following the Equator* as an abridged variant of it."[5]

This book will, I hope, offer pleasant reading. Although I have checked facts and quotations (which are extensive), I have modified capitalization at the beginnings and punctuation at the endings of quotations in order to avoid extensive or clumsy use of brackets. Because newspapers are often subject to typographical error, and since, moreover, Twain's "actual" words were not penned by him in the version

---

4. Allan A. Kirk, "A case of 'slight exaggeration' by Mark Twain," *Star* (Auckland), 25 July 1967.

5. Dennis Welland, *Mark Twain in England* (London: Chatto and Windus, 1979), pp. 181–182.

found in the articles, I have also silently corrected spelling mistakes, turned letters, and in a very few instances internal punctuation within newspaper quotations. I have not, however, modified acceptable variant spellings, most notably in words like *humour, humor, analyse, analyze* for they reveal a language changing, imbibing both English and American influence. Every effort has been made to provide full bibliographical information for all materials used; page numbers that are omitted were unavailable to me because I had to rely on a clipping or a previous scholar's report; or—in a few cases—I quote from the hand-written copy provided by the newspaper's archivist.

A book containing material so widely scattered generates much debt on the part of the author. Several require specific, and grateful, acknowledgment. The J. William Fulbright Foundation and the Australian-American Educational Foundation, under the direction of Ms. Noeline Milson, provided the opportunity for my family to reside in Australia in 1984. Professor Harry Heseltine, head of the English Department of the Royal Military College, University of New South Wales (now University College, Australian Defense Force Academy), and Professor Joseph E. Milosh and Dean Edward C. McGlone of the College of Arts and Sciences, Mississippi State University, were able to secure additional financial support, especially in the form of research funds. Professor Alan Gribben (University of Texas at Austin) and Dr. Robert Hirst (Mark Twain Project, University of California) were especially helpful in encouraging me to pursue this study by answering questions and otherwise making resources available to me.

Librarians, scholars, and editors from Adelaide to Gisborne scoured their collections, answering correspondence and questions, often drawing on their own knowledge where normal research procedures came up short. Although these custodians of our cultural heritage were uniformly courteous and helpful, several who went beyond normal expectations must be named: Anne Burrows, South Australian Collection; Debbie Gregory, *Gisborne Herald*; Professor Roger Collins, University of Otago; Moira Long and Janet Sorenson, Alexander Turnbull Library; T. Dowman, Wanganui City Council Library; Kathleen Stringer, North Otago Museum; and Jane Marshall, South Canterbury Historical Museum. I also wish to thank the staff in the newspaper collection of the Australian National Library for help over many months.

The support I received from the larger community fully justified Twain's designation of Australia as "the cordial nation": Alex Stone of the Bendigo Branch of the Royal Historical Society, Mrs. John Tait of Sydney, and the Honorable John White of Dunedin helped identify local residents and family members who met Twain. Robyn Lehmann of Melbourne and Mr. and Mrs. Bob Moore of Geelong were especially kind in entertaining my family overnight while I searched Victorian newspapers. I also wish to express thanks to the staff of the English Department at the Royal Military College, who were specifically helpful on portions of this work: especially Graham Barwell for making helpful suggestions on the New Zealand chapters, research assistant Trish Barton, Trish Middleton for typing, handling correspondence, and being my friend; and Malcolm Smith for computer assistance. Any errors are, however, my own.

I regret that the late Barry Andrews of the Royal Military College was unable to see this book in print. Through his published scholarship, his wide and deep knowledge of colonial Australian culture, his infectious enthusiasm for research and interpretation, his unfailing generosity in promoting the study of Australian literature, and his unabashed enjoyment of the discoveries recorded here, his contribution to this book is far greater than the notes would indicate. I am also especially grateful to Peter Shillingsburg, the only scholar hardy enough to read the entire manuscript, persistent enough to take it from Apple Macintosh to typesetting by computer, and patient enough to live with me.

June 1987

AT HOME ABROAD

Mark Twain in Australasia

CHAPTER ONE

The Fiery Furnace

"Straight Downhill toward Sure Destruction"

When, in April 1894, the publishing firm of Charles L. Webster and Company declared bankruptcy, part-owner Samuel L. Clemens, known to the world as Mark Twain, resorted to the lecture platform to repay his creditors. Although under bankruptcy proceedings Clemens the publisher and speculator was required to repay only a portion of the debt, Twain the writer determined to pay back "one hundred cents to the dollar." With the encouragement of his wife Olivia and the skillful guidance of his friend and financial advisor Henry Huttleston Rogers, vice-president and director of the Standard Oil Trust, he repaid the debts in a fraction of the four years he projected when he departed on a worldwide lecturing tour that brought him at the halfway point to Australia and New Zealand.

That Twain undertook his "talking tour round the world" because he was in dire need of money had been clear from the beginning. The obvious and immediate necessity was to repay the creditors of the publishing company. But the debt and bad investment had been accumulating for nearly fifteen years, and the final collapse of the publishing house on 18 April 1894 was only one in a series of reverses that would extricate Twain from business speculation—at least temporarily—and throw him back into writing and lecturing. In fact, a strictly chronological look at Twain's finances indicates that the most devastating loss—and the crushing of his last hope—was the failure of the Paige typesetting machine in the northern winter of 1894–1895. As early as 1881, Clemens had begun investing in an automatic typesetting machine designed by James W. Paige and "improved" by Charles E. Davis. By August 1885, he had invested $13,000 in the invention; early in 1886, he became the sole financier for its development; and by December 1887, it was costing him $3,000 a month in salaries and expenses, an investment by then of about $50,000. Several times Twain and various business associates tried to buy the entire Paige enterprise but the inventor would not sell. Finally, Twain exchanged his stock for future royalties and the Clemenses, in an effort to reduce expenses, moved from Hartford, Connecticut, to Europe—never to return to their big home.[1]

Simultaneously, Twain was involved in the then-successful Charles L. Webster and Company publishing business. After a tiff with his publisher James R. Osgood for selling less than fifty thousand copies of *Life on the Mississippi*,[2] and a later dispute over costs for *The Adventures of Huckleberry Finn*, Twain had, in May 1884, set up his nephew Charles L. Webster in the publishing business to bring out *Huck Finn* and other Twain titles. Thanks in part to being condemned by the Concord, Massachusetts, library committee as "trash and suitable only for the slums," *Huck Finn* sold fifty-one thousand copies in 1885 within three months of publication;[3] Twain was elated, not only as author, but also as publisher. The company also published General Ulysses S. Grant's *Personal Memoirs* in December 1885.[4] Flushed with these successes, Twain and Webster added another partner and enlarged their offices. After publishing a series of now-forgotten works, the Webster company in 1887 paid an advance of $5,000 for the autobiography of

---

1. *Mark Twain's Notebook*, ed. Albert Bigelow Paine (New York: Harper & Brothers Publishers, 1935; rpt. Scholarly Press, 1971), pp. 187ff. Twain described the original investment of $2,000 and, after he had seen the machine at work, another $3,000: "I was always taking little chances like that, and almost always losing by it, too" (A. B. Paine, *Mark Twain: A Biography* [New York: Harper & Brothers Publishers, 1912], pp. 903–904). On 21 October 1889, he wrote to William Dean Howells that he had spent "more than $3,000 a month on it for 44 consecutive months" (*Mark Twain's Notebooks and Journals, III, 1883–1891*, ed. R. P. Browning, M. B. Frank and L. Salamo [Berkeley: Univ. of California Press, 1979], p. 480).

2. Justin Kaplan, *Mr. Clemens and Mark Twain* (New York: Simon and Schuster, 1966), pp. 249–250. Kaplan's fascinating biography provides a detailed and readable account of this period of Twain's life to which I am indebted for the outline of this introduction.

3. *Notebooks and Journals, III*, p. 64; Kaplan, p. 269.

4. *Notebooks and Journals, III*, pp. 141–144.

Harriet Beecher Stowe's brother, Henry Ward Beecher, the extremely popular preacher with whom Twain had considered lecturing. He anticipated a profit of $300,000 if the preacher "heaves in just enough piousness"; but three weeks later Beecher was dead, and Twain, left with an unfinished manuscript, reckoned he had lost $100,000.[5]

At this time it was also discovered that the bookkeeper for the Webster firm had embezzled $25,000, and the company began a slide "straight downhill toward sure destruction."[6] In December 1888, Webster sold out his interest in the publishing house to Fred Hall, their honest and industrious partner, but by this time the business was irretrievably mismanaged, though it was another five years before it would become bankrupt. In a passionate account in his *Autobiography*, Twain blamed his nephew, who died in 1891 at the age of forty, for disastrous decisions.[7]

The most devastating decision, according to Twain's version, was the publication of Clarence Stedman's *Library of American Literature*, a handsome ten-volume anthology with lavish portraits of many of the writers represented. Twain claimed that Webster's enormous pride caused him to reject any book brought to Twain and to accept "worthless books ... because they had been offered to him instead of to me."[8] Webster accepted Stedman's book "on an eight per cent royalty, and thereby secured the lingering suicide of Charles L. Webster and Company."[9] It was Twain's intention in 1889 that the publishing company "must be brought to an end Feb. 1 at all hazards. This is final."[10] However, in that year Twain began to "use the publishing house as a private bank to finance the machine; he drew off the profits, demanded more, and left the firm undercapitalized, overexpanded, and fatally committed to publishing a ten-volume *Library of American Literature*."[11] Although

5. Kaplan, pp. 256, 289-291; *Mark Twain's Letters to His Publishers, 1867-1894*, ed. Hamlin Hill (Berkeley: Univ. of California Press, 1967), pp. 221-222.

6. *Notebooks and Journals, III*, pp. 283–285, 431.

7. *The Autobiography of Mark Twain*, ed. Charles Neider (London, Chatto and Windus, 1969), pp. 271–288.

8. Ibid., p. 278. See also *Mark Twain in Eruption*, ed. Bernard DeVoto (New York: Harper & Brothers, 1940), pp. 165–195.

9. *Autobiography*, ed. Neider, p. 280; *Mark Twain in Eruption*, ed. DeVoto, p. 192. See also Kaplan, p. 290.

10. *Notebooks and Journals, III*, p. 431; see also Alan Gribben, "Mark Twain, Business Man: The Margins of Profit," *Studies in American Humor*, n.s. 1 (June 1982), 24–43.

11. Kaplan, p. 291.

the company was reorganized in 1890, it seems clear that Twain was no longer interested in it, or perhaps he was merely suppressing his anger with its failure. Instead he turned his attention to the typesetter.[12]

"In the Poor-House Sure"

On 5 January 1889, Twain recorded in his notebook, "I have seen a line of movable type *spaced & justified* BY MACHINERY! This is the first time in the history of the world that this amazing thing has ever been done."[13] In December of the same year, Twain signed an agreement to manufacture the typesetter by which he would "pay Paige about $160,000 plus $25,000 a year for seventeen years" for all rights in the machine. Twain believed he could sell two thousand machines a year, earning $20,000,000 annually for the life of the patent. All he had to do was raise the money to build the 350 machines he thought he could sell immediately in New York City, the 600 he could sell in the United States, and the 800 in Europe. The typesetter became an obsession with him. In 1890, the "cunning devil" was costing $4,000 per month.[14]

In October 1890, Twain was writing (and typesetting) a pamphlet to be used in marketing the Paige machine and still calculating speed, accuracy, and expected sales. In December, he recorded:

About 3 weeks ago, the machine was pronounced 'finished,' by Paige, for certainly the half dozenth time in the past twelvemonth. Then it transpired —I mean it was discovered—that North had failed to inspect the *period, & it* sometimes refused to perform properly. But to correct that error would take just one day *& only* one day .... Well, the best part of 2 weeks went by. I dropped in (last Monday noon) & they were still tinkering. Still tinkering, but just *one hour*, now, would see the machine at work, blemishless, & never stop again for a generation.[15]

---

12. An excellent short account of the details of Twain's troubles with the typesetter may be found in *Notebooks and Journals, III*, 478-481 and 571-574.

13. *Notebooks and Journals, III*, pp. 441–442.

14. Kaplan, p. 301; Paine, *A Biography*, p. 912; *Mark Twain's Correspondence with Henry Huttleston Rogers*, ed. Lewis Leary (Berkeley: Univ. of California Press, 1969), p. 108. On 13 August 1890, Paige tried to sell all rights to the machine for a quarter of a million dollars to be paid in six months (*Notebooks and Journals, III*, p. 571). Twain projected as many schemes for making his fortune with the machine as he envisaged for selling his Australian material.

15. *Notebooks and Journals, III*, p. 596.

This became the story of the typesetter—Paige would get it working so that he could give a demonstration to Twain or some other amateur, or to a potential financier; then he would take it all to pieces trying to get it to do one more thing, and it would not work for months.[16] While Paige and his assistants fiddled with the machine, Twain scurried around trying to obtain small and large investments from friends, relatives, bankers, and famous people.

In the depths of the 1893 depression, when the creditors of the publishing company could be stalled no more and Twain could not borrow from anyone for either the typesetter or the publishing house, a mutual friend introduced him to Henry Huttleston Rogers. Rogers, who had admired Twain's books for many years, provided $8,000 to cover the immediate demands of a creditor who would not renew a Webster note. Rogers told Twain upon meeting him:

> I was one of your early admirers. I heard you lecture a long time ago on the Sandwich Islands. I was interested in the subject in those days, and I heard that Mark Twain was a man who had been there. I didn't suppose I'd have any difficulty getting a seat, but I did; the house was jammed. When I came away I realized that Mark Twain was a great man, and I have read everything of yours since that I could get hold of.[17]

A few months later (October 1893), Rogers suggested to his son-in-law, William Evarts Benjamin, also a subscription publisher, that he take over the *Library of American Literature* from Webster and Company for $50,000.[18] Twain also managed to interest Rogers in the typesetter sufficiently for him to travel to Chicago and to pledge an advance of $150,000 to the newly formed company that now was financing Paige. Through some fast talking, coached by Rogers, Twain managed to get Paige and his investors to accept Rogers's terms—to take twenty percent of face value for their stock in the company. On 15 January 1894, Twain could write in his notebook, "Yesterday we were paupers with

---

16. Kaplan describes the machine "in its most advanced state" as having had "eighteen thousand separate parts, including eight hundred shaft bearings. The patent application he filed in 1887 contained 275 sheets of drawings and 123 pages of specifications, and it was pending for eight years . . . . Eventually, in the hands of an operator of average skill, it could set twelve thousand ems an hour, compared with the 1890 average of eight thousand ems an hour for a practiced Linotype operator" (p. 285). Other typesetters of the period are described in *Notebooks and Journals, III*, p. 529*n*.

17. Paine, *A Biography*, p. 970.

18. *Correspondence with Rogers*, ed. Leary, p. 11; Paine, *A Biography*, p. 971.

but 3 months' rations of cash left and $160,000 in debt, my wife and I, but this telegram [from Chicago] makes us wealthy"; he cabled his wife on their twenty-fourth wedding anniversary, "Our ship is safe in port."[19]

But his financial troubles were far from over. For one thing, Webster and Company was now in a financial disaster; Twain decided to tell Rogers about these other worries on 15 February 1894. As late as 14 April, Rogers was "much encouraged about Websterco's probable ability to pull through alive,"[20] but four days later, the company filed bankruptcy when one of its creditors demanded repayment of two notes of $5,000 each that were due. When Rogers could not persuade the creditors to let the company continue business in an effort to repay the debts, he arranged to protect both Mrs. Clemens's position as a "preferred creditor" and Twain's by requiring him to pay back only fifty percent of the debts. However, Livy advised Twain, "don't be afraid. We shall pay a hundred cents on the dollar yet."[21] Rogers said neither Mrs. Clemens's house nor Twain's books were "an asset of Webster and Company, [but] that the creditors could have everything that belonged to Webster and Company."[22]

Leaving Rogers in New York to negotiate the settlement for Webster's creditors, Twain returned to France, where he wrote with some dedication on *The Personal Recollections of Joan of Arc*, apparently relieved of his worries over Webster and elated with the apparent success of the typesetter. He refused offers to lecture in the United States in January and—even after the bankruptcy—to lecture in London in May and June 1894, and he wrote several pieces for the magazines. In short, relief from Webster allowed him to return to writing, but its indebtedness did not yet force him to return to the platform.

In the northern autumn of 1894, the Paige typesetting machine was to undergo a two-month competition with Mergenthaler's Linotype and the McMillan typesetter. In October, Twain was writing to Rogers that "some day the Mergenthaler people will come and want to hitch teams with us. And we'll do it if they've got a long-life patent left then, on an essential feature .... With their machine suppressed, we should have

---

19. *Notebook*, ed. Paine, pp. 235–236; *Correspondence with Rogers*, ed. Leary, pp. 20–21.

20. *Correspondence with Rogers*, ed. Leary, p. 23.

21. *Autobiography*, ed. Neider, p. 281.

22. Ibid., p. 282.

no competition but hand-composition—5 and 6 cents against 45 and 50."[23] Its commercial value was clear to Twain, for it never tired and its accuracy seemed phenomenal. The erstwhile printer reckoned that "when we come to turning out perfect machines," newspaper compositors "will turn out 12,000 [ems] solid per hour, and their AA1 stallions 15,000 .... [The best hand-compositors] set 1,500 ems an hour. I have seen them do it. On the machine they will multiply that by ten."[24] Encouraged that Rogers was "pretty well pleased" with what he had seen of the Paige machine in action, Twain referred to the Mergenthaler Linotype as "a bastard cripple," and plans were proceeding for Rogers to lend the money for manufacturing. But by 28 November, the machine, in its public test, was proving "not nearly in condition for business yet." The next day—Thanksgiving—Twain responded to Rogers's assessment: he had told himself that "if Mr. Rogers finds it wise and best to remove his supports from under that machine, your fine ten-year-old dream will blow away like a mist and you will land in the poor-house sure."[25]

"Business Has its Laws and Customs"

Perhaps it is not fair to blame Twain too harshly for his obsession with the typesetter. The fact is the machine *did* work— occasionally—and very well. As early as 1889, Twain had saved two examples of its composition in his notebook. He believed that certain columns of Chicago's *Times-Herald* were set by the Paige machine and that they were "healing for sore eyes." Perhaps the major problem with the machine was that its inventor never could leave it alone. Twain recognized this and noted more than once, "No more experiments (on the machine). Definite work alone left to do .... No new devices or inventions."[26] This was just after Paige had installed a device to keep the keys from jamming, after adding an automatic justifier to the original machine; then they added "the final touch, the air-blast" to keep dust off the types; finally, Paige and his assistants—all on Twain's payroll—were ferreting out "even the triflingest defect," making the

---

23. *Correspondence with Rogers*, ed. Leary, p. 83. Ironically, when Twain got to Sydney a year later, he found the daily papers being typeset on the Linotype.

24. Ibid., pp. 88–90.

25. Ibid., pp. 99–100.

26. *Notebook*, ed. Paine, p. 207.

machine "perfecter than a watch."[27] Fed up with the breakdowns, delays, and improvements, Twain wrote to "these frauds and liars!" (as he privately called Paige and Davis) that he considered himself "as released from any further effort or expense in behalf of the machine."[28] Still, Twain could not keep away from the prospect of instant wealth. Besides, Paige was—next to H. H. Rogers himself, whom Twain did not yet know—"the smoothest talker I ever saw .... He could persuade a fish to come out and take a walk with him."[29] Twain wrote to his partner Hall on 9 August 1893, "I used to watch for the telegram saying 'the machine's finished—but when next week *certainly*' suddenly swelled into 'three weeks *sure*' I recognized the old familiar tune I used to hear so much."[30] A part of Twain saw through the charade, knew that "it is worth billions; and when the pig-headed lunatic, its inventor, dies, it will instantly be capitalized and make the Clemens children rich."[31]

In addition to the partial success of the machine in the late eighties, Paige's smooth talking, and Twain's own inability to resist a chance at a fast buck, there was at least one other circumstance that should mitigate a harsh sentence on Twain's judgment. Twain did, in fact, interest Henry Huttleston Rogers, vice president and director of the Standard Oil Trust, in investing $150,000 in the company that would manufacture the machine for the world market. In a series of complicated maneuvers, along with some fast talking, Rogers was able to consolidate the finances for manufacturing the machine, take control of the stock, secure Twain an additional $75,000 in stock (with the possibility of another $75,000), and promise to invest up to $150,000 in the company himself. A man who would tell a government commission investigating him that "we are not in business for our health ... but are out for the dollars" must surely be the man to trust.[32] In any event, Twain did trust Rogers, calling him "a great man" who for "foresight, wisdom, accurate calculation, good judgment and the ability to see all sides of a problem" was the only person who could match Mrs. Clemens.[33] But for once, Rogers apparently miscalculated.

---

27. Kaplan, pp. 302–304.
28. *Notebook*, ed. Paine, p. 211.
29. Ibid., pp. 231–232.
30. Paine, *A Biography*, p. 968.
31. Kaplan, p. 306.
32. Ibid., p. 321.
33. *Autobiography*, ed. Neider, pp. 283–284.

"Apparently" miscalculated, for—to read Twain's fond exposition of his relationship with Rogers, written in 1909—the financier seemed incapable of miscalculation where his friends were concerned. Twain explained that he had always "been the easy prey of the cheap adventurer. He came, he lied, he robbed and went his way, and the next one arrived by the next train and began to scrape up what was left. I was in the toils of one of these creatures sixteen years ago and it was Mr. Rogers who got me out."[34] The check for $8,000 and the "homeopathic powders" sent to relieve Twain's head colds surely fall into the category of friendly gestures for a tycoon like Rogers; buying the *Library of American Literature* was a business deal, however risky. But how could Rogers repay Twain's debts, which by a literary man's standards were exorbitant at about a quarter of a million dollars?[35]

Even though by Rogers's standards the debts might have been trifling, there was still Twain's pride to consider. Perhaps, then, Rogers did not so much miscalculate his investment in the Paige invention as he decided to become involved in it himself so that he could with authority call a halt to the endeavor at the appropriate moment. Perhaps, also, the invention might work; if it did, not only would Rogers make money, having taken over most of the stock at twenty percent, but also Twain would receive a commission of $150,000 in shares when Rogers had lent the entire pledge of $150,000. But Rogers actually gambled—or paid—only $72,000 for the privilege of closing down the business, thereby extricating Twain from the psychological strain of speculation, not to mention the drain on his bank account. Rogers effectively returned the writer to writing—the thing he had admired Twain for in the first place. Whatever the motive, whatever the method, Twain believed that Rogers

> dragged me out of that difficulty [the bankruptcy of Webster] and also out of the next one [with the Paige machine]—a year or two later—which was still more formidable than its predecessor. He did these saving things at no cost to my self-love, no hurt to my pride; indeed, he did them with so delicate an art that I almost seemed to have done them myself. By no sign, no hint, no word did he ever betray any consciousness that I was under obligations to him ... it belongs among the loftiest of human attributes.[36]

---

34. Ibid., p. 283.

35. The firm owed $60,000 to Twain, $65,000 to Mrs. Clemens, and about $100,000 to 96 small creditors (Ibid., p. 282).

36. Ibid., p. 282.

What Twain saw sixteen years later in the situation was that Rogers had rescued him financially and had possessed the wisdom to value the literary man's reputation. Rogers "was the only man who had a clear eye for the situation and could see that it differed from other apparently parallel situations. In substance he said this: 'Business has its laws and customs and they are justified; but a literary man's reputation is his life; he can afford to be money poor but he cannot afford to be character poor; you must earn the cent per cent and pay it.' "[37]

Even though—so Twain said—he overheard some of Rogers's friends remark that ninety-eight percent "of the men who fail at fifty-eight never get up again,"[38] he trusted his wife's judgment and began to cast around for another scheme that would bring in sufficient money to discharge all his debts. This scheming, which resulted in the world tour, began in January 1895, just after the collapse of the Paige enterprise. Later, when Twain sailed from North America on 23 August, he issued a statement that linked the tour with the publishing house's failure. This was reprinted in the papers around the world, and in Twain's mind it, rather than the Paige failure, became the impetus for the tour. In fact, the long diatribe against Webster and the complete omission of Paige from his posthumous autobiography (at least the portions of autobiographical dictations thus far published) may indicate how thoroughly Twain had suppressed the episode in his mind. The Paige failure was not generally known since there were no legal proceedings against the company; Twain was merely a stockholder and lost his investment, but no creditors made public claims against him for that fiasco.

On the other hand, the proceedings against Webster, of which Twain was two-thirds owner, resulted not only in losing his cash investments but also in at least one court summons and the resultant public record. Twain could not, therefore, hide the Webster embarrassment but he could obscure the Paige one. So for the public record Twain's tour became one solely of honor: "Honor knows no statute of limitations," declared Twain's nephew Samuel E. Moffett, and the statement was printed around the world.[39]

Twain wrote to Rogers from Paris on 3 February 1895 that he was on his way to New York to consult with him about contracts for *Joan of*

---

37. Ibid., pp. 283–284.
38. Ibid., p. 284.
39. Ibid., p. 284.

Arc and for a new uniform edition of his works to be published by the Harpers. The same letter says:

> Also to consult with you about another project, which is—(take a breath and stand by for a surge)—to go around the world on a lecture trip.
>
> This is not for money, but to get Mrs. Clemens and myself away from the phantoms and out of the heavy nervous strain for a few months. By the urgent help of the doctor I have got her more than half persuaded—provided Susy or Clara will go with us.

He implied that Rogers and his son and daughter should come along because they also needed the break and then continued, "I suppose I can hire myself out to Mrs. Clemens as a platform-reader and thus escape trouble from my creditors." He planned to sail west from Europe, lecture across North America, "and sail for Australia about Oct. 1. Read 60 times in Australia, New Zealand and Tasmania," continuing to India, Africa, England, then back to the United States.[40] By 3 February, he had already "discussed the matter with Stanley [the explorer] and got all the items. Also I have to-day written his lecture-agent in Melbourne and asked him to make me a proposition and send duplicate (signed) contracts for consideration, together with his guess as to how much my profits might exceed my expenses." A few days later, Twain wrote to Rogers that because some of Mrs. Clemens's interest had defaulted, "Apparently I've *got* to mount the platform next fall or starve; therefore I am examining into this thing seriously .... This is our last chance to go around the world. If we don't do it now we never shall." He had found out that the voyage from San Francisco to England via Australia was "delightful—also much cheaper than I had supposed;—$600 for one first-class the whole trip."[41]

This approach to the Melbourne agent R. S. Smythe became the subject of a short article that Twain sold to *Harper's Magazine*; it was reprinted in various Australasian newspapers as a part of the publicity for his tour:

> More Mental Telegraphy. About the end of January I wrote and asked Stanley for the name and address of his Australian lecture-agent, and he told me R. S. Smythe, Melbourne. So I wrote Smythe nine days ago—*and got a letter from him from Melbourne last night answering my questions!*

---

40. *Correspondence with Rogers*, ed. Leary, pp. 125–128.
41. Ibid.

There—how's that! It is true that his letter left Melbourne Dec. 17 and went to America and then back to Paris—still it was odd that he should take a notion to write me just about the time that I was going to write him. I hadn't thought of Australia away back there in December; so I conclude that his mind telegraphed the idea into mine across the ocean.[42]

The full record includes excerpts of the letter from Smythe dated Melbourne, 17 December: "It is so long since Archibald Forbes and I spent that pleasant afternoon in your comfortable house at Hartford that you have probably quite forgotten the occasion."

So the Clemenses determined to make a lecturing tour around the world, at the same time collecting information and observations for another travel book, perhaps like *Innocents Abroad* or its companion, *A Tramp Abroad*. Twain would be "a novelty in one way down there in Australia and the Cape of Good Hope—the only Yank that ever appeared there or in India on the platform."[43] Twain wrote, "Mrs. Clemens and Clara and I started, on the 15th of July, 1895, on our lecturing raid around the world. We lectured and robbed and raided for thirteen months. I wrote a book and published it. I sent the book money and lecture money to Mr. Rogers as fast as we captured it."[44] The title of that book as it appeared in the British Commonwealth was *More Tramps Abroad*, although it was published in America as *Following the Equator* (1897).[45]

When Twain celebrated his seventieth birthday in 1905, Rogers was close at hand, as were other business and literary friends. Among them was steel tycoon Andrew Carnegie, who praised Twain's mettle in overcoming his bankruptcy. The public did not know, said Carnegie, "that he was a man of strong convictions upon political and social questions and a moralist of no mean order." Carnegie prophesied that "what our friend had done as a man would live as long as what he had written

---

42. Quoted from "Mark Twain and Mental Telepathy," *Australasian*, 5 Oct., p. 650 (reprinted from *Harper's Magazine*, Sept. 1895). However, the first appearance of the anecdote was in a letter to Rogers on 12 February 1895.

43. *Correspondence with Rogers*, ed. Leary, pp. 127, 129. Twain was in fact not the first "Yank" to take to the platform in Australia: Californian Henry George had lectured on land reform in 1889, and Dr. Thomas De Witt Talmage, a popular and prolific New York preacher, had toured two months with Smythe early in 1895.

44. *Autobiography*, ed. Neider, p. 287; *Correspondence with Rogers*, ed. Leary, p. 130.

45. Welland discusses the extensive differences between the English and American editions.

.... Our friend, like Scott, was ruined by the mistakes of partners, who had become hopelessly bankrupt."

> Two courses lay before him. One the smooth, easy, and short way—the legal path. Surrender all your property, go through bankruptcy, and start afresh. This was all he owed to creditors. The other path, long, thorny, and dreary, a life struggle, with everything sacrificed .... There are times in most men's lives that test whether they be dross or pure gold. It is the decision made in the crisis which proves the man. Our friend entered the fiery furnace a man and emerged a hero. He paid his debts to the utmost farthing by lecturing around the world.[46]

"A Harder Master than the Law"

By the time Twain and his party arrived in Sydney aboard the *RMS Warrimoo* a little after eleven on the night of 15 September 1895, he had been lecturing off and on for nearly thirty years. This professional experience, his fame as a humorous writer whose works the Australasians had already read, and the unstinting promotional efforts of his Melbourne managers, the Smythes, ensured the success of the fifteen-week season of "Mark Twain at Home" in Australia and New Zealand.

Twain's earliest lecturing experience had been in the northern fall and winter, 1866–1867, just after he had returned from the Sandwich Islands.[47] That season is not unrelated to the Australasian tour of three decades later, for, in addition to the practical experience he gained in voice control, audience handling, and stage presence, some of the jokes he made about the Sandwich Islanders were also told to the Australasians in the heat of the southern summer of 1895.

His first major tour occurred in the 1868–1869 season when he lectured in New York, Pennsylvania, Ohio, Indiana, Michigan, Wisconsin, Illinois, and Iowa.[48] This tour was extremely important for several rea-

46. Andrew Carnegie, *Autobiography of Andrew Carnegie* (Boston: Houghton Mifflin, 1920), pp. 283–284.

47. Walter F. Frear, *Mark Twain and Hawaii* (Chicago: Priv. Print., 1947); Paul Fatout, *Mark Twain on the Lecture Circuit* (Bloomington: Indiana Univ. Press, 1960); Fred W. Lorch, *The Trouble Begins at Eight* (Ames: Iowa State Univ. Press, 1968); Lorch, "Mark Twain's 'Sandwich Islands' Lecture and the Failure at Jamestown, New York in 1869," *American Literature* 25 (1953), 314–325.

48. Fred W. Lorch, "Mark Twain's Lecture Tour of 1868–1869: 'The American Vandal Abroad,'" *American Literature* 26 (1954–1955), 515–527.

sons and set a life-long pattern for his lecturing. First, it provided him a quick and extremely profitable way of earning a living, which he resorted to on later occasions when he needed money. This was the single most important motivation for undertaking the world tour in 1895— that he needed to raise a lot of money rather quickly. He also showed in 1869 that he could please audiences other than the boisterous and perhaps unsophisticated ones in the American Far West. During the tour to Australasia, Twain certainly pleased both kinds of crowds: in Sydney and Melbourne the urbane, sophisticated, worldly-wise racecourse set, interlarded with clergymen and ladies, and in northwestern Victoria the gold miners and pastoralists and farmers. The judgment that he discovered he could rely on in developing his humorous material held up in 1895. Some of the same subject matter, from *Roughing It* and especially from *Innocents Abroad* (which was in press during the 1868 tour), became old stand-bys in 1895. Throughout the entire 1868–1869 season Twain seems to have gone "without a single lapse into bad taste," something he apparently strove for in the Antipodes, although, as it turned out, he did offend one audience.

The 1868–1869 tour also set Twain's professional manner and look on the stage: "Well-dressed and trim looking, he had ... a thick shock of curly, reddish brown hair, a well-defined mustache, sharp twinkling eyes, and intelligent features."[49] This is obviously the same figure the Australian critics described in 1895: "The bushy head of hair is there, and the deep set, closely drawn eyes look out kindly and gently from a strongly intellectual face ... this intensely civilised looking person does not strike one as being the author of *Roughing It*" (*Age* [Melbourne], 28 Sept., p. 7). And finally, the experience of this American tour taught Twain the value of good management. Although the humorist may have been trying to shake the "emasculating influence" of his literary guide Mary Mason Fairbanks, he opened the season in her hometown, where her husband, the publisher of Cleveland's *Herald*, printed several of his wife's notices about the forthcoming lecture, reprinted three of Twain's stories, and published his wife's "completely favorable" review of the lecture.[50] Under the management of Australasia's most experienced lecture agents, R. S. and Carlyle G. Smythe, a similar pattern of announcement, reprinting, and review can be seen. Moreover,

49. Ibid., p. 523.
50. Ibid., p. 521.

under Smythe's tutelage, but also because Twain seemed to want as much favorable publicity as possible, the humorist was more willing and gracious in giving interviews than he had perhaps been in the past. Whereas earlier in his career Twain had felt that journalists often misrepresented his remarks, in Australia and New Zealand he not only complimented the reporters and their journals as being truthful but cultivated their company in part as a means of promoting the book he would write about the tour when he got home.

Twain took the matter of his early lectures—the Sandwich Islands and the Nevada silver mines—to England in 1873, where he gave thirty performances, mostly in London, and a few more in the early weeks of 1874 back home in the United States. In the main, this tour received extremely favorable reviews. However, a general criticism in London's *Daily News* of the "new and odd school of American humorists" of which Twain was "a leading professor" shows a reservation among the British that was, twenty years later, not shared by Twain's Australasian reviewers. Though the new humor was "fresh, original, and amusing ... at best it is irresistible," the London reviewer doubted "whether it is destined to amuse the world for long; or that anything more than ashes will be left when its fire goes out."[51] Although this is not necessarily a typical opinion of the successful season, it might be briefly contrasted with the judgment more than two decades later reiterated by nearly all Twain's Australasian reviewers: his "books are read and sayings quoted wherever the English language is spoken, whether in the nasal twang of the American, the throaty drawl of the Britisher, or the word-clipping, metallic tone of the Australian" (*Adelaide Observer*, 19 Oct., p. 15, reprinted from *South Australian Register*, 14 Oct.).

The last lecture circuit Twain had undertaken before coming to the Antipodes was in the winter of 1884–1885 when he performed from Connecticut to Missouri. Advertised by his new agent, J. B. Pond, who would later be the manager for the American phase of the world tour, as "Twins of Genius," Twain shared the billing with George Washington Cable, a well-known writer of New Orleans local color stories. The most important lesson learned in that season was the effectiveness of mixing humor and pathos, supplied mainly in this instance by alternating readings by Twain and Cable. As one critic noted, "Mr. Cable

---

51. Fred W. Lorch, "Mark Twain's Public Lectures in England in 1873," *American Literature* 29 (1957), 297–304.

was humorous, pathetic, weird, grotesque, tender, and melodramatic by turns, while Mr. Clemens confined his efforts to the ridicule of such ridiculous matters as aged colored gentlemen, the German language, and himself."[52]

In Australia, the critics nearly always noted that the entertainment "comprised exceedingly humorous and pathetic stories," and that "Mark Twain has two sides to his nature: the humorous and the pathetic, and, he has by no means let the one smother the other" (*Courier* [Ballarat], 23 Oct., p. 4; *Leader* [Melbourne], 12 Oct., p. 18). With Cable, Twain also perfected the mannerisms he had been cultivating: "he sauntered to the reading desk, felt for it with his right hand, and began." Another critic noted his use of the pause "that is more suggestive than words. His face is immovable . . . , his right hand plays with his chin and his left finds its way to the pocket of his pants."[53] How like the Australian performances a decade later: in Stawell, "he lounges on to the platform, takes his place beside a small table on which there is not even the usual decanter and tumbler" (*Stawell News and Pleasant Creek Chronicle*, 19 Oct., p. 2). In his "opening Australian 'At Homes,' " he "dresse[d] in the regulation evening-clothes, with the trouser-pockets cut high up, into which he occasionally dives both hands . . . . His characteristic attitude is to stand quite still, with the right arm across the abdomen and the left resting on it supporting his chin" (*Critic* [New York], 25 Apr. 1896, p. 286, reprinted from *Sketch* [London]). And in Adelaide, his "almost indolent delivery, peculiar accent, unmoved demeanour, dry style of saying things, and mannerisms all stamp him as an original" (*Adelaide Observer*, 19 Oct., p. 15).

But Twain was not satisfied just to make the audience laugh. Cable told about waiting in the wings as "tides of laughter gather[ed] and roll[ed] forward and [broke] against the footlights" while Twain spoke. Back in the hotel, "Clemens groaned and seemed writhing in spirit and said: 'Oh, Cable, I am demeaning myself. I am allowing myself to be a mere buffoon. It's ghastly. I can't endure it any longer.' "[54] In Melbourne and throughout Australasia reviewers declared, "He is not alone the laughter maker that his books would pronounce him to

52. Guy A. Cardwell, *Twins of Genius* (East Lansing: Michigan State College Press, 1953), p. 20.

53. Ibid., pp. 20, 23.

54. Paine, *A Biography*, p. 786.

be .... The sense of proportion between tears and laughter is nicely gauged" (*Leader* [Melbourne], 12 Oct., p. 18).

Among the stories Twain would bring out in the Southern Hemisphere were the favorites of the tour with Cable: Uncle Dan'l's ghost story about the woman with the golden arm; the German fishwife, grandfather's old ram, and the jumping frog. But the most important new material was, of course, introducing Huck Finn and Jim to audiences. Selections from *The Adventures of Huckleberry Finn* were appearing in *Century* for December, January, and February 1884–1885, and the forthcoming book publication by Webster and Company was announced in February.[55] Therefore, not only did reading from the manuscript provide good publicity for subscription sales, but also sections like the King Sollerman passage and Tom and Huck's "rescue" of Jim were good platform pieces. These were used often in the world tour as well as Huck's fooling Jim in the fog and Jim's decision to steal his child. The tour with Cable was very successful, for Twain generated the publicity needed to help sell fifty thousand copies of *Huck Finn*, and, of course, the tour itself was lucrative. But when it was over, Twain intended never to undertake a circuit again. Nevertheless, under adverse financial circumstances and great psychological and physical stress, the Clemens family left Europe on 15 April 1895 to travel around the world.

Like his first tour, the world tour officially opened in Cleveland, Ohio, on 15 July 1895, where after only two tryouts—one in the House of Refuge, the other in the Elmira Reformatory in New York—Twain gave the "Morals Lecture," which would be the staple of the next year. Lecturing twenty-three times as he moved across southern Canada and the northern United States, Twain, Olivia, and their daughter Clara departed Vancouver, British Columbia, on 23 August 1895, bound for Australia via Honolulu.[56] As is well known, the tour, from the time he

---

55. Cardwell, p. 75. The book was published in England on 10 December 1884, and in the United States on 18 February 1885. Twain recalled that he and Webster had withheld it until they could secure sufficient subscribers. Walter Blair records, however, that publication was delayed in order to correct the electrotyper's indecent addition to an illustration of "Uncle Silas with his pelvis thrust forward, Aunt Sally looking sidewise at her spouse and grinning" (*Mark Twain & Huck Finn* [Berkeley: Univ. of California Press, 1960], pp. 364–367).

56. Fred W. Lorch, "Mark Twain's 'Morals' Lecture during the American Phase of His World Tour in 1895–1896," *American Literature* 26 (1954), 52–66.

had left his residence in London, had been plagued by bad luck. The tryout at the boys' refuge Twain thought a failure, and at Cleveland his curtain time was delayed forty minutes by the repeated encores of a violin and flute concert prior to his program. In Cleveland, he claimed to have been in bed sick for over seven weeks, arising only five days earlier. He had already been suffering from the carbuncle that would recur until he left Australasia, and he spent most of his free time from New York to British Columbia resting in bed.[57] As if that were not enough, as the *Warrimoo* left Vancouver on 16 August, it struck a reef in the dense smoke from forest fires. Delayed a week waiting while the ship was being repaired, Twain took the opportunity to lecture in Victoria, where the governor-general and his party attended.[58]

On 17 August, Twain wrote to Rogers that he had promised to pay his creditors one hundred percent of his debt, "a promise which I could have made a year ago just as well and with more advantage."[59] However, as he wrote Rogers, "as long as the promise must be made, it was necessarily well to make it *public*; and so I have made it public." Though it was not just a cheap publicity stunt, Twain saw the "advantage" in telling a reporter for the New York *Times*, "The law recognizes no mortgage on a man's brain, and a merchant who has given up all he has may take advantage of the rules of insolvency and start free again for himself; but I am not a business man, and honor is a harder master than the law."[60]

The interview was reprinted and excerpted many times in big papers and small all through Australasia. With Australia's economic hard times and outright fraud, no doubt Twain's admission that "if it had not been for the imperious moral necessity of paying these debts, which I never contracted but which were accumulated on the faith of my name by those who had a presumptive right to use it, I should never have taken to the road at my time of life" struck sympathetic chords in those Victorians whose life savings had been squandered by unscrupulous bankers in land speculation. He inspired his potential auditors and piqued their interest with his confidence that, "if I live I can pay off the

---

57. Fatout, *Mark Twain on the Lecture Circuit*, pp. 241–259; Lorch, *The Trouble Begins at Eight*, pp. 184–223.

58. Paine, *A Biography*, p. 1005; Fatout, *Mark Twain on the Lecture Circuit*, p. 251; *Correspondence with Rogers*, ed. Leary, p. 186.

59. *Correspondence with Rogers*, ed. Leary, p. 181.

60. Ibid., p. 182.

last debt within four years, after which, at the age of sixty-four, I can make a fresh and unincumbered [sic] start in life."[61]

Twain's stop at Honolulu, which he had visited three decades before, was to have allowed him to be "At Home," and five hundred seats were sold. His notebook entries as he rocked offshore at the end of August reflect his affection for the islands: "Just as silky and velvety and lovely as ever. If I might I would go ashore and never leave. The mountains right and left clothed in rich splendors of melting color, fused together. Some of the near cliffs veiled in slanting mists—beautiful luminous blue water; inshore brilliant green water."[62] But when the *Warrimoo* arrived, its passengers discovered the island was infected with cholera. No shore leave was allowed, and Twain's performance was canceled at a widely reported loss of $600.

---

61. Paine, *A Biography*, p. 1007.
62. *Notebook*, ed. Paine, pp. 249–250.

CHAPTER TWO

Sydney

"Important Questions of Our Time"

On 23 April 1895, Twain wrote from Paris to his New York publisher, J. H. Harper: "To-day I shall sign a contract which has just arrived from Melbourne, for a six to nine months' tour next fall and winter in the Sandwich Islands, New Zealand, Australia, Ceylon, Madras, Calcutta, Bombay and other Indian cities, then South Africa and the Mauritius."[1]

Impresario Robert Sparrow Smythe wasted no time in announcing the Twain visit, and, on 1 May 1895, the *Sydney Daily Telegraph* columnist "Outis" opined that after the lecturers Smythe had recently brought to Sydney, Twain would be "a blest relief" and would be ensured "a royal reception" wherever he went. The columnist noted that there was "probably no other man living, except, perhaps, Mr. Gladstone, so universally known," or who has given so many people "something to think and talk about." Some believed Twain "has rendered better service to the world than any imaginative writer of our period, not only by making it smile at clean inimitable humor, but in prompting deep and serious thought on many important questions of our time." This newspaperman named *A Connecticut Yankee* and *Pudd'nhead Wilson* as books that "give abundant proofs that the writer has a better grasp of some of the great problems of the world than many of the specialists who have dealt with them" (*Sydney Daily Telegraph*, 1 May, p. 8).

If this attitude—that Twain had a good grasp on morality and on the conflicts and foolishness that can arise when monarchy clashes with

---

1. *Correspondence with Rogers*, ed. Leary, p. 143.

nineteenth-century democracy—was generally held by Australians it is little wonder that his visit to the Antipodes was such a success. The newspaper record bears out the early assessment that Twain and the Australasians felt a certain kinship, if not always about the great problems of the world, at least about the ordinary problems of human experience. Nevertheless, in his early remarks Twain found himself— unintentionally and apparently naively—caught in the middle of a great debate over protection and free trade. Although his early remarks in Sydney stirred feelings and provoked editorial comment, he soon learned not to express to interviewers opinions on politics or, for that matter, on certain literary personalities.

The week before Twain was to arrive in Sydney Harbour, Smythe unleashed a barrage of publicity about the visit, setting the pattern for the entire Australasian tour. Pictures adorned any available post or flat surface; advertisements appeared in classified sections; and news releases along with portraits were supplied to obliging editors. Shortly before Twain would arrive, nearly every town he visited would be apprised of the unstinting efforts expended in getting the humorist to Australasia. In 1882, while escorting war correspondent Archibald Forbes through America, Smythe had called on Twain in his comfortable home in Hartford, Connecticut. Two or three years later—so the publicity went—"an eminent Melbourne journalist," sending up his card, had briefly visited Twain in Hartford "lying comfortably in bed .... very late one morning." Twain promised the journalist, "I'll call over at your place some day." About 1889 another "attempt to capture the popular novelist" was made when "a little Melbourne syndicate secretly sent an agent," but Twain replied that "if he ever did visit Australia, it would be under his friend Mr. Smythe's guidance." Finally, explorer H. M. Stanley had told his friend that "in almost every town he visited he was frequently asked whether he thought Mark Twain would ever come to Australia" (*Sydney Daily Telegraph*, 16 Sept., p. 4; *Table Talk* [Melbourne], 27 Sept., p. 5), and when financial necessity demanded it, Twain asked Stanley to recommend an agent.

Despite damage sustained in running aground off British Columbia, the Canadian-Australian Company's 3330–ton mail steamer fully loaded with 1150 tons at Vancouver, had made the "fastest passage on record—five and a half days" on its last leg between Suva and Sydney (*Australian Star*, 16 Sept., p. 5). Even before the Clemenses had disembarked, the newspapers had hired a "little launch" to anchor in Watson's Bay alongside the *RMS Warrimoo*, which had docked at 11:00 p.m. on Sunday, 15 September, still under the command of Captain R. E. Arundel. "Don't forget my soulful eyes," Twain is supposed to have said as he leaned over the ship's rail. The *Sydney Morning Herald* and Melbourne's *Argus* on the morning of 16 September carried similar but not identical reports of that interview, and it seems most likely that there was only one reporter present in the "little Post Office launch" hired by the *Sydney Morning Herald*. Asked his ideas and impressions on coming to Australia, the papers reported, Twain merely quipped, "I don't know. I'm ready to adopt any that seem handy. I don't believe in going outside accepted views" (*Sydney Morning Herald*, 16 Sept., p. 5).

About that time a hawser pipe drowned out Twain's remarks, but afterwards the humorist explained that he was going to start writing his Australian book right away because "you know so much more of a country when you haven't seen it than when you have. Besides, you don't get your mind strengthened by contact with the hard facts of things" (*Sydney Morning Herald*, 16 Sept., p. 5). The hardest facts for the foreign visitor who intends to write a travel account, Twain explained, "are the local liars. They come out and stuff you with information you don't want, and then they asperse your memory ever after" (*Sydney Morning Herald*, 16 Sept., p. 5). Coming prepared for these local liars seems to have allowed Twain to join in their fun, for he certainly played to them on stage and in interviews, and if his book can be believed, he used their yarns when he got home.

This very first interview from the boat reported that Twain claimed to be unwilling to duel his French literary rival Max O'Rell (Paul Blouet) because "I can disgrace myself nearer home, if I felt so inclined, than by going out to have a row with a Frenchman. The fact of the matter is I think Max O'Rell wanted an advertisement, and thought the best way to get it was to draw me. But I'm far too old a soldier for that sort of thing" (*Sydney Morning Herald*, 16 Sept., p. 5). This supposed reply about Max O'Rell, along with remarks about fellow American writer Bret Harte and others about New South Wales politics made the next day, stirred objections from Sydneysiders and Melbournians alike.

However, it turns out that one of the "local liars" was the newspaperman himself, reporter Herbert Low, who recalled over a decade later that the conditions under which this interview was conducted were impossible.

> After a few attempts at questions, I gave it up—I could neither be heard nor hear. I bawled out, "Mr. Twain, I'll have to imagine this interview," to which he screamed in a lull of the winch, "Go ahead, my boy; I've been there myself!" ... Well, I imagined an interview, which, although not true, ought to have been; and no one was more pleased than Twain. [*Worker* (Sydney), 2 Apr. 1908, p. 11.]

The Sydney that Twain and his family encountered the next day was a city of about 380,000 inhabitants including its suburbs. It contained about 2,600 acres stretching nearly three and a half miles from north to south, and almost three miles west. There were several large hotels and public buildings, some of which—like the School of Arts and the Protestant Hall where he spoke—still stand. The most worrisome news item in the papers Twain would have read on 16 September concerned widespread drought, unbroken for six months and extending back even further with only minor relief. This, in turn, particularly in the country towns of Victoria, resulted in a general economic sluggishness to which even Twain became victim. Prayer meetings for rain had been held especially on the Sunday afternoon before Twain's arrival; the next day there was light rain widely scattered across the continent, and Twain may have been aware of heavy thunderstorms just north of the city. But the drought was far from over.

Among the main issues in politics were the union movement, manifested in meetings to discuss "sweatshops" in both Melbourne and Sydney, the debate over trade protection in New South Wales, and railway scandals, strikes, and suits in Victoria. A major social concern was the "new woman" question, accompanied by new styles in clothing so that she could indulge in the newest fad—bicycle riding. The business pages most often reported on shipping, mining, and the wool trade. Spring sports included the America's Cup from which England's *Valkyrie* soon would withdraw, cricket, the inevitable horse racing, and the beginnings of bicycle racing. The entertainment circuit in the capital cities was also full that season with the Russian pianist Mark Hambourg and the English mesmerist T. A. Kennedy, lecturers Michael Davitt on Irish nationalism and the Reverend Haskett Smith on the Holy Land, several melodramas including *Joseph of Canaan* and Marcus Clarke's *For the Term of His Natural Life*, and a wide variety of continuous annual spring shows, lectures, and concerts. As the season progressed, Christmas choral concerts and charity benefits filled any lull in entertainment.

"The Average Globe-Trotter"

The fun would not begin until Wednesday evening at a private dinner at the Athenaeum Club. In the meantime there was the problem of publicity, most readily solved by co-operating with Sydney's reporters. From Brisbane to Adelaide, papers carried excerpts from early interviews with the great man. In Adelaide it was reported that on his first day in Sydney he was "made the target of numberless interviewers, to all of whom he poured out any amount of confidences, though never venturing a serious opinion on a serious subject."[2] Although it is not true that Twain expressed no serious opinions, and it may not have been true that he was "besieged by interviewers," such notices served the useful purpose of keeping his name before the public.

As the *Warrimoo* tied up at Circular Quay a little after 7:00 Monday morning, 16 September, it had too much way and crashed into the wharf but without damage, and scarcely noticeable on board where the Clemenses were having their breakfast. A reporter accosted Twain as he finished and extracted some interesting comments. Twain claimed they had had good weather for the whole trip (although others said not), and he complimented the harbor, which he had been able to see since 6:30. He said that, although he had come to Australia "to get money to pay [his] creditors" and lecturing was "rather hard work," it was "the quickest way to pay" and he did like lecturing after he was "on the platform" (*Evening News* [Sydney], 16 Sept., p. 4).

He told the reporter that "the average globe-trotter," while he may provide pleasant reading, seldom is accurate in his "impressions." He was thinking of Max O'Rell, the Frenchman who had recently been to Australia and was then being announced to lecture in the United States. In addition to Twain's dislike of Frenchmen, O'Rell had attacked Twain's unfavorable article on Paul Bourget's globe-trotting opinions of America. When O'Rell challenged Twain to a duel, the American passed it off as "twaddle" and a cheap publicity stunt, but he did tell the

---

2. *Express and Telegraph* (Adelaide), 17 Sept., p. 3. If this notice was actually wired as its dateline says, on 16 September, it must have been sent out by the interviewer himself, for its language appeared the following morning in the *Sydney Daily Telegraph*, 17 Sept., p. 5.

reporter that Bourget, in spite of his misunderstanding Twain's home-land, was "a man of great literary reputation and capacity," while O'Rell had "no rank whatever" as a literary man (*Evening News* [Sydney], 16 Sept., p. 4). Here Mrs. Clemens covered Twain's mouth and asked the reporter to omit a line. Two weeks later a reader, writing as "Attrape," agreed with Twain's opinion of O'Rell, that his reputation "is not even a cypher" because of the "notoriety for the most deliberate falsehoods, the most exaggerated statements, the most glaring inaccuracies, and the most shallow observations" about Australia (*Herald* [Melbourne], 30 Sept., p. 2).

The *Sydney Morning Herald* and Melbourne's *Argus*, the same papers that had sent out the little launch on Sunday night, interviewed Twain later that morning. Although there may have been two reporters, it seems more likely that a single journalist wrote both, despatching one by telegraph to Melbourne for the morning paper on 17 September. The *Argus* report, called "A Further Interview," was surely by the same writer as the launch interview. The similarities in the Tuesday reports are striking: both, for example, gave Twain's views on General Grant ("a grand figure and ... a noble nature" (*Argus* [Melbourne], 17 Sept., p. 5), the coincidence in Twain's first acquaintance with Rudyard Kipling in Elmira, New York, and the anecdote about a London visit with H. M. Stanley and a hundred friends. It was at Stanley's dinner that Twain met Mrs. Cyprian Bridge, wife of the commander of the Australian Naval Station.

Years later, journalist Herbert Low took credit for the *Morning Herald* report on Twain, writing that before the Post Office launch left, Twain called out, "I'll meet you at the Australia to-morrow at 11 o'clock." Low emphasized in the *Sydney Morning Herald* the "Wit and Humour" that he asked Twain to distinguish. "It is easy enough often to say what [humor] is not; but an exact scientific definition—it seems like trying to transfix a sunbeam," Twain explained. Both the *Herald* and the *Argus* reported that Twain said life is a serious matter enlightened occasion-ally by a humorous slip, a "contribution which the gods have sent," according to the *Argus* (17 Sept., p. 5). Editorials and letters refuted some of Twain's notions on wit, humor, comedy, and pathos, especially before the writers had seen him in the flesh. But even the angriest usu-ally came around to the view that Twain was master of conjoining humor and pathos in a superior way.

Most of the conversation on wit and humor seems to have taken place before Twain, entertaining Low and another friend, or perhaps his agents Robert S. and Carlyle G. Smythe, was joined by a reporter from the rival morning paper, the *Sydney Daily Telegraph*. That report devoted only a small portion to literary theory, although a substantial part reported Twain's tastes in contemporary literature. It is possible, even likely, that Low was the only reporter with Twain that morning and that he sold articles to all the major morning papers except the *Age* in Melbourne, with which he had only recently parted company. He may even have wired Adelaide and Brisbane with portions of the *Daily Telegraph* interview.

Although the *Sydney Daily Telegraph* article was titled "A Ramble with Mark Twain," the reporter omitted a significant part of the "ramble" that Low recorded over a decade later in his "Australian Press Reminiscences." Low said that he took Twain around the city "at his request."

> The picture posters that the much-travelled Smythe had placed on every boarding to herald Twain's arrival, made his identity unmistakable. And this circumstance led to the recognition of an unpleasant feature of Australian city life that I had previously not suspected. We were encountered and blocked by a veritable race of genteel cadgers as we wandered towards Cooper's wharf. Men would pause, in affected abruptness, as Twain approached, then rush up to him, shake hands enthusiastically, saying something like this: "You are Mark Twain; I know it. Sir, it is the glory of my life to have shaken hands with you." Then, drawing the penitant author aside, prefer a request for half-a-crown. [*Worker* (Sydney), 2 Apr. 1908, p. 11.]

But soon "This sort of thing became so frequent that at last Twain invented the remedy."

> Approached by an enthusiastic literary admirer with a borrowing eye, he did not disclaim his identity, but after acknowledging it he would say rapidly, "Yes, indeed, I am Mark Twain; but I regret to say after all my labors in the literary vineyard I have arrived here in very distressed circumstances. Could you oblige me with half-a-crown till I get back to the States." It was a complete cure. [*Worker* (Sydney), 2 Apr. 1908, p. 11.]

Surely Low, between jobs in September 1895, was seeking to keep his free-lance markets viable at least in the same city, by varying the emphasis in his articles. It is hard to believe that the *Sydney Daily Telegraph* reporter—if not Low—could have failed to report this anecdote.

"So Long as They Are the Best Men"

The *Sydney Daily Telegraph* representative wrote that about noon Twain and two friends were drinking a whiskey cocktail at the bar of the Australia Hotel. Twain "mightily amused" his listeners, moving his hands "up and down like two ships at sea" to illustrate "a narrative spoken with extreme 'deliber-ation.'" Ready to leave for Falk's studio, then owned by Mr. Barnett, where he was to have his portrait made, Twain invited the *Sydney Daily Telegraph* reporter to "go along." The resulting article recorded, among other things, some Twain remarks on politics that would provoke a diatribe the next afternoon from a rival paper, the *Australian Star*, the only "protectionist" paper then in Sydney. Twain admitted, "I don't profess to be learned in matters of this kind ... but my instinct teaches me that protection is wrong. Surely it is wrong that on the Pacific Slope they should be compelled to bring their iron from the east when they might get it landed at a much lower price direct from foreign ships at their own door" (*Sydney Daily Telegraph*, 17 Sept., p. 5). Twain added that the chapter in *A Connecticut Yankee* on free trade "was penned at a time when one of the New York papers was publishing a great deal about the progress of New South Wales under freetrade" (*Sydney Daily Telegraph*, 17 Sept., p. 5).[3]

After sending for Olivia and Clara Clemens to take their pictures, Mr. Barnett displayed a photograph of Sir Henry Parkes, "a magnificent specimen of photography," the reporter wrote, "for all the world like a perfect etching, if, indeed, it would be possible for the human hand to trace lines so fine and so soft. Mr Clemens was delighted with the work, and, commenting upon the subject, said that Sir Henry had a truly splendid head, and that it was hard to believe that he could make the bitter speeches that he had heard attributed to him."

Twain did not realize the depth of emotion that the issue of free trade versus protection was then arousing in New South Wales. Sir Henry Parkes, four-time premier of New South Wales off and on from 1872 to 1891, in the 1880s had become known as the "high priest of free trade." He had marshalled up the merchants and professions to oppose the squatters and landowners, and had been kept in office because of his personal charisma and the excellent content of his speeches on free trade. But during the early nineties, the overseas price of wool fell, and the squatters who owned vast tracts of land from Queensland to

---

3. *A Connecticut Yankee* was written between February 1886 and May 1889.

South Australia began to see the burgeoning unionization of shepherds, shearers, drovers, and other pastoralists as a threat.[4] In 1895 Parkes, though mostly retired from public office, announced his candidacy late in the year, running as a protectionist.

While Twain had not intended to comment on partisan politics, his remarks were interpreted by the rival paper as precisely that. Although the afternoon paper, the *Australian Star*, had on Saturday pointed out that "probably in no land outside his own country is Mark Twain more appreciated than Australia," in an angry editorial on Tuesday it denounced Twain's remarks: The *Sydney Daily Telegraph* had trapped Twain into saying

> slanderous matter concerning Sir Henry Parkes .... It is understood that he came to Australia to lecture for money, and not to discuss party politics, and if he had a tithe of the common sense he is credited with possessing he would have decided to leave the subject of party politics severely alone. Nor would he have been guilty of the meanness of making disparaging remarks, on hearsay, concerning Sir Henry Parkes, who is not nearly so black as he has been painted by Mark Twain's malicious mentor. [*Australian Star*, 17 Sept., p. 4.]

But Twain had roused further ire. *Progress and Poverty* by Californian Henry George had been published in a Sydney newspaper. He had visited Australia in 1889, lecturing to large ready-made audiences. Although some Australians may have perverted George's ideas into their own hope for land nationalization (as, indeed, Twain seems to have done in Sydney) and though they may have confused his notions with what would be known in Australia as the single tax doctrine, his work nevertheless had a great influence in the debates of the early nineties.[5]

Twain said he had read George and some others on land nationalization and their idea to "let the Government own the land, and lease it to people who would work it, and not leave it lying idle" seemed to contain "a measure of justice. But I do not see," he continued, "how so prodigious a revolution like that could be brought about without stopping dead and starting again; and to do that would mean a sort of revolution that is not to be brought about in this world except by bloodshed" (*Sydney Daily Telegraph*, 17 Sept., p. 5). The *Australian Star*

---

4. Vance Palmer, *The Legend of the Nineties* (Melbourne: Melbourne Univ. Press, 1954; rpt. 1980), pp. 70–74.

5. Ibid., pp. 74–77.

editorial advised that "having cursed Parkes and protection and flat-
tered the single-taxers Mr. Clemens should go a step farther and boom
Mr. Reid [then premier who was running for reelection], and his general policy. A[t] any rate he ought to ask the Premier to preside at
his first lecture." Besides, the *Australian Star* pointed out, "nobody has
fought harder for an international copyright law [than Twain] .... He
wants plenty of protection for his own books" (17 Sept., p. 4).

That was Twain's first and last sally into Australian politics. He did
tell Low that "it seems to me that you've got right at the basis of things
if you have that strong third party with the best men in it. It doesn't
matter what their views are, so long as they are the best men. And
having thoroughly established my reputation for humour by talking of
politics seriously, I shall stop" (*Sydney Morning Herald*, 17 Sept., p. 5).
Twain met the great Sir Henry two evenings later at the Athenaeum
Club, where the two exchanged toasts and public compliments. After
the *Australian Star*'s angry editorial the only thing reporters were able
to induce Twain to say about politicians was that "it is easy to see that
they are able men, and remarkable men, or they would not be in these
positions" (*Sunday Times* [Sydney], 22 Sept., p. 4).

Mostly the latter part of the conversation concerned contemporary
literature, especially humorous literature—Sydney's *Bulletin*, London's
Punch, and New York's *Puck* magazines, as well as contemporary
"greats" like Kipling, Du Maurier, and Stevenson. To the question
whether Twain considered his works "to be more correctly described as
'witty' or 'humorous,'" the author responded "without hesitation that
he did not think them witty, but that he did think they were humorous.
Wit, he thinks, is something that flashes itself upon the hearer; humor something that scintillates and meanders. Wit need not be funny;
humor must be funny" (*Sydney Daily Telegraph*, 17 Sept., p. 5).

When Low said, "Mr. Clemens, it has been said more than once
that you are the laziest man in the world," Twain revealed a personal
attitude toward work.

> I think that is a mistaken notion. I don't think there ever was a lazy man in
> this world. Every man has some sort of gift, and he prizes that gift beyond
> all others. He may be a professional billiard-player, or a Paderewski, or a
> poet—I don't care what it is. But whatever it is, he takes a native delight
> in exploiting that gift, and you will find it is difficult to beguile him away
> from it. Well, there are thousands of other interests occupying other men,
> but those interests don't appeal to the special tastes of the billiard cham-

pion or Paderewski. They are set down, therefore, as too lazy to do that or do this—to do, in short what they have no taste or inclination to do. In that sense, then, I am phenomenally lazy. But when it comes to writing a book—I am not lazy then. My family find it difficult to dig me out of my chair. [*Sydney Morning Herald*, 17 Sept., p. 5.]

Of this leisurely interview and stroll Herbert Low later recalled, "I was in Twain's company nearly every day that he was here, and always, when the subject was broached, he disclaimed all knowledge of even familiar, standard books. This was not affectation, I am sure; he had read a little, and relied upon his immense powers of observation and sense of contrast for the rest" (*Worker* [Sydney], 2 Apr. 1908, p. 11).

Discovering that Twain did not eat lunch and therefore had nothing to do until three, when he "had promised to meet a gentleman at his hotel"—possibly from the Sunday *Truth*—the reporters strolled with Twain to Town Hall, where he tried out the acoustics, around the Domain with Twain commenting on the wood-cobbled streets, around Mrs. Macquarie's Chair, and finally back to the Australia Hotel.

A "Quite Unwarrantable Attack"

This attitude about laziness and work, recorded by both the *Sydney Morning Herald* and the *Argus*, perhaps helps explain another opinion held by Twain which was reported only in Melbourne, and which raised "a chain explosion of protest" in the Victorian capital.[6] The Melbourne paper printed Twain's comments about his former friend, fellow Californian, and fellow exile to Britain, Bret Harte: "But mind if I speak strongly it is merely a personal opinion."

I detest him, because I think his work is "shoddy." His forte is pathos, but there should be no pathos which does not come out of a man's heart. He has no heart, except his name, and I consider he has produced nothing that is genuine. He is artificial. That opinion, however, must be taken with some allowance, for, as I say, I do not care for the man. It is purely a personal criticism. I dare say, when I go to London, I shall meet him, but what of that? I am most moderate in my dislikes. There are only three or four persons in the world to whom I have had any antipathy, and the Almighty has removed most of them. It does seem wonderful that I should not have been allowed to get at them before they died. [*Argus*, 17 Sept., p. 5.]

---

6. Coleman O. Parsons, "Mark Twain in Australia," *The Antioch Review* 21 (Winter, 1961–1962), 455–468, quotation p. 458.

Twain's outburst against Harte may seem a bit excessive, particularly without context or explanation. That it was a "personal opinion" and was based as much on a dislike of Harte's personal life and habits as on the "shoddiness" of his literature requires emphasis. In his autobiographical dictations some ten years later, after Harte's death, Twain said: "Bret Harte was one of the pleasantest men I have ever known. He was also one of the unpleasantest men I have ever known."

> He was showy, meretricious, insincere; and he constantly advertised these qualities in his dress .... He hadn't a sincere fiber in him. I think he was incapable of emotion, for I think he had nothing to feel with. I think his heart was merely a pump and had no other function. I am almost moved to say I *know* it had no other function .... When he died in London, he had been absent from America and from his wife and daughters twenty-six years.
>
> This is the very Bret Harte whose pathetics, imitated from Dickens, used to be a godsend to the farmers of two hemispheres on account of the freshets of tears they compelled. He said to me once with a cynical chuckle that he thought he had mastered the art of pumping up the tear of sensibility .... When Bret Harte started east in his newborn glory thirty-six years ago [1870] with the eyes of the world upon him, he had lived all of his life that was worth living. He had lived all of his life that was to be respectworthy. He had lived all of his life that was to be worthy of his *own* respect. He was entering upon a miserable career of poverty, debt, humiliation, shame, disgrace, bitterness, and a world-wide fame which must have often been odious to him, since it made his poverty and the shabbiness of his character conspicuous beyond the power of any art to mercifully hide them.
>
> There was a happy Bret Harte, a contented Bret Harte, an ambitious Bret Harte, a hopeful Bret Harte, a bright, cheerful, easy-laughing Bret Harte, a Bret Harte to whom it was a bubbling and effervescent joy to be alive. That Bret Harte died in San Francisco.[7]

Twain's opinion of Harte was mainly colored, according to the record in the *Autobiography*, by his having abandoned his wife and children, his doing sloppy editorial work in his various newspaper assignments, his sponging off friends including Twain's family, his refusing to pay debts (including a debt of fifteen hundred dollars to Twain), his failing to honor writing contracts for which he sometimes had even received an advance, his drinking excessively, and, finally, his allowing himself to be "kept" by various women throughout his life and at the time of

---

7. *Autobiography*, ed. Neider, pp. 136–138.

his death.[8] In short, it was his inability, as Twain saw it, to "persuade himself to do a stroke of work until his credit was gone, and all his money, and the wolf was at his door; then he could sit down and work harder—until temporary relief was secured—than any man I have ever seen."[9]

Yet the Australians either were not aware of these transgressions against Twain's sense of decency or else they did not care. Of course, Twain had no way of knowing how popular Harte was in Australia, that his books were widely admired, and that several of his stories, especially "The Luck of Roaring Camp," had appeared on the stage in Sydney and Melbourne off and on for two decades prior to 1895. The next day the *Argus* published a letter from "Forty-niner" defending Harte. "Fortunately," he said,

> the position Francis Bret Harte occupies in the estimation of all who love the beautiful in fiction is too secure to be affected by the spiteful utterances of Mark Twain . . . . [Twain] must be indulging in one of those obscure jokes which pass current as American humour. Only those who have lived as I did for years in the mining camps of California in the palmiest days of the gold-fields know how true to nature, how exact in every detail, are those wonderful word-pictures handed down to us in . . . *Outcasts of Poker Flat* [and other stories]. There is no writer of English fiction at the present day whose works have enjoyed a wider circulation than those of Bret Harte, and in my humble opinion they will continue to delight posterity long after such samples of slipshod English as The £1,000,000 Note and the *Yankee at the Court of King Arthur* have been forgotten. Bret Harte is a child of genius, a scholar, and, above all, a poet. Mark Twain is—well a humourist. [*Argus*, 18 Sept., p. 6.]

"Melburnian" wrote the next day that " 'Forty-niner' has hit out very straight from the shoulder; [Twain's was a] quite unwarrantable attack on a most delightful and popular writer . . . . I hope Mark Twain is not going to stud his coming lectures with ill-natured notices of his literary *confreres* [including, no doubt, Max O'Rell], most of whom are very great favourites with us benighted Englishers" (*Argus* [Melbourne], 19 Sept., p. 6).

But this was not the end of the matter. Controversial interviews had appeared on 16 September and in three papers on Tuesday, 17 September; letters and editorial comment followed them on Wednes-

---

8. Ibid., pp. 325–327.
9. Ibid., p. 323.

day and Thursday. On Friday a letter from "Croppy" good humoredly charged that neither "Forty-niner" nor "Melburnian" had a sense of humor. Rather, Twain had engaged in "a mild, and additionally seductive, form of advertising" in slandering Harte, and it had come out "pretty neatly, and very cheap, in the guise of an interview with a press representative." Harte "*may* shoot him ... but ... in all probability they would go round the corner, hunt up Mr. Marratta, their genial consul, and over gin cocktails or some other equally abominable American invention, have 'some laughs'" (*Argus* [Melbourne], 20 Sept., p. 6). This was certainly the effect of Twain's comments—to generate interest in him and to justify in people's minds why they liked one or the other or both writers—even if that was not the intention.

In Saturday's editions both the *Argus* in Melbourne and the *Australian Star* in Sydney carried editorials discussing Twain's comments on humor that had appeared in the *Sydney Morning Herald* and on Bret Harte that had appeared in the *Argus*. The *Australian Star*, possibly because it was still piqued with the supposed insult to Sir Henry Parkes, was rather severe with Twain, implying he was ill-humored and lacked taste in literature.

The *Argus*, whose reporter had elicited the remarks about Bret Harte, was kinder. Admitting there are many kinds of humor, not all appealing to all tastes, it found nothing unusual in some liking Harte, some Twain, some both, and some neither. Citing a literary historian, Scotsman John Nichol, who had said that "Mark Twain ... has done more than any other writer to lower the tone" of written English, the *Argus* suggested that taste in humor has cultural biases: Twain's

> preference of [New York] *Puck* to [London] *Punch* is in no way astonishing. Each represents phenomena which appertain to its own country .... The gulf at this point cannot be bridged. But what seems to have amazed many of our readers is the fact that, in the opinion of the author of the *Tramp Abroad* and the *Jumping Frog*, the author of *Truthful James* and the *Luck of Roaring Camp* is a writer of "shoddy." To hold the critic guilty of personal animosity for entertaining this frank opinion is to be unjust. The work of Mr. Clemens is everywhere characterised by penetrating good sense and by an uncompromising contempt of shams and cant. [21 Sept., p. 6.]

Twain had the opportunity to redeem himself in the brouhaha over Harte when he talked with an interviewer from the *Sunday Times* on Friday. In general, Twain stuck by his "spiteful utterances" against Harte: "I said that a criticism of Bret Harte from me could have no value, as it would be tainted with prejudice." He did, however, apologize to the "unoffending public" and expressed a willingness to "modify my language, not my opinions. I have a full right to my opinion concerning anybody's literature, and concerning the writer of it also, but I have no right to state those opinions publicly in unparliamentary language" (*Sunday Times* [Sydney], 22 Sept., p. 4). When Mrs. Clemens entered the room, she scolded her husband's "great mistake .... I think it would be better if your wife saw your interviews in print before they were published." Although Twain would again be asked by reporters about Harte, he had made peace with his readers, who apparently were willing to believe "that you in the rush of talk intrude your private feelings upon the public, and no one has a right to do that" (*Sunday Times* [Sydney], 22 Sept., p. 4).

Even so, the following Saturday a Sydney weekly agreed with a reader that his use of "sham and shoddy ... showed bad form and if possible worse judgment." Admitting that there may be two opinions on the subject, the editor wrote, "For our own part we think there is little comparison as humourists ... between the two writers; but of course that has nothing to do with the 'Jumping Frog' order of humour, where doubtless no one would be readier [than Harte] to grant the 'greatest American humourist' the easy pre-eminence" (*Freeman's Journal*, 28 Sept., p. 14). Twain finally ended the matter nearly a month later when he asked reporters in Adelaide to let it drop.

The youthful Sydney reporter Herbert Low, whose interview for the *Sydney Morning Herald* and Melbourne's *Argus* had elicited the outbursts from both Twain and the Australians, recalled a dozen years after the episode that Twain "was a great-hearted, great-minded, man, his one tinge of bitterness—or, perhaps, it was a natural defect—becoming apparent in his dislike of Bret Harte, to whose genius he could not be brought to grant praise of any sort" (*Worker* [Sydney], 2 Apr. 1908, p. 11).[10]

"The Great Hi Ham"

On Tuesday and Wednesday, the family apparently rested and went sightseeing. Columnist "Asmodeus" from the Sunday paper,

---

10. For an extended account of Twain's criticism of Harte, see Sydney J. Krause, *Mark Twain as Critic* (Baltimore: Johns Hopkins Press, 1967), pp. 190–224, and Margaret Duckett, *Mark Twain and Bret Harte* (Norman: Univ. of Oklahoma Press, 1964).

the *Truth*, claimed to have "strolled round to interview the man" on Tuesday. That garrulous reporter printed a full three columns of jokes, mainly about Australian journalism and politics, subjects Twain had blundered into on Monday. Admitting that "my recent interview with Mark Twain ... was something of a failure," the "interviewer" did not quote any remarks by Twain (*Truth*, 22 Sept., p. 1).

Another article in the same issue began by stating that Twain "was a stranger and we took him in. He asked to be taken in." Twain is supposed to have been "weary to death of the interviewer and the garrulous newspaper man .... I went for a walk t'other day, round your Do-main; round Man o' War Bay or whatever you call the place, and con-found me if I didn't have half-a-dozen newspaper reporters strolling round with me all the time .... Then I went to a photographer, and I'm blessed if the whole press gallery didn't come too" (*Truth*, 22 Sept., p. 5). The newsman quoted Twain as having said, "I had a look in at a very charming Australian comedy on Monday night—'Joseph of Canaan,'" but if the Clemenses did see that play—an extravagant and extremely popular pageant—this is the only record of it. "To this hour," concluded the article, "we don't know whether we saw 'Mark Twain' in the flesh or whether we were had by some mad wag." It seems more likely that readers of the *Truth* were "had" by "some mad wag" of a reporter, for most of the "quotations" from Twain could easily have been patched up from reports in the *Sydney Daily Telegraph* and *Sydney Morning Herald*.

It is possible that Twain spent Tuesday evening in the smoking room of his hotel "with a few attentive listeners" telling an anecdote printed in the *Australian Star* on 16 December, the day before he was scheduled to return from New Zealand. According to that report, Twain asked companions if they knew anything about someone who had impersonated him as a lecturer and who was buried in Melbourne around 1879. But he found no clues to the mystery in Sydney, nor did he when he asked journalists in Melbourne a few days later. He also told a short joke about the relative popularity of his books and those of Thomas Bailey Aldrich in Rome: "Oh, yes, [said the bookseller], I have heaps of [Twain's books] in stock; the cellar is full of them .... I can't sell a blessed volume at any price" (*Australian Star*, 16 Dec., p. 20).

At two o' clock on Wednesday, Twain met a different representative from the *Evening News*, an inexperienced interviewer who said he "had no business attempting an interview" and kept apologizing for his lack of expertise. The young man, who had discovered a few days ago that Twain had read the book he had once written, was probably Australian writer Louis Becke, not formally affiliated with any newspaper at that time. In other interviews Twain repeatedly praised Becke's volume *By Reef and Palm*, and before he left Sydney he wrote to Becke encouraging him to collect and publish all the stories of the Sandwich Islands he could find.

Becke asked him about his collaboration with Charles Dudley Warner on *The Gilded Age* and about the prototype of Colonel Sellers, who Twain said "was a very real personage, and, indeed, the man could not be exaggerated" (*Evening News*, 21 Sept., p. 3). These two writers gossiped about American authors Thomas Nelson Page, George Washington Harris, Artemus Ward, and especially Twain's friend and former lecturing partner George Washington Cable, and their relative popularity and literary merit. On Monday, Twain had told the *Sydney Daily Telegraph* that when he served in the Civil War, he had mainly spent his time in retreat. On Wednesday he elaborated on this, explaining that while in the Confederate army he "was engaged in retreating the whole of the fortnight [that he served]. Then my company became so fatigued that we couldn't retreat any more .... I should have got fatigued earlier had the company marched in the other direction." He also talked briefly about his career as a Mississippi River pilot, a subject he usually avoided while in Australasia.

It appears that later that same afternoon (18 September), Admiral Cyprian Bridge, commander of the Australian Fleet, had a tea aboard the warship *Orlando* to which the Clemenses were invited. On Wednesday evening, Twain was entertained at the Athenaeum Club by about a hundred members and guests including Irishman Michael Davitt, then lecturing to large audiences on home rule for Ireland, and Sir Henry Parkes, who presented Twain with his book of poems.[11]

Parkes, now eighty years old, born on 27 May 1815, the son of a tenant farmer in Warwickshire, had migrated to Australia in 1839. His biography sounds enough like Twain's to leave little wonder that the two found instant companionship. Parkes had tried his hand at various businesses, all of which had gone bankrupt. He had been a journalist—the editor and proprietor of the New South Wales paper the

---

11. *Sonnets and Other Verse* (London: Kegan Paul, Trench, Trubner, & Co., 1895).

Empire (which also went bankrupt); it was through his powerful editorializing on behalf of "the little man" and his masterful speeches—despite his thick northern brogue—that he became one of the colony's most important politicians. When Twain was in Australia, Parkes, whom the *Bulletin* had long called "the Great Hi Ham," was the subject of almost weekly cartoons on free trade and protection. He is always recognizable by his white mane and effulgent beard, which he had begun wearing in 1862 and which had been white at least since 1872 when he first became premier of New South Wales.

Twain's hair also fascinated the Sydneysiders as his most striking asset and became the feature—in addition to his "Murkan" accent, or "twang" as they often called it—usually satirized in the press. In the letter to "Moorabinda," a weekly gossip columnist writing as "Sappho Smith" crooned:

I'd love to run my fingers reverently through Mark Twain's silky grey hair .... He might think it's the custom of the country which almost grew the veteran Parkes, and bear with me in consequence as one upon whom hair had an unforseen effect. I prefer Mark's pretty hair to his eyes, which he kept half-closed at his first 'at home' .... I think Mark quite fills the eye as a lion. Small, spare, nervous, and thickly-maned, with a platform manner quite his own, he really looks Mark Twain. Thank heaven! [*Bulletin* (Sydney), 28 Sept., p. 12.][12]

Like Twain, Parkes was also—intermittently—an author, not only of political material, but of poems; in 1862 one critic had written of him: "We read of great men amusing their leisure hours with carpenter's tools, and we never imagine that the results of their handiwork displayed much skill. Mr. Parkes has amused himself with iambs and anapests instead of saws and chisels."[13]

The *Sketch* (London) had called his latest work—the one that he gave Twain—"a valiant little book, full of fresh, youthful enthusiasms, and evidence of mental and physical health." On 19 October, after Parkes had announced his intention to marry, the *Bulletin* quoted this remark from the *Sketch* and the verse used to illustrate the youthful enthusiasms:

---

12. W. E. FitzHenry's unpublished history of the *Bulletin* identifies the twenty-seven-year-old Alexina M. Wildman as Sappho Smith (National Library of Australia, Canberra).

13. Quoted in A. W. Martin, *Henry Parkes* (Melbourne: Oxford Univ. Press, 1964), p. 6.

> I count it the mercifullest part of all
> God's mercies, in this coil of eighty years,
> Is that no sense of being disappears
> Or fails.

The *Bulletin* joshed that "there is a shriekingly funny lie current just now about the evident non-failure of *one* sense of the virile old gentleman's being" (28 Sept., p. 13). However, Parkes was not yet married, and the *Bulletin*'s cartoon depicting the meeting between him and Twain suggested the affinity between the two elderly gentlemen without the retrospective raciness that Parkes's marriage lends it.

At the Athenaeum Club the toast was proposed by the chairman, Edmund Barton, QC, who would become first prime minister of Australia upon federation on 1 January 1901. It was "responded to in an extremely felicitous speech by Mr. Clemens, who concluded by moving the sentiment, 'Advance Australia.' " The slogan is commonly attributed to Parkes who was a prime mover in the Australian federation movement then being considered in the colonies. In *More Tramps Abroad* Twain wrote, "About the best humourous speeches I have yet heard were a couple that were made in Australia at club suppers—one of them by an Englishman, the other by an Australian" (p. 78). It is tempting to believe that one of them was by Sir Henry Parkes at the Athenaeum Club. Unfortunately, no record of Twain's remarks seems to have survived, nor of the responses to Twain's toast offered by Sir Henry, who had a "magnificent reception," Justice William Windeyer, and Attorney General J. H. Want, QC. The latter two were principals in the notorious Dean Case, that was at the moment dormant but that would again flare into public display within the week before Twain left Sydney. Three weeks later Twain would become satirically involved in the case. Barton visited privately with Twain in Melbourne, promising to provide him with a complete file of the Dean Case.[14]

Meantime, the newspapers were advertising Twain's first appearance the next evening, and shrewd entrepreneurs were promoting them-

---

14. Notebook 35, Mark Twain Papers, Bancroft Library, University of California. All previously unpublished words by Mark Twain quoted in this book are ©1988 by Edward J. Willi and Manufacturers Hanover Trust Company as Trustees of the Mark Twain Foundation, which reserves all reproduction or dramatization rights in every medium. They are published here with the permission of the University of California Press and Robert H. Hirst, General Editor of the Mark Twain Project at Berkeley. Hereinafter they will be noted as MTP:NB35.

selves and their wares under Twain's ads. One of these unlabeled advertising columns—a feature of Australasian newspapers Twain found annoying—announced on the front page of a Sunday paper among other gossipy notes, the following: "Mark Twang (see it) while in town dines at the John Bull Catering Co.," "Outside the States, says Mark Twang, the John Bull Catering Co. beats them all in charges," "Mark Twang says, for breakfast, dinner, or tea try ...," and "Mark Twang on food—Try the John Bull .... Do you more good than my lectures. Don't forget now." Booksellers, not so cleverly perhaps, simply advertised lists of their Twain titles, and *Samuell's Guide to Sydney* printed a recent letter from Smythe endorsing it as one of the best guide books Twain had seen. Arnott's biscuits was also not slow to see the advertising potential of Twain's popularity.

"This Boomerang Recital"

The first "At Home," as Twain's performances were called, was held in the Protestant Hall, billed in Smythe's advertising as "the best hall in Sydney," easily seating 2000. The auditorium, at 236–240 Castlereagh Street, was variously described as "crammed from floor to ceiling" (*Argus* [Melbourne]), with the "many unable to find seats ..., spread out against the wall like the unfortunate Mr. Wheeler, who getting mixed up in the machinery of a carpet factory, was returned to his widow in 14 yards of three pile carpet" (*Sydney Daily Telegraph*, 20 Sept., p. 5). The numbers did not lessen as the week continued.

It was Twain's popularity as an author that roused the Sydneysiders, but his presence did not disappoint them. Virtually everyone in the audience felt "that an old friend—a personal friend, who had been speaking words of wit and wisdom to them from away back—had come to town" (*Sydney Daily Telegraph*, 20 Sept., p. 5). All five dailies reporting on the performance recorded a "burst of applause that hailed him when he first stepped out on to the platform," calling it "instinct with affectionate recollection ..., a spontaneous expression of love and admiration" (*Sydney Daily Telegraph*, 20 Sept., p. 5). The *Australian Star*, that on Tuesday had editorialized against Twain's political views, reported "such an ovation, such an outburst of uncontrollable enthusiasm as but rarely comes within the experience of the average man. The man's work and the feeling of it was evidently in the hearts of his audience, who not only cheered but waved hats and handkerchiefs as he stepped out from behind the Stars and Stripes" (20 Sept., p. 8). The *Sydney Morning Herald* said few could "remember anything more spontaneous, heartier, or more prolonged" than the "roars of welcome" (20 Sept., p. 5).

Twain's response was genuine—the ovation "quite overcame the lecturer, and some moments elapsed before he had recovered sufficiently to proceed," as the *Argus* put it (20 Sept., p. 5). When he did recover himself, he "said in tones of evident emotion how deeply he felt the warmth and cordiality of the reception, that was but a continuation of the friendliness and hearty welcome extended en masse and individually since his arrival" (*Australian Star*, 20 Sept., p. 8).

The only thing conventional about Twain was his clothing: he wore a black claw-hammer evening suit with patent leather shoes, but even that could not obscure his personality. Laying his watch on the small table that was his only stage furniture, he planted his feet "some little distance apart, a hand sometimes in his trousers pockets, some times [sic] placed up against his cheek, and the elbow supported by his other arm, whilst his eyes ... had the appearance of being closed .... [He] never once raised his voice above a conversational pitch." He walked "with a 'toddling motion,' not in itself an indication of age, but like the lines on his face, part and parcel of his drollery" (*Sydney Daily Telegraph*, 20 Sept., p. 5). These mannerisms, along with his "pince nez for style and spectacles to see through, as he puts it" (*Evening News* [Sydney], 20 Sept., p. 4), would be characteristic throughout the Australasian tour.

The lecture, which lasted an hour and a half, was a "medley of anecdotes and personal experiences, to which were appended some moral put in the quaintest way" (*Argus* [Melbourne], 20 Sept., p. 5), a "string of inimitably funny stories" (*Sydney Daily Telegraph*, 20 Sept., p. 5), told "in his own peculiar drawl ...., long-drawn and strangely-punctuated" (*Australian Star*, 20 Sept., p. 8). There were three somewhat distinct lectures, and the one that became known as the "First 'At Home'" began with the tale of the young boy who, returning from a truant fishing excursion, finds a corpse in his father's office. Huck Finn's struggle with his conscience over freeing Jim was called "the crowning effort of the evening ...., the choky bit," which came in the middle of the lecture. Other tales reported by the papers included the buck-jumping horse, the German language lesson, and the lost dime story (also called grandfather's old ram). Twain claimed that he was working on a moral discourse that "will some day take the lecturer a week of Sundays to deliver" (*Melbourne Punch*, 26 Sept., p. 203). "Anecdote, story, sketch, reminiscence, and the dryest aside tumbled over each other" (*Sydney Morning Herald*, 20 Sept., p. 5).

And the reaction of the crowd set the standard for Australasian audiences. They hung "trembling all the time between tears and laughter" (*Australian Star*, 20 Sept., p. 8). A well-known lawyer, so the *Sydney Daily Telegraph* said, "shook from the shoulders downwards from beginning to end," while a "popular comic artist, sat, as he invariably does when he is entertaining particularly humorous thoughts, without a smile on his face" (20 Sept., p. 5). It is tempting to guess that this was "Hop" from the *Bulletin* who would do several cartoons of Twain in the next few days. Livingston Hopkins, an American to the end of his life, credited America's "austere" Puritan stock with producing the finest humorists, including Twain. "Humour thrives best," "Hop" wrote, "under hard conditions .... The cheerful image stands out best against a dark background."[15] Presumably the audience were not disappointed, for at the next performance the building was again packed, and Twain was greeted "with a cordiality scarcely less demonstrative than that accorded him on the occasion of his debut" (*Sydney Daily Telegraph*, 23 Sept., p. 3). And by Saturday the papers were advertising an added show "in compliance with many requests."

The second entertainment took place two evenings later, on Saturday, 21 September. Again the hall was filled; many who could not find seats "seemed quite content with standing room," and they gave the speaker "another tremendous burst of applause ... as he came quietly on to the platform" (*Australian Star*, 23 Sept., p. 3). Tuesday's bitter editorial in the *Australian Star* may have still been fresh in Twain's mind, and on Tuesday morning the *Argus* and the *Sydney Daily Telegraph* had printed editorials, which, although not bitter, were not entirely favorable. Moreover, on Friday Twain had talked with the interviewer from the *Sunday Times*, who informed him of the press coverage of his remarks about Bret Harte and through whom he apologized to his public. When he stepped onto the stage, greeted "by a storm of applause ... from floor and gallery" (*Sydney Daily Telegraph*, 23 Sept., p. 3), Twain said:

---

15. Dorothy June Hopkins, *Hop of the "Bulletin"* (Sydney: Angus and Robertson, 1929), pp. 8–9.

[he] hoped he would never do anything to lose their good will which he understood was not merely the good will of a day or two—not merely the good will of, say, the day before yesterday—but of a good long standing. (Loud applause.) He hoped he would never do anything to forfeit it, but he should always strive to do his best to be worthy of their kindness. [*Australian Star*, 23 Sept., p. 3.]

Promising to get up a "sermon on morals—he did not know anything about morals—(laughter)—except good ones—(loud laughter)—but he could rectify that difficulty" (*Australian Star*, 23 Sept., p. 3), he began with a tale about his first interview in which he cast the journalist into a trance from which he never awoke. The *Sydney Daily Telegraph* found it to be "the most successful and the most enjoyed" sketch of the evening. Perhaps it was because of the recent tiff in the press over Twain's opinion of Bret Harte that his audience especially enjoyed his saying that Australian interviewers, compared to American ones, were "as truthful as *Hansard*," the official record of Parliament. He let his audience in on a secret, which, he said, "he didn't wish to go any further than a newspaper" (*Sydney Morning Herald*, 23 Sept., p. 6).

He told different stories in the second "At Home," giving his adventures as a Nevada editor who nearly got into a duel, the tale of the negro Henry searching for his mother, and Uncle Dan'l's ghost story. "The introduction of gold field 'slang' terms in the history of the death and burial of Buck Fanshawe was effected without allowing the 'slang'— so often objectionable—to be anything except very amusing" (*Evening News*, 23 Sept., p. 4). The program was made up "largely [of] readings from memory .... The humorous pieces were agreeably varied by selections which evinced his power of touching the deeper sympathies" (*Sydney Daily Telegraph*, 23 Sept., p. 3). All the reviewers pointed out that in the usual sense of the term, "Mark Twain doesn't lecture at all. He rambles on with the set purpose of rambling .... he starts out ... stops halfway through ... digresses a little more, and at the widest circle of this boomerang recital drops back of a sudden on the tag, or the moral, or the lost point of his anecdote" (*Sydney Morning Herald*, 23 Sept., p. 6).

"If Your Rhymes Rhyme Then There Is No Sense in It"

The "Third 'At Home,'" given on Monday night, became the favorite on Twain's tour throughout Australasia. An overcrowded house of sweltering listeners heard a "sort of continuation of the [lecture] preceding it" (*Sydney Daily Telegraph*, 24 Sept., p. 3). Laying his spectacles, his watch, and a book on the table—apparently a new flourish—Twain began what would become known as the "Morals Lecture," with some off-handed comments about how the events of boyhood "crop up later on in the form of maxims to guide his future life" (*Sydney Daily Telegraph*, 24 Sept., p. 3). This introduced the stolen green watermelon story followed by Adam's diary in Eden, which Twain read from his book. Jim, Huck, and Tom contemplating a crusade to the Holy Land, "The Notorious Jumping Frog of Calaveras County," which was "funnier still," and the blue jay story followed, and the reviewers from the morning papers—no doubt meeting a deadline—gave rather detailed reports of these.

All the papers commented on the transitions between his anecdotes. They form

the most painless kind of progression. The transitions pass unnoticed, and if you forget just exactly the point where the *raconteur* began that is only because ripple after ripple of laughter has obliterated the first impression .... He doesn't give you breathing-space to take his good things up critically and examine them; but each time invites you to come along and listen to his next, which is always better than the one before. [*Sydney Morning Herald*, 24 Sept., p. 6.]

The transition between the stolen watermelon and Adam's diary was "the sort of connection that there is between an apple and a watermelon" (*Sydney Daily Telegraph*, 24 Sept., p. 3). The reviewer for the afternoon paper *Australian Star* stayed until the end of the performance, and he emphasized the portion that the morning papers had omitted. He reported, nearly verbatim, the first rendition of Twain's "Australian Poem," which was destined to become a favorite for the remainder of the tour, even in India and Africa.

If I am going to write a book about this trip round the world, why a book of such a character ought to have some poetry in it. I felt that. So I was looking round for a subject .... Then I thought of the fauna of Australia .... I made a list of them and began .... I can say now that the most difficult thing in the world to do is to write poetry when you don't know how. You see it is the rhymes that make the trouble, for if you get the sense right, why then there is no word that will rhyme with it. If your rhymes rhyme then there is no sense in it ....

> Land of the ornithorhynchus
> Land of the kangaroo,
> Old ties of heredity link us.

And there you are. You see I am right against a dead wall. You can see there is nothing in the world that will rhyme with ornithorhynchus. Kangaroo? nothing rhymes with kangaroo. Of course you can slyly let it off without a rhyme, but it would fail.

I have got three more stanzas, but I wrote them on a separate piece of paper, not in my note-book. I was coming along and I met a man who said he was very hungry, and told me he had nothing to eat for two weeks, and really he looked as if he had nothing to eat for a good while .... He did look so hungry, so miserable, and I gave him the poem. [*Australian Star*, 24 Sept., p. 2; indentation of poem regularized.]

As Twain told this yarn around the continent it took on minor variations both in the poem and in the interpolated remarks. But not all his listeners agreed that it was impossible to find rhymes for use in an Australian poem, and several efforts were offered to the local papers. In Sydney, for example, the *Bulletin* carried a response to his reading in Melbourne:

I tried to make a poem about Australia, but gave it up in despair. I could get nothing to rhyme with kangaroo, *except* kangaroo.—Mark Twain.

> Why, says a man from Dandaloo,
> Does Mark make such a hullabaloo
> Bout finding a rhyme for kangaroo?
> Here's a rhyme—Tanmangaroo.

— ED. B. [*Bulletin*, 7 Dec., p. 28.]

The extra performance on Tuesday night filled the auditorium still at the rather high prices of five shillings for reserved seats down to two shillings for the chance that one would have to stand. The "First 'At Home'" was repeated, and the Lieutenant Governor and Lady Darley, along with a "fashionable company," sat in the front rows. Evidently not all the routine was from the first performance, for the *Sydney Daily Telegraph* said that stories of "previous evenings were repeated" while the *Sydney Morning Herald* (25 Sept., p. 5) mentions the "reference to 'burglars, lawyers, highwaymen—all that goes to make life happy,'" which was part of the "Second 'At Home.'" To the same welcoming ovation, Twain responded that he "knew he was a long way from home—that, of course, he knew—but ever since his arrival in Sydney he had been so kindly treated that he had never felt so" (*Sydney Daily Telegraph*, 25 Sept., p. 6). What the *Sydney Morning Herald* said of the second performance may sum up the entertainments: "He doesn't travel over the same ground; in fact, he doesn't travel over any ground. He mounts a balloon and throws out anecdote, story, incident, scraps of dialogue, short readings from his books, and spontaneous (at any rate they seem spontaneous) observation" (24 Sept., p. 6).

The assessments of the weekly press add little to the factual record. The *Bulletin* catered to the humorous with its hyperboles: Twain "presents a close, and perhaps, intentional resemblance to his portrait .... His head is like an amazed gum-tree" and his hair "gives him the wild expression of a man who has just found a baby's shoe in the soup." Even its criticisms were comic: his telling of the corpse story "lasted 15min., [sic] and in the Australian climate, where the deceased doesn't keep for any considerable period, this prolonged exposure was unwise." Overhearing two men claim willingness to give thirty shillings just to see him, "THE BULLETIN is of opinion that M. Twain could make a considerable sum by giving private back views of himself in his shower-bath at a guinea a head" (28 Sept., p. 8).

The regular Sunday column called "Our Telephone" carried a supposed telephone interview with Twain, satirizing several actual events that had occurred during the week—jokes about interviewers, his agent, the Australian "twang," Bret Harte, and, of course, Sir Henry. The thing that had most impressed Twain was "your parks."

Yes, we have some very beautiful parks ....

But you misunderstood me about the parks [Twain is supposed to have said]. No doubt you have ver' fine parks; but I was alluding to the old chap, your Sir Henry .... I have sort of prided myself on my mop, and reckoned on it staggering you some .... But your Sir Henry—he has the pull on me. I reverence that man's hair! ... I'm sure, had he lived his life in the States, he would have been President. That head of hair would have been irresistible. [*Sunday Times* (Sydney), 22 Sept., p. 5.]

One columnist quipped that since Twain's subject had been erroneously referred to as "The Knights of Wit and Humor," Twain "was doubtless for once amused by the way in which he received a title without any trouble" (*Sunday Times*, 22 Sept., p. 5). The *Sunday Times* said of the first performance that it "was somewhat thin and skimpy," and Twain's "repeated references to his watch" made it appear that he was trying to stretch out the entertainment and still save some for the next evening. Watching Twain himself "as he ambles through his chat" made the reviewer want to re-read his books (22 Sept., p. 7).

One emphatically dissenting voice was heard in a Catholic publication: "Peggy" saw Saturday's performance and found Twain no longer "a purveyor of coarse-grained fun," but instead "a quite uninteresting and almost insufferable old man—a tedious knifegrinder with no story to tell" (*Freeman's Journal*, 28 Sept., p. 6). After several humorous similes, "Peggy" said she "had sounded all the depths and shoals of endurance, but ... [Twain] flattened out all others in the sense of overwhelming weariness .... [He] doesn't make you laugh; he only makes you tired and cross." In nearly every town Twain would visit, some would dislike his performance, but so far as the printed record is concerned, it is decidedly a minority. The dissatisfaction, when it occurred, with the exception of Timaru, New Zealand, stemmed from the reviewer's having had a very high opinion of Twain's humor from reading his books. But in person Twain's slow pace, exaggerated accent, pointless stories, and in a few instances his age and frail health disappointed such readers. This was the case with "Peggy," although she did not emphasize that Twain was a writer not a speaker, as did most dissatisfied reviewers. Perhaps she would have liked the third performance, which contained the Australian poem, better.

"Paying Not Only Their Own Calls But ... Mine"

Mrs. Clemens and Clara attended almost all of Twain's performances. "Moorabinda" reported that, accompanied by Smythe, one could easily distinguish them at the theatre "partly because of the strong facial resemblance Miss C. bears to her father, and partly because they sometimes forget to smile at the lecturer's jokes" (*Bulletin* [Sydney], 28 Sept., p. 12). "Miss C. is a distinctly pretty girl, with ink-black hair and large dark eyes. She wore a black skirt with a yellow silk blouse and black gloves" while Olivia was in a black silk gown. Other reporters commented on Clara's "coal-black hair, *a la bandeau*, a style that suits about one in a thousand" (*Melbourne Punch*, 3 Oct., p. 222).

Of course, the Clemenses did not travel around the world solely for the purpose of earning money to pay off their bankruptcy. They also enjoyed the hospitality of individuals, as well as more formal entertainment such as that afforded Twain by the Athenaeum Club. Clara, for example, had barely arrived before she was joining a "numerous company" of the Society of Artists at a private showing of the works of Ethel A. Stephens, who was "at home" at her studio on Tuesday afternoon (*Sydney Morning Herald*, 18 Sept., p. 6).

At a dinner in London in April, Twain had met the wife of the commander in chief of the Australian Naval Station, "and she said her husband was able to throw wide all doors to me in that part of the world and would be glad to do it; and would yacht me and my party around, and excursion us in his flag-ship and make us have a great time"[16] Lady Bridge promised to write her husband so that he would be ready for the party, and the next week she sent Twain a letter of introduction to Admiral Cyprian Bridge. On Wednesday, 18 September, the Clemenses attended a tea given by Admiral Bridge at which they met visitors from Melbourne, including the vice-regal party and Miss Carter with whom Clara attended Saturday's horse race (*Melbourne Punch*, 3 Oct., p. 224). Admiral Bridge, Captain Fisher, and the officers were again "at home" to a large party at luncheon on the twenty-third when the *Orlando* was "gaily decorated with flags and evergreens" (*Evening News* [Sydney], 24 Sept., p. 3; *Sydney Morning Herald*, 24 Sept., p. 6). Aboard the flagship for a dance until six that afternoon, Mrs. and Miss Clemens met the lieutenant governors' wives and daughters, Lady and the Misses Darley and Lady and Miss Madden; Mr. and Mrs. S. M'Culloch, whom they would later visit in Melbourne, and numbers more. The programs bore "the Admiral's flag above the name of the ship and the date, and the band of *H. M. S. Oriana* played music" (*Australasian* [Melbourne], 5 Oct., p. 663).

They were also entertained at a rather private luncheon by Sir Henry Parkes not long before he announced his planned third wedding. Olivia described the old man to her adopted sister, Susan Crane: Sir Henry's second wife "had been his mistress. So she was not received in Society." His daughters by his first wife would have nothing to do with her, but since he had been widowed about three months when the Clemenses met him, the older daughters had "returned home and kept house for the father, and took care of the young children." Olivia guessed that the oldest was about fifty years old while the youngest was about two and a half. (Parkes had two separate families, the first six children born in the forties, and the last five born since 1889.) Sir Henry married

---

16. *Correspondence with Rogers*, ed. Leary, p. 138.

Julia Lynch in Parramatta on 24 October 1895, to the amusement or horror of almost everybody in Australasia. Livy's assessment was that "the other morning all this part of the world was startled by reading in the newspaper that [he] had married his housemaid, and that the daughters had again quitted the paternal roof. He said he could have married more advantageously from a worldly point of view but he preferred to marry for love."[17] The newspapers reported that even the little children's governess left!

On Friday afternoon, the Clemenses were luncheon guests of H. Pateson, the manager of the New South Wales Fresh Food and Ice Company; on being shown the premises, Twain "expressed surprise at the extent of the works" (*Sydney Daily Telegraph*, 21 Sept., p. 5). Refrigeration was only about a dozen years old at this time; it had made it possible for Australia and New Zealand to ship meat to England, and the colonists were understandably quite proud of this new industry. Twain marveled at its "flourishing in so comparatively small a community" (*Sunday Times*, 22 Sept., p. 2).

On Friday evening in Sydney, the family attended the second ball of the season at Government House. The occasion marked the social debut of Sir Frederick and Lady Darley's youngest daughter Sylvia and five other young ladies. The papers, listing the names of quite a few guests including the Clemenses, reported that six hundred attended. It was possibly because of the lieutenant governor's meeting the Clemenses at this ball that the extra Tuesday performance was scheduled to accommodate the vice-regal party, which had previously been totally committed to huge social functions, including another one upcoming for Monday night.

The Australian Jockey Club was having its annual spring derbies at Randwick the week the Clemenses were in Sydney—Twain would later joke fondly about the Australian obsession with horse racing—and on Saturday Clara, "in a rather tiredlooking garment" of cream color, attended the last day of the event with Miss Carter and other young ladies (*Bulletin* [Sydney], 28 Sept., p. 12; *Sydney Daily Telegraph*, 23 Sept., p. 3). (To the governor's ball Olivia had worn "white figured silk" and Clara "buttercup satin, with cream lace" [*Sydney Mail*, 28 Sept., p. 636].)

---

17. E. Daniel Potts and Annette Potts, "The Mark Twain Family in Australia," *Overland* 70 (1978), 46–50, quotation p. 47.

Clara recorded in her book that they also attended polo matches;[18] and they might have seen the steeplechase in which a horse called Mark Twain was expected to place third.

Mrs. Clemens not only saw to the everyday needs of her family, but she also took over as much of Twain's work as she could. After the *faux pas* over Bret Harte she seems even to have sometimes "interrupted" interviews before her husband said something that might offend the public whose good will they had come to cultivate. Besides scolding him about the "great mistake you made," in voicing his opinion about Harte, it was reported that when he was asked about Max O'Rell, she "divined what he was going to say, smothered the word by placing a delicate hand over his mouth, at the same time telling the writer to be sure not to put that in" (*Evening News* [Sydney], 16 Sept., p. 4). During the interview with Louis Becke, Mrs. Clemens acted as receptionist for another visitor waiting in an antechamber. Twain wrote to his friend Rogers that his wife and Clara "slave away answering letters for me half the day and night and paying not only their own calls but as many of mine as can be brought within their jurisdiction."[19] Twain did write a few letters, including one to Becke, thanking him for the copy of his book on the Sandwich Islands, which, Twain said, "stands the sharp test of a third reading .... Don't stop; search out *all* the Island tales and print them."[20] Twain also wrote to twenty-two-year-old Ethel Turner, who would become a prolific writer of children's books, whose publisher hoped she could elicit a complimentary statement from Twain to be used in promoting her new book *The Family at Misrule*.[21]

---

18. Clara Clemens Gabrilowitsch, *My Father, Mark Twain* (New York: Harper, 1931), p. 144.

19. *Correspondence with Rogers*, ed. Leary, pp. 188–189.

20. Alan Gribben, *Mark Twain's Library* (Boston: G. K. Hall & Co., 1980), I, 55. Twain's copy of the third edition of *By Reef and Palm* still exists, inscribed by the author.

21. These letters are in the Mitchell Library, State Library of New South Wales, Sydney.

CHAPTER THREE

Melbourne

"Almost in Love with the Platform Again"

While Livy and the maid were packing up the luggage on Wednesday, 25 September, for the train trip from Sydney to Melbourne, Twain rested, trying to stave off an attack by a new carbuncle on his calf. He wrote to his business manager and friend Henry Huttleston Rogers: "We have had a darling time here for a week—and really I am almost in love with the platform again."[1] And well he should be, not merely because of the salvos and waving handkerchiefs from both audience and critics, but because he had made a lot of money—the reason he had, at nearly sixty, set out on the venture round the world. On 3 October he would send Rogers, £437.13.6; on 1 January he would write that he had sent "about two hundred pounds a few days ago in Sydney; and by this present mail Mrs. Clemens expects to send about £850 more."[2] All these proceeds must have been from the Australian tour, not the North American phase, because then he had a different manager.

Though the records to determine attendance are practically nonexistent, it is possible to make some guesses. The Protestant Hall in Sydney held over 2,000 seats and was filled to overflowing four nights at two, three and five shillings per seat; at a conservative average of three shillings per seat, Twain would have grossed about £300 for each night. In Auckland, nearly eleven hundred seats were paid for each of three nights; at an average of three shillings, that would amount to

---

1. *Correspondence with Rogers*, ed. Leary, p. 188.
2. Ibid., p. 190.

about £170 per night. In the country town of Horsham Smythe required a guarantee of £35 for the appearance, but this was reached days before the performance and additional seats were sold at a reduced rate; the estimated audience would be around 300. In Invercargill, "it was rumored that a speculator had ... bought the house for £40 and disposed of about £120 in tickets at one to four shillings each."[3] And in Adelaide Twain reportedly earned £210 in a night, "a record for receipts."[4] Although the terms of the contract with Smythe are not known, it seems probable that he took twenty percent, the same fee paid J. B. Pond, the North American agent; of course, there were other costs as well. The *Bulletin* had claimed that the reason Twain paused so often during his performances was that he "could hear Smythe in the back-room counting the proceeds" (28 Sept., p. 23).

Leaving the Australia Hotel at four-thirty, the family and Smythe took the evening train to Melbourne. Twain later described the train as "American" because it had "a most rational sleeping car; ... clean, and fine, and new .... But our baggage was weighed and extra weight charged for. That was continental. Continental and troublesome" (*More Tramps*, p. 91).

As soon as the train stopped for breakfast, the party was handed a copy of *Melbourne Punch*, Victoria's version of the *Bulletin*, which carried the portraits of Twain and Mrs. Clemens made by Falk's in Sydney. Olivia and Clara "read the paragraphs, asking questions about the local jokes and allusions, and the public men satirised in pictures and text, with keen desire to know all about us," reported *Melbourne Punch* (3 Oct., p. 216). The previous issue had contained a cartoon satirizing various Melbourne politics and politicians as "jokes" that would rival Twain himself. When asked by reporters, the American refrained from voicing his opinion on the newspapers—except to say he thought highly of the *Argus*—but of these weeklies he wrote in his diary, "Punch (Melbourne) & Bulletin (Sydney) good papers. Good & bright cartoons in both; Bulletin bright enough to hold its own in any country."[5] If he saw the *Quiz and Lantern* in Adelaide, he did not leave a record of his opinion.

---

3. Parsons, "Mark Twain in New Zealand," *South Atlantic Quarterly*, 61 (1962), 51-76; quotation p. 55.

4. Parsons, "Mark Twain in Adelaide," *Mark Twain Journal*, 21 (Spring, 1983), 51–55.

5. Gribben, *Mark Twain's Library*, II, 682. From MTP, 14.

"Aubrey," the journalist on the train, may have been Herbert Low; he had ridden up from Melbourne the day before and boarded after breakfast at Seymour, about 125 miles northeast. He seems to have sold articles to the *Evening News* and the *Herald Standard*, both Melbourne papers, on the same day, adding a few notes in each paper the following day. He was known to Twain from the interview in Sydney Harbour the night of the *Warrimoo*'s arrival, for he reported that Twain said, " 'You have been kind to me "Aubrey." You let me down so easily in your first *interview*.' ... You want to break through all precedent and gush. You *must* come out with: He *has* soulful eyes ... " (*Evening News* [Melbourne], 26 Sept., p. 2.) Low had just then finished his work in Melbourne and gone to Sydney for a stint on the *Sydney Morning Herald*, the paper that had printed Low's "soulful eyes" interview.

The Clemenses had to change gauges about five in the morning, and, despite Mrs. Clemens's "acute attack of rheumatism, the result of changing trains at Albury ... on a bitterly cold night" (*Melbourne Punch*, 3 Oct., p. 222), the venture lent itself to humor in the interview: "I must say I believe in early rising—for everyone but myself. Personally, I can always excuse myself for not getting up so very early .... I can't understand ... how it is that one has to change trains at Albury. Break of gauge, or something of that sort, isn't it?" (*Herald* [Melbourne], 26 Sept., p. 1 [2nd edition]).

"Aubrey" tried to explain to Twain. The "colonies are not yet civilised up to the federalising standard, and ... they have not learned to cooperate in trading and travelling affairs for the good of the whole community. But this is a political problem, and Mark Twain confesses: 'I am no politician .... ' So one—like the Australasian Premiers—drops federation" (*Herald* [Melbourne], 26 Sept., p. 1).

"Aubrey's" allusion was to one of the most vexing problems of the nineties. The first federation conference had occurred in Melbourne in 1890, the result of the almost single-handed effort of Sir Henry Parkes, then premier of New South Wales. His main argument in favor of federation was that the seven disparate colonies (including New Zealand) lacked adequate defense and were unable to raise such defense should it become necessary. Although the conference received extensive publicity in the press, the public practically ignored it, being more concerned with the looming conflict over unionization in western Queensland, protection versus free trade in New South Wales, the tottering banks in

Melbourne, and the growing numbers of non-English immigrants appearing in ports from Darwin to Adelaide. It is even possible that the conference did more harm than good in that it gave "the average man an impression that federation was an abstract thing, far removed from current realities."[6] In the early nineties, politicians were not sufficiently in touch with the public; and until the public could be enlisted in the federal cause, it would get nowhere.

But there was another problem, perhaps more serious: the petty jealousies among the politicians from the cities, especially Sydney and Melbourne. Their excuse for opposing federation was that England was actually attempting to extend her control, which had been minimal, over a unified Australia. The second convention, in Sydney in 1891, drafted a constitution, but one that was not yet democratic enough to distract the average person from more concrete problems. The constitution underwent several revampings before it was finally adopted in 1901. Sir George Grey, representative from New Zealand at the Sydney conference, and A. G. Stephens of the *Bulletin* were instrumental in "bringing the whole mass of the people into politics."[7] In the middle nineties when Twain arrived in Australia, the movement toward federalization was stronger among the people and the newspapers than among the constantly wrangling politicians, who seemed mostly to fear that New South Wales would "annex" the rest of the country. Twain became aware of this fear, for while he was in Melbourne, he was told that Sydney's Sir Henry Parkes "proposed that New South Wales be named Australia .... Resented here in Victoria" (MTP, p. 56).

When it came to *More Tramps Abroad*, Twain, humorously but mincing few words, used the gauge change as a parable: It was

> the oddest thing, the strangest thing, the most baffling and unaccountable marvel that Australasia can show. At the frontier, between New South Wales and Victoria, our multitude of passengers were routed out of their snug beds by lantern-light in the morning in the biting cold of a high altitude to change cars on a road that has no break in it from Sydney to Melbourne! Think of the paralysis of intellect that gave that idea birth; imagine the boulder it emerged from on some petrified legislator's shoulders.
>
> It is a narrow gauge road to the frontier, and a broader gauge thence to Melbourne. The two Governments were the builders of the road and are the owners of it.

6. Palmer, p. 135.
7. Ibid., p. 151.

One or two reasons are given for this curious state of things. One is, that it represents the jealousy existing between the colonies—the two most important colonies of Australasia ....

All passengers fret at the double-gauge; all shippers of freight must, of course, fret at it; unnecessary expense, delay, and annoyance are imposed upon everybody concerned, and no one is benefited. [*More Tramps*, pp. 91–92.]

He then struck the same theme that had caused the *Bulletin* to quip: "Mark Twain's 'instinct teaches him that Protection is wrong!' A man's instinct teaches him a good many things that he has afterwards carefully to unlearn with the help of his reason—when he has any!" (28 Sept., p. 16). Twain continued:

Each Australian colony fences itself off from its neighbour with a Custom house .... We have something resembling it here and there in America, but it goes by another name. The large empire of the Pacific coast requires a world of iron machinery, and could manufacture it economically on the spot if the imposts on foreign iron were removed. But they are not. Protection to Pennsylvania and Alabama forbids it. The result to the Pacific coast is the same as if there were several rows of Customs fences between the coast and the East. Iron carted across the American continent at luxurious railway rates would be valuable enough to be coined when it arrived. [*More Tramps*, p. 92.]

Comparing railroad travel in Australia and America, Twain expressed disappointment that the outside car was no longer used in Australia, even though he himself seldom rode in it anymore. (He would remark on the romance of its existence in New Zealand.) Reminded that the seat covers were buffalo, Twain reminisced:

but not buffalo-buffalo. There are no buffaloes in America now, except Buffalo Bill .... I can remember the time when I was a boy, when buffaloes were plentiful in America. You had only to step off the road to meet a buffalo. But now they have all been killed off. Great pity it is so. I don't like to see the distinctive animals of a country killed off. [*Herald* (Melbourne), 26 Sept., p. 1.]

Being told the kangaroos were going the way of the buffaloes, Twain agreed: "Ah! I suppose so. And what a queer animal the kangaroo is. I haven't seen one, but I suppose it is." Then he made a joke about a favorite native bird, the kookaburra:

"I did see one of your native creatures while I was in New South Wales. That was the laughing jackass. It sat on a tree, and I stood looking at it.

But it wouldn't laugh for me. I tried to make it laugh; indeed I did; but it respectfully declined."

"Probably it didn't think you were funny," put in Mrs. Clemens who was sitting in the opposite corner.

"Probably not; but I did my best." [*Herald* (Melbourne), 26 Sept., p.1.]

This joke captured the fancy of the press and was illustrated by cartoonists in both Sydney and Melbourne. Later in the Adelaide zoo and other places he did see several kookaburras that *were* laughing.

Then Twain told about having his palm read from an unidentified photograph by four "experts."

Three of [the reports] were of no consequence whatever. They were right out of it. But the fourth one made a remark that made me think deeply. She said, "The owner of those hands has no sense of humor!" Well, you know, this made me wonder whether I haven't been deceiving the public for the last thirty years or so; and, worse still, deceiving myself! It is things like this that make a serious man muse. [*Herald* (Melbourne), 26 Sept., p. 1.]

"Obliged to Stick to Possibilities"

Saying that the family had a wonderful time in Sydney, Twain complimented the weather and the harbor and described it as Marcus Clarke had described Hobart:

The way it is broken up, with its hundreds of little forks and tongues of water breaking into the land—fringed round with blue inlets ... reminded me of a figure used by Marcus Clarke ... the way the water spread round and indented the land was like "melted lead spilt in water." That is, I say, one of the most perfect figures I have ever read. You know how melted lead, when you drop it in water, shoots in all directions—radiates—and that figure came forcibly to my mind when I was looking at Sydney Harbor. [*Herald* (Melbourne), 26 Sept., p. 1.]

Twain said Clarke's novel *For the Term of His Natural Life* was read by some in America; "but it is a work that is bound to be one of the most read as it becomes known, because it is a great work of art." Indeed, several times reporters noted Twain reading Clarke, whose collected works he bought while in Australia; and in one of his "lectures" he praised Clarke publicly. In December, back in Sydney, the family would be delighted with the melodrama made from that novel.

Mark Twain was greatly impressed with the Blue Mountains, "the most felicitously named of any natural object he has ever seen."

They are of a blueness not to be paralleled in the world. They are of a blue
that is a blue. So many of the so-called "blue" mountains are not blue at all.
They lack the quality of intensity, or something, and they are only a name.
The blueness of your Blue Mountains has life in it. It seems to have a light
from behind, and is endowed with spirituality. [*Evening News* (Melbourne),
26 Sept., p. 2.][8]

"Your gum trees," he said, in answer to a question, "require long
study. I think I should grow fond of them. I know I would try to very,
very hard. They look so reproachful, and grave, and serious. I am to
be introduced to some of them one day before I leave. So far I have
not made any nearer approach than an acquaintance with Bosisto's Eu-
calyptus oil." On his way between Melbourne and Adelaide he again
remarked on the gum trees.

After describing in *More Tramps Abroad* the change of trains at Albury, Twain then said they had breakfast "at the station." This error,
though misleading, would not be serious, but it was compounded when
he placed a New South Wales town somewhere in Victoria, south of
Seymour. After the breakfast, Twain wrote, "The air was balmy and
delicious, the sunshine radiant; it was a charming excursion. In the
course of it we came to a town whose odd name was famous all over
the world a quarter of a century ago—Wagga-Wagga" (*More Tramps*,
p. 94). The train did indeed go through Wagga Wagga, but, since that
town is in New South Wales, it would have passed there around midnight. Twain apparently kept no notes on this train trip, and therefore
he would have been relying on his memory when writing the seven
pages of *More Tramps Abroad* about the Tichborne claimant. He had
followed this case as it went through the courts in London, and he
claimed actually to have met the man. No doubt Twain was reminded
of the episode upon seeing pieces about it in the Sydney newspapers
during his stay there.[9]

This tale of intrigue, though repeated at length in his travel book,
is, after all, not used to give a lesson in geography but rather to sub-
stantiate the axiom that truth is stranger than fiction, or, as Twain and

8. In *More Tramps Abroad*, p. 92, Twain placed the Blue Mountains in the "early sun"
near Albury; but it is more likely that he saw them in the setting sun the evening
before. One Australian reviewer drew attention to this error.

9. Louis Budd, *Our Mark Twain* (Philadelphia: Univ. of Pennsylvania Press, 1983),
pp. 119–129, notes Twain's addiction to reading newspapers, from which he got some
lecture material.

Pudd'nhead Wilson put it, "Fiction is obliged to stick to possibilities; Truth isn't. Truth can outrage all the possibilities, and get off unrebuked; but there is a fine fuss whenever Fiction ventures to make even the poorest little try at the miraculous" (*More Tramps*, p. 97). He sets out the facts—the posh existence in France and England of the Tichborne heir, his visit to South America and subsequent disappearance at sea; the bereaved mother who advertises worldwide for the return of her son; the impostor, a fat Wapping butcher who knows neither French nor English, but who has been to South America and now plies his trade in Wagga Wagga; the reunion in France with the indulgent mother; the supposed recognition of all his old friends whose language (French) he has forgotten (but not Spanish); and eventually the expensive London trial that concluded only when the baronet's betrothed brought forward a sealed envelope deposited with his banker these many years ago. Any self-respecting fiction writer would "lose his courage" before inventing such implausible facts (*More Tramps*, pp. 94–100).

The mystery of the Tichborne claimant made a good introduction to the mystery about Twain's own funeral (or that of an impostor) for which he had hoped to find the answer in Australia. Unfortunately, "the Sydney journalists had never heard" of it; but Twain was confident he would have it cleared up when he got to Melbourne, where the funeral was supposed to have taken place around 1881 (*More Tramps*, p. 102). Twain left his readers hanging for over fifty pages before spinning out the rest of that yarn.

"The Much-Travelled" at Home

The party was met in Melbourne at the Spencer Street Station by about 200 people; the official greeting party made up of members of the Institute of Journalists, American consul Daniel W. Maratta, and other Americans had trouble getting through the crowd. Institute members who welcomed Twain included the vice president, S. V. Winter, owner of the Melbourne *Herald*, and John Lamont Dow, former minister of works, former *Age* journalist, and now editor of the *Leader*, an agricultural weekly owned by Melbourne's *Age*. Although Winter seems not to have been caught in the recent land "bust," Dow was not so lucky—in 1893 he had gone bankrupt to the tune of about £26,000. Dow himself was acquitted of fraud, but most of his cronies were not, and when his party was swept out of office in the 1894 elections, Dow began a crusade in the *Age* to keep banks from foreclosing on farmers.[10] Though Twain probably did not know of Dow's financial embarrassment, nearly everybody else must have, and they certainly knew of Twain's.

For Twain's manager, Robert Sparrow Smythe, the triumphant entry into Melbourne with Mark Twain in tow must have been particularly gratifying. He had first come to Melbourne in 1855 and after working as a music and drama critic for newspapers in New South Wales and South Australia he made his home for many years at "Highgate-on-the-Hill" in Deepdene, Melbourne. He was born in March 1833, in Lambeth, London, making him even older than Twain, about whose great age at the time of the Australasian tour the newspapers and later scholars have remarked. Smythe had worked in London as a proofreader on such works as John Timbs's *Curiosities of London*, Alexander Dyce's *Shakespeare*, Thomas Carlyle's later books, and his edition of Ralph Waldo Emerson's *Essays*. He seems to have studied law reporting, for he was competent in shorthand. When he immigrated to Australia searching for better health, he was quickly employed as parliamentary reporter on the *Register* in Adelaide. He soon founded and edited the *Illustrated Post*, the first illustrated paper in Australia, and he had journalistic practice with the *Age* in Melbourne.

Smythe's first experience as a theatrical manager came in 1862, when he accompanied the tenor and soprano team, the Bianchis; that was followed by a five-year tour with French violinists Poussard and Douay, in whose singing company he met Amelia Bailey, a popular Melbourne coloratura soprano who became his wife during that tour. He also managed the French pianist Boulanger and the eccentric German tragedian Daniel Bandmann. In 1863 he had begun touring abroad, in Asia, India, and South Africa, he became the first manager to conduct a company in Japan after the port treaty, and the first to take professionals into the Himalayas (in whose foothills his son was born) and into the Transvaal.

His first Australian "discovery" was the Reverend Charles Clark, a popular Baptist preacher in Melbourne who occasionally read Dickens at the Athenaeum Hall; Smythe piloted him around Australasia annually for four years, eventually going to America, Canada, and South

---

10. Michael Cannon, *The Land Boomers* (Melbourne: Melbourne Univ. Press, 1966), p. 33.

Africa. After the success with Clark, he began to specialize in lecture management about 1872, taking Australians to Europe and America, and bringing to Australia scientists, explorers, and literary personalities. He squired around the likes of English astronomer R. A. Proctor, journalist G. Augustus Sala, litterateurs Annie Besant and Moncure Conway, preacher Dr. Thomas De Witt Talmage (whose visit to Sydney and Melbourne earlier in the year was not successful), and explorer Henry M. Stanley, who recommended Smythe as Twain's manager. It was in the company of war correspondent Archibald Forbes that Smythe had first approached Twain at his home in Hartford, Connecticut, in 1882.[11]

In the nineties, with his son Carlyle G. Smythe, he was agent for Max O'Rell, whom Twain so thoroughly disliked, baritone Charles Santley, and Sir Charles and Lady Halle. Although there were other managers in Australasia, Smythe was widely respected as one of the best, and was a sought-after companion for his varied experience, genial disposition, and excellence as a raconteur. In September 1895, he announced tour management as his full-time occupation, using as his trademark "the much-travelled." When he was quarantined aboard the *Cuzco* (returning from Adelaide to book Twain's Melbourne farewell), his son the "more-travelled" started accompanying Twain, beginning in Ballarat.[12]

Melbourne was the largest city in Australia in 1895, boasting about 490,000 residents, sprawled over a vast land area. The central downtown portion already had, as a result of the land boom of the early nineties, many of the buildings that still form its center. Some of the buildings were as tall as twelve stories and had high-speed lifts. Melbourne had a brand new fish and meat market built for £210,000, which was the subject of several political jokes. It had four daily papers and over twenty weeklies or monthlies, several of which still publish.

The Clemenses resided at the Menzies Hotel while in Melbourne, and on the afternoon of his arrival Twain rested. He had slept poorly

---

11. *Referee*, 30 May 1917, p. 14; *Argus*, 24 May 1917, p. 6; *Town and Country Journal*, 30 May 1917, p. 47, *Some Melbourne Notabilities*, pp. 198–199.

12. The *Bulletin* (21 Sept., p. 13) wrote: "R. S. Smythe and his two sons are now all in the entertainment business. They are known respectively as the Most, the More, and the Much Travelled." However, the only evidence I can find that Smythe had a second son is that on 18 October, while the senior Smythe was quarantined aboard the *Cuzco*, "Mr. Clemens was introduced to the Mayor [of Stawell] by Mr. Robert Smythe" (*Stawell News . . . and Chronicle*, 19 Oct., p. 2); and *Tasmanian News* calls Carlyle Smythe "a" son of R. S. Smythe (2 Nov., p. 2).

on the train and suffered from the pain of the carbuncle that soon would confine him to his room. In a parlor he entertained an interviewer from the *Age* amid "clouds of tobacco smoke" (27 Sept., p. 6). "He had to pull himself together for next evening's lecture, so he rested for the day with the aid of a pipe and a book, which was no other than *For the Term of His Natural Life*."[13] He compared Australia with America rather than with Europe, this time for its "tall city buildings made possible by the use of the rapid hydraulic lift such as they have in America. It is not so in Europe yet, he tells us. 'They still stick to the old slow going lift that carries two people and a half, and you arrive at old age on your trip to the sixth floor'" (*Age* [Melbourne], 27 Sept., p. 6).

Twain complimented the Australians for having both the ability to adopt the "swift lift and the electric wire, and the sentiment that preserves the old plough that turned your first sod." No doubt this was something the Australians appreciated, especially at this time when they were conscious of a developing national identity.

As the conversation turned to Twain's own works, the author said that "a humorous book has not the same chance of life as a narrative . . . for it depends on its style, in which the taste changes." He professed to believe that his book "which is likely to have the most permanent effect" was *A Connecticut Yankee*, in which—the reporter interpolated—"some very powerful, political and social lessons are cleverly interleaved . . . . [It is] a power wherever it was widely read, especially in the democratic colonies of Australia." Twain once more expressed disapproval of those who, having seen only the fringes of a country, write travel books "out of their colossal incapacity for the job" (*Age* [Melbourne], 27 Sept., p. 6).

"Is He Dead, Mark?"

Melbourne's "First 'At Home'" was the next evening, Friday, 27 September, at the Bijou, which had been closed but was reopened, as the *Bulletin* put it, "for a short season of Bret Harte—no, Mark Twain" (28 Sept., p. 8). It was not the largest theatre in Melbourne, and, before the week was over, people not only were filling the orchestra pit but were sitting three rows deep around the back and

---

13. Twain's copy of this book still survives; see Gribben, *Mark Twain's Library*, I, 145. According to the *Bulletin* (19 Oct., p. 13), Twain acquired all but one of Clarke's books while he was in Melbourne.

sides of the stage itself. The newspapers had reported that an hour before the box office was to open on 24 September, people had begun
to queue up to buy "the more desirable positions" and that "to prevent
crushing and inconvenience, the management resorted to the expedient
of distributing numbers .... Half an hour after the first seat was marked
off the greater portion of the dress-circle and nearly the whole of the
stalls had been reserved, and the cry was 'Still they come' " (*Evening
News* [Melbourne], 24 Sept., p. 1).

Among those no doubt in the "more desirable positions" were various political and social luminaries, Olivia and Clara Clemens, Edward
FitzGibbon, who would preside during Twain's visit at the Yorick Club
the next evening, and the Honorable James Service and Sir James Patterson, both former premiers.[14] There was also a large contingent of the
clergy of several denominations; evidently some parishioners thought
it inappropriate to attend such frivolous entertainment, for later in the
week both the Catholic and the Anglican papers defended such innocent pleasure.   The Protestant paper answered the criticism that
Twain's material was old, out of his books: "Is there any reason why
we should have a brand new lecture all to ourselves?" The thing that
really puzzled "John Quill," however, was that "people with no pre-
tence to a sense of humour have ventured to hear Mark Twain." He
overheard an old woman on the tram who objected to Twain's moral
principles advocated on Monday and Tuesday nights; she "thought
they were calculated to do a great deal of harm." Her companion
agreed that picturesque lying was "positively awful, and said the young
men of Australia were inclined to go astray quite fast enough without wickedness being made attractive to them." In fact, the two old
ladies "didn't believe there was no such thing as an ornithorhynchus.
That was only another of his fairy tales" (*Australian Weekly*, 4 Oct.,
p. 8).

Unlike the old ladies in the tram, most Melbournians knew what to
expect before they bought their tickets. Even if they had not read the
Sydney papers, Melbourne publications had published interviews and
reprinted snatches of the reviews. On the day before Twain's first Melbourne show, an original review appeared of his opening night from
"A Correspondent" in Sydney. The intimate details and personal style

---

14. Patterson, the subject of a cartoon welcoming Twain to the city, died quite
suddenly on 30 October, before Twain left Melbourne.

in the short essay indicate it was probably by young Herbert Low. The "genial Smythe was all beams and smiles" at the packed hall and the "spontaneity of the warm greeting such as is given, or received, by a lover to his lady after an absence" (*Melbourne Punch*, 26 Sept., p. 203). The humorist was so "unnerved" and "impressed" that "after the show the writer heard him ask his manager if his wife and daughter were there to hear it." The correspondent said the anecdotes were "told in such a natural manner—as if he were in a smokeroom .... [It was] a lecture in which there is only pure amusement—nothing of an educational nature—he teaches us to be merry for an hour or so; but there is only the memory of having laughed to carry away" (*Melbourne Punch*, 26 Sept., p. 203).

The first Melbourne "At Home" mainly used the material of the "First" entertainment in Sydney but with some alterations. The lecture began with the truant fishing excursion and concluded with the German language lesson. Both these illustrated some moral, but, as one reporter pointed out, the "illustrations overbalanced the moral principles" (*Age* [Melbourne], 28 Sept., p. 7). In between came Huck's struggle with his conscience over freeing Jim, the man who fell into the carpet machine, the buck-jumping Mexican plug, and grandfather's old ram. He also told the jumping frog story and Adam's diary, which he had told in the "Third 'At Home'" in Sydney. And he told as part of the old ram yarn, the story "of the maiden lady who lent her No. 6 glass eye to another maiden lady who was 'excavated' for No. 7" (*Australasian* [Melbourne], 5 Oct., p. 655). Melbourne's "Second 'At Home,'" given the next night, was announced to be a repetition of this performance, but reporters who heard it both times liked it just as well the second time as they did the first.

The newspaper reviews of the Melbourne performances were highly appreciative, emphasizing the fact that Twain was like "a friend who has accompanied them on many a journey ... to make their life the happier with his humorous philosophy and wholesome wit" (*Age* [Melbourne], 28 Sept., p. 7). The *Age* commented on the "originality, the freshness, and above all, the abundant humor," the "quaint expressions and jests," saying that only twice did Twain bring out the pathetic. Melbourne's *Evening News* reported that only once did Twain reach "an impassioned ring"—in Huck's struggle with this conscience. Rather he

spoke "in slow, weary American accents that [fell] with limpid clear-
ness upon every ear ..., the same calm, languid, slightly monotonous
drawl, a medley of quaint anecdote, humorous sketch, and bizarre reflection, culled from his written works, and strung together by the very
slightest of threads" (28 Sept., p. 4).

There was, however, an innovation to the "At Homes" in Melbourne.
On the first night, "someone from the gallery cried out twice, 'Is he
dead, Mark?' "

> The lecturer did not catch the remark the first time; the next time he heard
> but did not understand. After the lecture he made special inquiries what
> that interjection meant .... It was an admirer paying back on him the mys-
> tification he inflicted on the poor guide who showed him the statute [sic]
> of Christopher Columbus. "Is the gentleman dead?" [*Argus* (Melbourne), 28
> Sept., p. 7.]

While in New Zealand he recorded in his notebook that the "Larrikins
of Sydney and Melbourne used to hail me 'Hello, Mark; good night,
Mark' and of course I responded."[15] But when he put the idea in *More
Tramps Abroad*, he not only wrote a more elaborate account but also
included an illustration in the Hartford edition, *Following the Equator*.

Saturday's repetition of the "At Home" was similarly well received,
although there was "a stray gap here and there in dress circle"—the
five-shilling seats. One reporter provided illuminating details about
Twain's performance: Unlike Dickens, who read his stories, Twain
"re-tells some of his best and funniest stories, revised and amplified
according to the humor of the moment, and containing many subtle
touches and vocal asides which would be ineffective in print, but which
on the platform are instinct with humor."

> For instance in telling the half humorous, half pathetic story of Huck. Finn's
> dilemma in sheltering a runaway slave, the author gives us in much greater
> detail than in the book the terrible struggle which goes on between Huck.'s
> sound heart and his "deformed conscience." The audience fairly roared with
> laughter at Huck.'s naive remark, "The truth is plenty good enough in ordi-
> nary places, but when you get into a tight place you can't rely on it," just as
> they accentuated with their perfect silence the pathos of the hunted slave's
> cry across the water, rendered with tears in his voice by the author, "Dah
> you goes, de ole true Huck., de bes' frien' poor Jim ever had, de ony frien'
> poor Jim has now." [*Age* (Melbourne), 30 Sept., p. 6.]

---

15. *Notebook*, ed. Paine, pp. 256–257.

The reporter said also that "it was worth much to hear Mark Twain tell with such dry humor the story of the jumping frog. Mrs. and Miss Clemens, who occupied one of the boxes, and to whom the story must be as familiar as a household word, could not restrain their merriment as he told it" (*Age*, 30 Sept., p. 6). Of this collection of stories the weekly *Melbourne Punch* wrote:

> he rambles on to the stage, bringing all his wealth of hair with him .... [and] composes himself to sleep, like a horse standing up. He closes his eyes, rests his head lightly on his right hand, which in its turn is supported by the left arm folded across his chest, and then – commences to talk in his sleep .... For nearly two hours he keeps in that sleep .... Such are the impressions that we feel after seeing and hearing Mark Twain, the greatest humorist and entertainer (not lecturer) of the present day. [*Melbourne Punch*, 3 Oct., p. 218.]

About eighty-five members and guests of the Yorick Club, an organization of professional and literary men, entertained Twain at supper after his performance on Saturday night, 28 September. Members of the medical profession, the bench, the bar, journalism, academia, public service, the military, and the dramatic arts were all there. The guest's health was proposed by the chairman, E. G. FitzGibbon, CMG, and Twain was welcomed "with a storm of applause." He expressed "his gratification at the warm welcome and generous hospitality with which he had been received in Sydney and Melbourne, although he modestly admitted that it was thoroughly deserved," reported the *Argus* (30 Sept., p. 6).

Twain made a rather lengthy address, which was reported verbatim in the *Australasian*, the weekly paper owned by the *Argus*, and which was reprinted in several other papers. He was of the opinion that Australia "should be branded and trade-marked as 'the cordial nation.'" His audience cheered agreement that

> there is one fact ... which stupid people who speak the English language all over this world are prone to overlook or to ignore, and that is—let us chaff and jaw and criticise one another as we please, when all is said and done, the Americans, and the English, and their great outflow in Canada and Australia are all one .... Oh yes! blood is thicker than water, and we are all related .... We do belong together, and we are parts of a great whole—the greatest whole this world has ever seen—a whole that, some day, will spread over this world. [*Australasian* (Melbourne), 5 Oct., p. 615.]

Little did he suspect that before he left Australasia, England and America would be tottering on the brink of war over a border dispute in South America.

Most of the speech was devoted to his Mississippi River experiences, the only time on his Australasian tour that he would talk publicly about them. Laughter interrupted the speech throughout; when it was concluded, the evening "proved the best ever enjoyed by the members since the club was founded in 1868." Mr. Kaye sang a song especially adapted from "Tommy Atkins," as follows:

> Oh, Markie, Markie Twain,
>> You're a good 'un heart and hand,
> You're a credit to your calling
>> And to your native land.
> May your heart be ever faithful,
>> May your love be ever true,
> God bless you, Markie, Markie Twain,
>> Here's our country's health to you.

Toasts to the "Stars and Stripes" by Mr. Deakin, MLA and one of the younger federation politicians, who would subsequently become Australia's second prime minister; to "Literature" by *Herald* director Theodore Fink, MLA; to "Guests" and to the "English Language" by Judge Molesworth, who within the fortnight would again rule on J. L. Dow's £26,000 bankruptcy; and to "The Chairman" by Professor Kernot concluded the evening.

"Packed Like Sandwiches"

On Monday night, 30 September, "people were packed like sandwiches into the boxes, the gallery was brimming over, there were two perspiring rows of spectators in the orchestra, and a side glance at the wings showed a background of eager faces." Even the minister for mines, Harry Foster, had to sit on the stage; yet money had to be returned to those who could not get into the theatre (*Argus*, 1 Oct., p. 6; *Evening News* [Melbourne], 1 Oct., p. 6). That night and Tuesday, 1 October, the performances included the stories that in Sydney had been known as the "Second 'At Home.'" The *Age* called the prologue "a delightful piece of dry humor, something complete in itself, and one of the smartest and neatest of his inventions in that particular class" (1 Oct., p. 6). This referred to the introduction to the morals sermon, recorded for the first time in this third Melbourne performance, although he had used it in Canada and the United States in another form and perhaps in Sydney.[16]

With variations during the rest of the tour, the introduction claimed that its author had a little scheme for the moral perfection of the world. Every

> sin or crime had its moral value towards building up a character. It should be stored up as a lesson and a bulwark against the commission of that particular sin again. Hence to arrive at moral perfection it was necessary to go on and commit every known sin, so as to be strengthened against the repetition of it. There are only 354 crimes altogether, and an industrious man with strict attention to business could commit them all in a year. His character would then be complete. [*Age*, 1 Oct., p. 6.][17]

Although the "Morals Lecture" frame was probably used just to give an excuse for stringing together some of his favorite stories, it is tempting to think Twain actually had in mind writing a burlesque sermon when he began putting it together. When the *Age* interviewer discovered that Twain had contemplated "writing a burlesque on [Dr.] Talmadge," he said it "would no doubt have been appreciated in Melbourne after our own experiences of that eccentric individual." Twain continued by saying that, after reading the sermons in the New York papers, he thought he "could burlesque some of his performances without any impropriety" and so he bought the sermons. But Twain found "they were altogether different .... He had edited the book carefully, and it was quite a reasonable sermon .... Yes he cheated me badly" (*Age*, 27 Sept., p. 6).[18]

The stories that illustrated this character building included, as usual, first the stolen watermelon, followed by Huck and Tom's crusade to rescue the Holy Land. The decline in the art of picturesque lying was lamented and an example that "American humor alone can invent" was cited here for the first time. It was "the yarn about the meanness of the company that docked one of its men for absence while he was up in the

---

16. Lorch, "The American Phase," p. 61; a version of the introduction also appears in MTP, pp. 53–55.

17. The number of sins apparently changed at Twain's whim; however, in India he gave a little girl "a signed declaration ... that there were only 354 sins, and all the experts in the penitentiaries of the world had not been able to invent any more" (Carlyle Smythe, "The Real 'Mark Twain,'" *Pall Mall Magazine* 16 [Sept. 1898], 35).

18. Three of Twain's volumes of Talmage's works survive. See Gribben, II, 685.

air after being blown up by a premature blast" (*Age*, 1 Oct., p. 6). The worker "dematerialised from a man to a boy, to a doll, to a bee, and after being out of sight altogether he came back in the same proportions. 'Now,' said Mark, 'that man was only away from his work 15 minutes, and that champion mean man docked him his wages'" (*Evening News* [Melbourne], 1 Oct., p. 1).

In the Catholic weekly, "Tapley" defended Twain's humor against the apparent criticism of church-goers, reporting that his seatmate, "a stolid Englishman, who listened impatiently all through that most amusing story of the Incorporated Company of Mean Men .... turned to me and said,—'Well, that is about the most barefaced lie I ever heard. If he expects us to believe that he must take us for gulls'" (*Advocate* [Melbourne], 5 Oct., p. 14). Although other papers also reported that some humorless people attended but that they nearly always broke down and laughed, Melbournians generally liked these stories, probably because of the current political interest in issues like land reform, taxation, and the practice of "sweating."

Twain told the blue jay story, and the large number of clergymen "appeared to greatly relish" the christening story whose moral was not to jump to conclusions on insufficient evidence (*Evening News* [Melbourne], 2 Oct., p. 4). The pathetic tale of the slave mother separated from her son was relieved by the Australian poem, his duel while a Nevada editor, and Uncle Dan'l's ghost story. Twain had now begun to tease his audiences with the promise of improvements and additional stanzas to his poem, for "hitting on the golden secret of making all the ends of the lines words of one syllable he succeeded [in a rhyme], and the glorious result sent the house into convulsions" (*Argus* [Melbourne], 1 Oct., p. 6). On the next night, a rainy Tuesday, the audience knew what to expect, and when "he began to inform them that the poetic inspiration, 'which only attacked him every 30 years,' had just seized him, and caused him to commence a poem on the fauna of Australia, the audience went into convulsions of laughter" (*Age*, 2 Oct., p. 6).

The Bijou was "much too small to provide accommodation for all who sought admission" to the added performance on Wednesday night. The *Age*'s review of Tuesday's show, the so-called "Second 'At Home,'" promised, "To-night Mr. Clemens will make his last appearance in Melbourne, when he will repeat the greater portion of last night's At Home and add several of the most popular pieces from the first entertainment." No doubt, Smythe had provided the newspaper with this information when he had placed the advertisements, possibly thinking that the most popular pieces from each show would keep the audience up. That morning both the *Argus* and the *Age* had advertised "Second Mark Twain 'At Home' Introducing 'The Boy and the Corpse,' [from the first] &c." Twain was apparently not consulted about this advertising, for he complained in his notebook, "Got through this prodigious bill between 8.03 & 9.45 or 50. It was a sweater! And all because of an idiotic advertisement mixing the 2 lectures" (MTP:NB35). A few pages later, apparently referring to this fifth night (for nowhere else did he give five performances), he wrote that the "first 4 audiences take it [the watermelon story], for they know me through my books; but the 5th fights shy—don't quite know what to do" (MTP:NB35).

He opened by praising Australian author Marcus Clarke's *For the Term of His Natural Life*, regretting "that a book possessing so many attractions should now be out of print" (*Sydney Daily Telegraph*, 21 Oct., p. 5). The performance was "a repetition, more or less of those previously given" (*Age*, 3 Oct., p. 6). He mixed the watermelon story, examples of picturesque lying, and the German language lesson from the first series with the Nevada duel, the separated slave family, and the Australian poem from the second series of tales. Evidently, however, he did not tell the "boy with the corpse" (often called the truant fishing excursion) as promised by the paid advertisements. The *Age* said that the way the stories were received "suggested that from his lips they would well bear telling twice, indeed were as welcome as if redemanded"—forgetting that the audience, except for the reporters, was probably different each evening (*Age*, 3 Oct., p. 6).

In Melbourne Twain's carbuncle began to get the best of him and curtailed his activities. No doubt it was the carbuncle that caused Rolf Boldrewood, who called on Twain in Melbourne, "the greatest difficulty in the world to persuade him to take a drive" (*Critic* [New York], 25 April 1896, p. 286). By Saturday night at the Yorick Club, he was joking that the carbuncle "reminds me of its company occasionally. I have a greater respect for it than for any other possession I have" (*Australasian* [Melbourne], 5 Oct., p. 615). Furthermore, he lectured five consecutive evenings (skipping only Sunday), a far more grueling schedule than the one Smythe had planned for him in Sydney, and for a while he and Smythe were considering a matinee, apparently before leaving for Bendigo on 3 October.

Probably he continued reading Marcus Clarke's *For the Term of His Natural Life*, whose "dramatic power and vigor of writing" had "greatly charmed" him into thinking the book would "win for its author lasting fame" (*Sydney Daily Telegraph*, 21 Oct., p. 5). He evidently spent some time reading Louis Becke's *By Reef and Palm*, which he called "one of the best books that has been produced in recent years" (*Bulletin* [Sydney], 5 Oct., p. 16). Or he may actually have been reading *Seven Little Australians*, the book Ethel Turner had sent him, of which he had "had a glimpse" but explained "the days *are* so short ever since they made the mistake of arranging them in groups of 24 hours to accommodate the long-lived idlers of the dawn-time of creation."[19]

The *Bulletin* claimed that "Mark Twain is not much of a humorist to his wife and daughter. One who spent an evening with the trio in Melbourne" claimed,

> I was very much amused by the conversation of the Tramp Abroad. His quaint turns of expression and his sparks of wit kept me in a continual titter of merriment. But I noticed that the Mark-ess and Miss Mark took no live interest in pap's talk. Madame lolled in her chair and put on a faraway look, whilst Miss read "Love in Idleness"—a shilling's-worth of fiction in blue covers. Perhaps it is rather trying to spend a lifetime with a professional humorist, who is expected to be funny all the time. [12 Oct., p. 13.]

On the other hand, the polite ladies may have been trying not to eavesdrop on the reporter's conversation.

Meanwhile the Melbourne papers as well as the country papers were advertising that the humorist was leaving on Thursday, 3 October, to lecture at Bendigo for two nights. It seems he must have been planning to leave Livy and Clara in Melbourne for a few days because "Mrs. S. M'Culloch gave a tea and chatter party, to meet Mrs. and Miss Clemens at Oakdene, Toorak-road, Toorak" on Thursday, 3 October. Clara, who would become a concert pianist, "charmed everyone with her two well-executed pianoforte solos" (*Australasian* [Melbourne], 5 Oct., p. 663). At the last moment it became clear that Twain was too ill to travel, much less to work. A cancellation notice appeared in Bendigo's evening pa-

19. Samuel L. Clemens to Ethel Turner, 24 September, Mitchell Library of the State Library of New South Wales, Sydney.

per, and handbills were distributed to people as they arrived at the theatre where the performance was to have been held.

On 4 October, Dr. N. T. FitzGerald lanced the carbuncle and prescribed plasters, which Olivia solicitously applied for several weeks; Twain recovered sufficiently for the family, accompanied by Smythe, to take the overnight express train for South Australia on 11 October. During the enforced stay in Melbourne, Twain kept strictly out of the public eye. He read the newspapers and entertained callers, including on 10 October Justice William Windeyer, who had spent the night of 9 October in the Menzies Hotel on his way to Adelaide; Sydneysider and future prime minister Sir Edmund Barton; the Wagners, whose guests they would be when they returned from Adelaide; the Smythes; and several ladies (MTP:NB35). Evidently they were also dinner guests; for Twain noted the "table, table-ware & decorations beautiful & in perfect taste. No disposition to put the host's millions on exhibition" (MTP:NB35). In the meantime, Smythe had rearranged the country tour schedule for the last two weeks in October on the return from Adelaide to Melbourne.

CHAPTER FOUR

Adelaide

"Not Likely That Adelaide Will Be Behind"

The Clemenses and Smythe left Melbourne on the overnight express for Adelaide at 4:30 p.m. on 11 October. The trip took seventeen hours, and Twain claimed that they met several Sydney friends and some Americans on the train (*More Tramps*, pp. 112, 118).[1] Not far outside Melbourne the train stopped "to let out Dr. FitzGerald ... [at] one of those mighty estates" where the surgeon lived (MTP:NB35). On his return to Melbourne Twain offended Dr. FitzGerald "by asking for his 'bill' as if it were a tradesman's" (MTP:NB35). Traveling through the level countryside until dark, Twain remarked on the characteristic gum trees. In the morning passing through the "first 'scrub' I have seen" he saw for only half an hour "gums with lower half of each [a] bunch of foliage [of] a rich brown (stem), upper half a deep rich vivid assertive aggressive green," calling them "perfectly beautiful" (MTP:NB35).

Adelaide had four daily papers, two news weeklies, and another eight special-interest weekly or monthly papers. Saturday's morning paper carried, in addition to Smythe's advertisements, an appreciative editorial, or "leader" as the Australasians called it, welcoming Twain to

---

1. One was "a judge who was out on circuit, and was going to hold court at Broken Hill." This seems to refer to Judge William Windeyer; but he was in Adelaide attending a luncheon on 11 October; probably Twain was telescoping into the train trip a visit Windeyer paid him in Melbourne on the tenth when he gave Twain a "luminous & deeply interesting" story of the Dean poisoning case. Interestingly, Twain never mentioned Dean in *More Tramps Abroad*, although he told about Judge Windeyer's going to Broken Hill.

Adelaide. The editorial reminded that "Sydney and Melbourne have flocked in turn to hear the various good stories that have amused for so many years retold with the quaint manner and the 'Yankee' accent that add a fresh point to them. It is not likely that Adelaide will be behind the other colonies in her welcome." It continued, "There is something particularly fascinating in the oral delivery by a great writer of his own works .... Now, an increase of public curiosity as to the personal appearance and private life of public favorites is admittedly one of the marked characteristics of this age, and ... an author possessing the gifts required for a satisfactory appearance on the platform" should be highly successful (*Advertiser* [Adelaide], 12 Oct., p. 4).

Readers were perhaps reminded by this article that they might catch a glimpse at the railway station of the man whose appearance promised so much. However, Twain disappointed the crowd waiting there, for his party (along with American consul, C. A. Murphy) had left the train at Aldgate, some twenty rail miles southeast of the city, and instead meandered by open carriage for about two hours along the last twelve road miles through the wooded hill country, "which did *not* remind Mark Twain of the Sierra Nevada or the Pacific Slope" (*South Australian Register*, 14 Oct., p. 6). In *More Tramps Abroad*, Twain described how

> The road wound around through gaps and gorges, and offered all varieties of scenery and prospect—mountains, crags, country houses, gardens, forests—colour, colour, colour everywhere, and the air fine and fresh, the skies blue, and not a shred of cloud to mar the downpour of the brilliant sunshine. And finally the mountain gateway opened, and the immense plain lay spread out below and stretching away into dim distances on every hand, soft and delicate, and dainty and beautiful. [p. 119.]

At the South Australian Club Hotel, the party was informally welcomed by several local gentlemen, and Mr. Murphy's two young daughters presented the ladies with a flower basket (*Express and Telegraph*, 14 Oct., p. 2). Twain was particularly impressed with the flowers in South Australia, both native, like the wattle which he praised, and imported. Of the botanical gardens, he said, America "cannot have these paradises. The best we could do would be to cover a vast acreage under glass and apply steam heat ... in place of the Australian openness to the sky, the sunshine, and the breeze. Whatever will grow under glass with us will flourish rampantly out of doors in Australia" (*More Tramps*, p. 121). As his trip continued, he would be more conscious of the Australasian love of flowers and gardens, noting especially those in Hobart, Christchurch, Wellington, and, on his return, in the botanical garden in Sydney.

Shortly, Twain retired with reporters from the *Register* and the *Advertiser* into a private parlor where, from weariness after the "sultry" overnight journey, he reclined on a sofa "with an air of languor" explaining that he had smuggled "his carbuncle past the Customs officers .... It sits on me like the nation; ... it keeps quiet awhile, but at times it gathers itself together and gives an almighty hard twist. It's pretty vigorous" (*South Australian Register*, 14 Oct., p. 6). The carbuncle was well known to Twain fans since he had told the Yorick Club two weeks earlier that "I am entertaining a carbuncle unawares .... and it reminds me of its company occasionally. I have a greater respect for it than for any other possession I have in the world. I take more care of it than I do of the family" (*Australasian* [Melbourne], 5 Oct., p. 615).

The reporters were quickly impressed with his drawling accent, calling it "a constant protest against the hurry and worry of the nineteenth century." It was privately "even more pronounced than on the platform" (*Express and Telegraph*, 14 Oct., p. 2).

One of the yarns Twain used in the "Second 'At Home'" was about meeting

> an interviewer who desired to lay bare the soul of the humorist, and record the number of meals he ate in a day, and the size of his biceps, and the money he earned, and to that end put many torturing questions to the snared celebrity, and even suggested attractive replies. This didn't happen in this country, where the interviewers are as truthful as *Hansard*, but in America, where a shocking laxity prevails on this head. [*Sydney Morning Herald*, 23 Sept., p. 6.]

In Adelaide, Twain told the reporters that as long as a person had something to confess, interviewing was a good thing, but sometimes "the interviewed has nothing to say, and the interviewer does not know how to make him say it. Sometimes in despair they write up a lot the man never said, never intended to say, and couldn't say if he thought of it." The humorist claimed he had never interviewed anyone and warned against generalizing about the press: "there are all sorts and conditions of newspapers." Perhaps remembering the "interview" by Herbert Low in Sydney Harbour or perhaps the fanciful one in Sydney's *Sunday Times*, he said there are even some interviewers who work up half a dozen words into "a column of imaginative matter" (*South Australian Register*, 14 Oct., p. 6). Some unthinking people stamp "the whole Press with the character of the individual .... It is like the silly superstition that Americans habitually carry revolvers and shoot them off promiscuously for pastime, particularly in the Southern states .... I tell you it is not a fact" (*South Australian Register*, 14 Oct., p. 6).

Again Twain praised Kipling's writings; of his own books he liked *Huck Finn* best, but when asked about Australian journals he declined to "make comparisons, because it is about the worst way of forming an opinion" (*South Australian Register*). He had told the *Age* that Australian cities with their fast lifts and tall buildings were like American cities. And now that he had met more Australian people and actually spent time in their homes in Melbourne, Twain could say that the Australians were unself-conscious, frank, open, unreserved, independent, and not exclusive. "That is American and Australian, but not English. The Englishman has a sort of reserve, and a part of that reserve comes from native shyness and self-consciousness" (*Express and Telegraph*, 14 Oct., p. 2). Confined to his hotel in Melbourne, with sufficient time for visiting privately with several Australians, both men and women, he had first confided this opinion to his notebook. Evidently he was not merely trying to flatter his potential audiences with such a comment, and he would express similar sentiments throughout Australasia from Adelaide onward.

A question about racial feeling in America evoked a brief diatribe against "windy agitators and stump orators, [who do] not represent the real feeling .... I expect agitators are much the same breed all over the world." The Chinaman he felt was "a pathetic object, a poor hardworking industrious, friendless heathen, far from home, amongst a strange people, who treated him none too well" (*South Australian Register*, 14 Oct., p. 6). Twain may not have been aware just how suspicious and fearful of the "Yellow Hordes" Australians had been for at least a decade. At the time, the cartoons he would have seen in the *Bulletin*, for example, would not have revealed such a preoccupation, for elections were imminent and the issues were mainly economic. In Victoria Twain was quite aware that the main issue was the railroads, which were handed out as blatant political spoils. Still, readers of this interview probably agreed when he said:

Like most other Americans his views on the yellow question have undergone a change. At first the western states were strong in the assertion that the American Republic must be a shelter to all comers irrespective of race, but of later years they had come to see that the unrestricted influx of Chinese is a real danger, and now all are agreed as to the necessity for shutting the door on the Chinaman. [*Advertiser* (Adelaide), 14 Oct., p. 7.]

On the other hand, the Japanese Twain personally knew were "highly cultured gentlemen educated in our Colleges ..., superior person[s]" (*South Australian Register*, 14 Oct., p. 6).

The interview wound up with an exquisite tale about authorial intention and the composition of the jumping frog, which he would repeat to reporters in New Zealand. The story was, he claimed,

not a fiction but an anecdote taken from the lips of a resident of Calaveras country. The name "Smiley" was originally "Greeley," but the story appeared in a tottering weekly called the *New York Saturday Gazette*—"in the last number; it killed it," said Mark, modestly—and as the printers had run out of capital G's the alteration had to be made. [*Express and Telegraph*, 14 Oct., p. 2.][2]

If Twain had seen Saturday's papers when he arrived, he would have known that the previous afternoon, Friday, 11 October, Lieutenant Governor Samuel J. Way had held a farewell luncheon at Government House for the Reverend W. H. Fitchett, president of the Victorian and Tasmanian Methodist Conference, who was returning to Melbourne. In addition to several parliamentarians, Justice William Windeyer (who had toasted Twain in Sydney at the Athenaeum Club) was also in attendance. A New South Wales judge, Windeyer was on his way from Sydney to Broken Hill to preside at a case, and he had to get there by going to Melbourne (where he called on Twain) and Adelaide.

Windeyer was the judge in the notorious Dean poisoning case. The papers all over Australia carried daily reports of the new developments, retrospectives of the entire case, pictorial displays of the principal actors, and finally cartoons satirizing the outcome. In April, George Dean, a popular ferry-boat driver in Sydney Harbour, on her testimony and that of his mother-in-law, had been convicted of poisoning wife. When the jury was slow in returning a verdict the justice had

---

2. Parsons, "Mark Twain in Adelaide," p. 55, explains that even this story is not right. However, in Wellington Twain again told about the failure of the newspaper that first published the story: " 'The Jumping Frog' got even with [the publisher]. After that Saturday that paper of his never appeared again" (*New Zealand Mail*, 12 Dec., p. 51).

admonished "that he could not understand their long deliberating, because to him the matter seemed very simple. If the poisoning were not accidental, it was done by design, and either Dean or the woman had done it" (*Argus* [Melbourne], 27 Sept., p. 5). When he threatened to lock up the jury over the weekend, it returned the guilty verdict seven minutes later.

The death sentence passed by Justice Windeyer was commuted to life imprisonment by the Executive Council of Parliament. After public demonstrations led by Dean's supporters, a Royal Commission discovered, among other things, that Dean's mother-in-law herself had a criminal record in her youth (not an uncommon situation in colonial Australia); in July the Royal Commission found against the verdict, and Dean was given a free pardon. With Dean back at work on the ferryboat, his wife petitioned for support and was awarded twelve shillings per week. By 19 September, rumors that Dean had confessed to the attempted murder were so rampant that it became a matter for parliamentary discussion. Dean requested an investigation of the rumors, and on 27 September the Attorney General Want "said that he was informed by Sir Julian Salomons some days ago that Dean was really guilty." Then the case erupted into the most important news of the next fortnight. When Dean "broke down" (*Sydney Daily Telegraph*, 10 Oct., p. 5) and signed a confession implicating his counselor, Dean was charged with conspiracy to perjure, along with the lawyer and his clerk.

Public sentiment, which had ostracized Mrs. Dean, now swung in her favor and public subscriptions were launched for the maintenance of her and her infant. The case dragged on for months longer; finally the attorney was convicted of perjury, and, as late as 1910, he was defending himself in a public lecture to the Athenaeum Club. Twain had only to pick up a current newspaper in any one of the capital cities to be informed of all the particulars of the case. On 12 October, after the judge had had lunch with the lieutenant governor, the *Advertiser* reported,

> The judge found himself in sympathetic company .... Mr. Fitchett ... congratulated [Sir William] upon the complete turn in public feeling which had now taken place. He who had been abused and vilified was right .... We gather from eye-witnesses that the judge was moved to tears. When the time came for him to respond he completely broke down .... Those who were present tell us that his utterance was choked with sobs, and there was not a dry eye round the table .... Other things were said which those

who were present decline to repeat as too sacred for the public eye, but the whole scene is referred to as one which can never be forgotten. Before the party broke up the Rev. John Watsford had them all on their knees, and gave God thanks for the past and invoked the Divine blessing on each and all—especially on the one whose recent experiences had been so hard to bear. [12 Oct., p. 5.][3]

Of course, Twain was not at the luncheon and he may not have even read this short notice; it is even less likely that he saw the cartoon the following week in Adelaide's satiric weekly *Quiz and Lantern*, in which his caricature punned on the episode.

"The One Treat of Their Lives"

Smythe had been advertising Twain's two scheduled lectures for a week, calling him the "king of humorists," "der einzige," "the funniest man on earth," and "the greatest celebrity of all." He used snippets from reviews in Sydney and Melbourne and advised that "everybody should hear Mark Twain, for everybody is better for it." Twain was billed as having "just concluded the most successful series of lectures ever given in Melbourne and Sydney, hundreds being unable to obtain admission," and seats were completely sold out at five shillings for reserved stalls and dress circle (early doors one shilling extra). As had become his practice, Smythe issued the "positively no free-list" announcement when he was satisfied the house was sold; this meant that "even the wearied pressman, deprived by managerial success of his accustomed seat, took his laughter standing, and joined with the rest in giving the lecturer hearty welcome" (*Chronicle* [Adelaide], 19 Oct., p. 17). And Smythe did not fail to capitalize on the lieutenant governor's announced intention to visit Twain "At Home" both nights.

Promotional pieces had appeared in Adelaide newspapers as early as 17 September, Twain's first day in Sydney, when he was reported to have been "the target of numberless interviewers, to all of whom he poured out any amount of confidences, though never venturing a serious opinion on a serious subject"—a journalistic oversimplification to say the least. This notice, datelined 16 September, must have been wired by Herbert Low, the young reporter who had come in a launch into Watson's Bay. The language is the same as that extracted from Twain on the sixteenth and published in the *Sydney Daily Telegraph* the

---

3. Similar reports were wired to the Melbourne and Sydney papers.

next morning: "Mark Twain's hands would move up and down like two ships at sea; but he speaks with extreme deliberation, and in tones that we are wont to describe as nasal" (*Express and Telegraph*, 17 Sept., p. 3).[4]

The "tremendous reception at his opening lecture in Sydney" assured that his audiences would "be numbered by thousands wherever he goes," predicted *Quiz and Lantern* (26 Sept., p. 13). "If Mark as a lecturer is only as funny as he is as a writer there ought to be no doubt as to his success on Australian soil. Australian humor approximates more closely to the humor of America than that of England. We are fond of anti-climaxes" (*Quiz*, 3 Oct., p. 3). Editors latched onto the Bret Harte and Max O'Rell gaffes made in Sydney, claiming that if Twain were not funny enough to suit the South Australians they "will hand him over to the tender mercies of Max O'Rell, who is very anxious to fight a duel." Twain and Artemus Ward were called the greatest humorists produced by America, but Bret Harte was in a different category with his unparalleled "pathetic and idyllic writings" (*Quiz*, 3 Oct., p. 12). Though his English may not be up to snuff, the sentiment of the theatre columnist was typical, especially of the more rural people Twain visited: "he is conferring an honor on we benighted South Australians by lecturing to us" (*Quiz*, 10 Oct., p. 4).

Pictures of the humorist had been distributed not only to the newspapers but also to shopkeepers for their display windows; Marshall's Department Store, where tickets could be secured, displayed a "splendid likeness ..., the largest photograph from life ever taken in Australia" (*Quiz*, 10 Oct., p. 12). On 12 October, the day of the arrival, both the *Adelaide Observer* (p. 25) and the *South Australian Register* (p. 7) printed a poem by "Ab-Original" saluting

> ... Mark Twain; no more than he;
> The charmer of nations, who doth scatter
> Clean mirth, while all the world laughs, and grows fatter.[5]

---

4. The *Courier* (Brisbane) carried similar wire releases or excerpts from Low's interviews.

5. "Ab-Original" was the nom de plume of thirty-five-year-old James Sadler, educator, journalist, and occasional poet, especially for the *Register*. His volume *Lyrics and Rhymes* (Adelaide, 1890), which contained light-hearted narrative verses, is the book Twain referred to when he thanked him and explained that Livy had pasted the newspaper clipping in the book to complete the works (Samuel L. Clemens to James Sadler, 16 Oct., Mark Twain Papers, Bancroft Library).

Even though Twain had ridden the train all night and had spent at least some of Saturday visiting with reporters and townspeople, his first performance in the Theatre Royal went as scheduled. "Every class of society, from his Excellency the Lieutenant Governor downwards" was in the theatre, which was "crowded to its last seat," including lawyers, clergymen, merchants, and especially ladies "who had come to disprove the calumny that they were not gifted with an appreciation of humor" (*Advertiser* [Adelaide], 14 Oct., p. 7). *Quiz and Lantern*, the South Australian version of the *Bulletin* and *Melbourne Punch*, reported that there "were more 'goody-goodies' in the Theatre Royal ... than have been for many a long day, and they do say that the bars were never better patronised," but it lamented that "some of the gallery boys sent a twisted-up programme into the vice-regal box .... This is a species of larrikinism that might very well be repressed" (17 Oct., p. 6). As the curtain went up and "about forty people arranged in a semicircle" stood on the stage behind him (*South Australian Register*, 14 Oct., p. 6), Twain discovered a bouquet of flowers on the small table that was his only furniture. He said he "presumed they were intended for him, but whether they were or not made no difference, for he accepted them very kindly just the same" (*Advertiser* [Adelaide], 14 Oct., p. 7).

The stories he used were the old ones well practiced in the other capitals: first the truant fisherman, then Adam's diary, followed by the Mexican plug, and the widow whose husband, having fallen into the carpet-making machine, was returned to her as "14 yards of 3-ply carpet"—she "could not bear the idea of 'rolling up the remains,' but boxed them at full length, and set the result up as a monument." The German language lesson "seemed to be as well appreciated by the Teutons present as by those who, like Mark Twain, had merely wrestled with that formidable tongue" (*Advertiser* [Adelaide], 14 Oct., p. 7). He seems to have changed his selection from *Huck Finn*, telling about the boy's "disgust at Jim's talk about hiring an abolitionist to steal his children" (*South Australian Register*, 14 Oct., p. 6) instead of Huck's struggle with his conscience about whether to return Jim to Miss Watson. He also explained that Uncle Lem's dog "was a 'composite dog,' made up of different kinds of dogs—a sort of syndicate, so to speak—a mongrel dog was made up of what was left. The suggestion of the syndicate tickled the fancy of the house—something akin to a composite dog and a mongrel, too, may be found on the mining corner any day" (*South Australian Register*, 14 Oct., p. 6).

As in Sydney and Melbourne, the papers zeroed in on the familiarity of the American's works, "wherever the English language is spoken." However, it seemed that a few people in this first audience might not have already read the stories judging by "the uncontrollable laughter—the abandonment of enjoyment, so to speak—with which they were greeted. Probably those few were raised in Central Australia or the Northern Territory, and came down for the one treat of their lives," sagely opined the *South Australian Register* (14 Oct., p. 6). But surely it was "his strong features, shaggy, grizzly hair, calculating, leisurely, almost indolent delivery, peculiar accent, unmoved demeanour, dry style of saying things, and mannerisms" that most tickled his auditors. He had

> a habit of carefully holding the one side of his head up with his right hand and propping his elbow up with his left palm, as though the great straggling thatch of hair had caught the wind and canted his massive head over. Now and then he takes a sort of quarter-deck walk along the stage—three steps to starboard, one to port, and a turn; but most of the time he is standing still. [*South Australian Register*, 14 Oct., p. 6.]

These are the same mannerisms noted by *Melbourne Punch* and the ones that would be captured in a drawing in New Zealand. They seem to be an integral part of the act, not the result of his "real and obvious pain" as has been suggested (*Advertiser* [Adelaide], 17 Oct., p. 4).

After the performance Twain enjoyed "rather a lively and congenial social ... amongst friends with whom wit was rampant, and flourished till the 'wee ama' hoors ayout the twal'" (*South Australian Register*, 15 Oct., p. 6). There seems to have been some petty journalistic rivalry among the press corps in Adelaide, for *Quiz and Lantern* disapprovingly reported that because Twain was not a journalist, some Adelaide reporters "declined to join in any demonstration to the American humorist" (10 Oct., p. 6). However, two weeks later *Quiz and Lantern* took obvious pleasure in reporting an impromptu fete, which the disgruntled must have been sorry to miss. There was a

> great gathering of the clans at Flecker's Hotel the other evening .... Some men who are literary, others who fancy that they are literary, and others again who hang on to the skirts of literature ... were present, and I am told that they bored poor Mark Twain almost to death. Two lawyers in particular made speeches of most inordinate length, and they showed not the slightest consideration for a man over sixty years of age, who had been engaged lecturing the same evening. At twelve o'clock the electric light ... went

out, but the bores would not take the hint. They waited until the room had been relighted, and then started once more to air their eloquence. Surely they were preparing a rod for their own backs. When Mark Twain's book on Australia comes out——well, I guess some people will smart. [*Quiz*, 24 Oct., p. 6.]

Possibly at this roast Twain received a book from Edward Planta Nesbit, one of Adelaide's Old Colonists, an educator, editor, and author. The next day (13 October) Twain wrote to Nesbit that he was in bed with his carbuncle reading a book Nesbit had given him.[6]

Twain's health curtailed his accepting invitations: during his four days in Adelaide, the appreciative editor of the *Advertiser* wrote, "he gave four lectures and attended several welcome meetings of a more or less public character, and in the intervals he hardly ever left his room, declining, with evident reluctance, invitations of a private nature. The programme prearranged was courageously gone through, but real and obvious pain prevented its being materially exceeded. Thus Adelaide had a somewhat tantalising glimpse of ... a great man" (17 Oct., p. 4).

One of the quasi-public gatherings was the official welcome by about a score of the city fathers on Monday afternoon at the Mayor's Parlor, along with Premier C. C. Kingston, Manager Smythe, and American Consul Murphy. Twain, in his response to Mayor C. Tucker's toast and invitation to make a second visit to Adelaide, complimented the city and its honest government. His reading had been confirmed that Adelaide, a city of 320,000 souls from every part of the globe, "was beautiful, its buildings fine, and its drainage excellent" (*South Australian Register*, 15 Oct., p. 6). Again he warned against generalizing, this time about city governments, for "one fly in the amber ... always gave the amber discredit" (*Advertiser* [Adelaide], 15 Oct., p. 5). Twain remained consistent in his refusal to make hasty generalizations, and when he returned to Sydney from New Zealand he made clear his position: "I don't think it is right to hurry through a place and form impressions .... That is what I object to so many people doing with regard to America. They just hurry through the place, and then venture an opinion on the nature of the country and the characteristics of

---

6. Samuel L. Clemens to Edward Planta Nesbit, 13 Oct., American Museum of Historical Documents, Las Vegas (copy in Mark Twain Papers). Twain's copy of *Christ, Christians, and Christianity. Book I* (London: Simpkin, Marshall, & Co., 1895) by Nesbit is extant. See Gribben, *Mark Twain's Library*, II, 499.

the people, and they just know nothing" (*Sydney Daily Telegraph*, 20 Dec., p. 6).

The lieutenant governor's announced intention to attend Twain's "At Home" again on Monday night may have contributed to his decision to use the "Second" performance, the one beginning with the scheme for moral regeneration, illustrated with the stolen watermelon story. Twain "soon had his hearers in fits of laughter over ... Tom Sawyer's projected crusade in the Holy Land"; he told about the incorporation of mean men who "docked an employee's wages for loss of time incurred while flying through the atmosphere after an accident." As on the first evening, the theatre "was filled to its utmost capacity by an audience anxious to do honor to the magician of the pen" (*Advertiser* [Adelaide], 15 Oct., p. 5).

Probably Adelaide—which struck Twain as being extremely religious with its sixty-four sects—especially appreciated his observation that there was "no need for a man to lie promiscuously unless business requires it." By the time he had gotten through his introduction to the Australian poem, the audience was in such fits "that the house spoilt his points by uncontrollable laughter" (*South Australian Register*, 15 Oct., p. 6). The blue jay story, the old slave woman searching for her son, and Uncle Dan'l's ghost story filled out the entertainment.

The third performance, a repetition of Saturday's show, was an extra one enthusiastically received by a packed house, presumably with another forty people sitting on the stage as on the first night. Even though the auditors already knew most of the stories, they responded in "fits of laughter" and "a burst of merriment" (*Advertiser* [Adelaide], 16 Oct., p. 6). That afternoon—Tuesday—Twain had lunched with the Ministry, and after the "At Home" he was entertained by the Adelaide Club on North Terrace.[7]

The full houses encouraged Smythe, "in compliance with numerous requests" for a repetition of Monday's show, to book a Wednesday matinee, apparently catering especially for young people. For this last performance, about twenty minutes shorter than usual, there were no reserved stalls and seats went on a first-come basis as second-class tick-

---

7. *Geelong Evening Star*, 24 Oct., p. 3: "During his stay he was on different occasions the guest of the Acting-Governor, the civic authorities, the Ministry, and of the Adelaide Club, altogether crowding a lot of work and entertainment into four days." See also Parsons, "Mark Twain in Adelaide," p. 52. Parsons notes an invitation from Adelaide's Baseball League.

ets. The house, though not overflowing, was quite full, and "a large number of the audience assembled on the platform of the rail-way station" to bid Twain farewell on the Melbourne express (*Express and Telegraph*, 16 Oct., p. 4). There an "enthusiastic crowd of persons . . . , many of them complete strangers to Mr. Clemens . . . , pressed forward . . . for the privilege of shaking hands" (*The Advertiser* [Adelaide], 17 Oct., p. 4). Others seeing off the Clemenses were the public works minister Mr. Jenkins, born and reared in Pennsylvania, and his wife; Sir E. T. Smith, and Mr. Murphy (*Express and Telegraph*, 16 Oct., p. 4). However, Livy and Clara had gone riding with the lieutenant governor and were not at the station with the luggage when Twain arrived.

The ladies, who had attracted attention in both Sydney and Melbourne, especially when they attended the horse races, were now sought after in their own right. The *South Australian Register* called Clara "a lively, self-possessed, frank, chatty young lady," and she was evidently a clever conversationalist, discussing with the reporter whether there was any danger of horses becoming extinct "owing to the domestication of the more docile and enduring bicycle" (*South Australian Register*, 14 Oct., p. 6). "Those steel substitutes for horseflesh did not satisfy her," she said. "In Melbourne and Sydney they were the craze, and she saw numbers of ladies riding about [on] them, but give her a live horse." It is true that in *A Connecticut Yankee* (1889)—one of Australia's favorite Twain books—Lancelot had led "five hundred mailed and belted knights on bicycles . . . [an] endless procession of webby wheels" to the rescue. But these were—as Dan Beard's drawings show—"penny-farthings." The modern bicycle was a new invention since 1893; and in the six months since Clara had left England, it had become rather popular. But the family did not join the fad until back in London, when Twain complained of Clara and Jean badgering him to get them bicycles. Of course, he tried to learn to ride one himself.[8]

While waiting for Olivia and Clara and the luggage to arrive, Twain was worried by one old bore who stuck "closer than a creditor," and received the homage of an over-large clergyman who bowed asking for the "honour of shaking hands with you."[9] The Clemenses left Adelaide

---

8. Welland, pp. 187–188. A. B. Paine dates Twain's fictional essay "Taming the Bicycle" to the early eighties; the bicycle Twain "tamed" was the penny-farthing.

9. Parsons, "Mark Twain in Adelaide," p. 52.

on the 4:30 train, arriving at Horsham, Victoria, at 2:30 Thursday morning. Most papers agreed that the triumph in South Australia surpassed both Melbourne and Sydney.

"He's a Wonner, Sir, and No Mistake"

The day after Twain had left Adelaide, the *Advertiser* expressed the cumulating appreciation of the humorist throughout Australia.

> Some people are of opinion that it is not well to seek for closer acquaintance with the fleshly trappings that enclose a genius one has greatly admired .... [But] no derogatory effect can possibly have been the result of a nearer knowledge of Mr. Clemens. There has been a general sense of anticipations realised, a feeling that the setting, so to speak, was appropriate to the jewel .... That drawling voice and elaborate amplification of a point characterise the man, it appears, as much in private life as elsewhere. He has ... the manner of one who is accustomed to be listened to with attention whenever he speaks. [*Advertiser* (Adelaide), 17 Oct., p. 4.]

It was to be admired, the editor wrote, that

> in all his successful efforts to amuse mankind, Mark Twain has never forfeited his claim to be seriously regarded as a literary man. He has introduced to Englishmen and Australians a whole vocabulary with which they were previously unfamiliar .... He has also maintained throughout a distinct literary style, founding thereby a school of imitators of whom not one has come near to rivalling him. And there is, further, a very frequent depth of thought, only partly concealed by some distorted phrase or daring expression of untutored slang. [*Advertiser* (Adelaide), 17 Oct., p. 4.]

The editor cited a Twain simile (taken from *Innocents Abroad*) to demonstrate "the combination of high charge and low quality" that Twain satirized: "the quiet remark concerning the wine of some Rhine district, that one might perceive by the price that it was dissolved jewellery—and might perceive by the taste that dissolved jewellery is not good to drink." The only possible disappointment was that he "was elderly and fragile beyond expectation" (*Advertiser* [Adelaide], 17 Oct., p. 4).

Of course, there were the minority in Adelaide, as there had been in the other capitals, who "profess to be disappointed." However, *Quiz and Lantern* answered this grumble by saying "it is something to have seen Mark Twain. It has been a privilege to sit at the feet of a master who, for over a quarter of a century, has been keeping the intelligent people of this bored world of ours amused .... As it is we have no reason to be dissatisfied" (*Quiz*, 17 Oct., p. 12). The satiric weekly pointed out that there were "overflowing houses on Saturday, Monday, and Tuesday evenings, and Wednesday's matinee attracted such a large attendance that Manager R. S. Smythe went about murmuring Mark Twainisms on his own account. Mark has packed the theatre as it has seldom been packed." Before it was all over, as Smythe deservedly "contemplated the Theatre Royal[,] his bosom heaved with pride, and he looked even more Napoleonic than usual" (*Quiz*, 17 Oct., p. 6).

Quiz and Lantern devoted three rather large humorous features to Twain's visit, more than he had received in Sydney's or Melbourne's comic weeklies. Evidently they worked all week on the satire of the George Dean case that was represented in a full-page cartoon whose last frame showed Twain's supposed opinion of the matter. They also printed a half-page spoof, appropriately set in the barber shop and written by "Close Shave." The fictional barber, like the report in the *Advertiser* and *Quiz and Lantern*'s cartoon, periodically verges on tears over having been "taken in" by Dean's protestations of innocence; now the barber is repentant over having been made such a fool—as many Australians were. In an effort to change the subject, the client asks the barber's "impressions of Mark Twain."

> "He's a wonner, sir, and no mistake .... Funny? I should just think he was. I'd like to pay him ten pounds a week just to sit in my shop and tell my customers stories. I guess I'd be able to retire in two years .... I heard one of his lectures, and I laughed fit to bust myself. I forgot how my shares had gone down. I didn't even think of George Dean. I just kept my eyes on Mark's face, and laughed and laughed .... " [*Quiz*, 17 Oct., p. 2.]

Quiz and Lantern's third feature was a supposed interview by "Little Boy Blue" in which the slim merits of Adelaide humorists were satirized. Little Boy Blue claimed to have met Twain "in Sacramento five-and-thirty years ago," to which Twain is supposed to have responded, "You're a liar," unless he was "alluding to our charming Northern township—Eurelia." Twain's interviews with the daily papers, the poetic tributes he had received, the jokes made at public meetings, and Twain's own whiskey cocktail (in the news since his first day in Sydney) were ridiculed. It was another case of the journalists' inability to resist joining in the fun Twain generated; this had become a hallmark, or as "Aubrey" of Melbourne said, the "twain mark," of his trip to Australasia.

It must have been while he was in Adelaide that a "big offer was made to Mark Twain to visit the Westralian goldfields, but declined. Mark says he wants information about the fields all the same. 'I'm writing a book,' said Mark, 'and I want information. I don't care if it's true or not'" (*Bulletin* [Sydney], 26 Oct., p. 13). Twain actually said to the city fathers in Adelaide that the American consul "knew all about the trees, and described everything about the country. He did not care whether the information was correct or not, for all he wanted was information and plenty of it" (*Adelaide Observer*, 19 Oct., p. 15; reprinted from *South Australian Register*, 15 Oct., p. 6). He had been credited with a similar joke while he was still on the *Warrimoo* in Sydney Harbour; it seems unlikely that he entertained the idea of actually going to the goldfields, although he did have to cancel a hoped-for visit to Broken Hill silver mines.

R. S. Smythe, who had accompanied the Clemenses throughout their visit so far, left them in Adelaide to make the trip back to Ballarat, Victoria, on their own. He left Adelaide at 1:15 p.m. on 16 October (before the matinee) aboard the *RMS Cuzco* to Melbourne to arrange for Twain's farewell matinee there on the twenty-sixth before sailing to New Zealand on 31 October. On 19 October, the *Cuzco* arrived in Melbourne at 5:00 p.m. and by 6:00 it was declared to have one case of smallpox among the crew. About 160 passengers got off at the quarantine station in Melbourne (*Age*, 19 Oct., pp. 6–7). Smythe stayed aboard, and when they got to Sydney half a dozen cases eventually were confirmed.

As the problem was reported in Dunedin, New Zealand, by "Our Own Correspondent" on the eve of Twain's arrival,

> Mr R. S. Smythe is fretting out his soul in quarantine in Sydney. He did the run round from Adelaide to Melbourne in the Cuzco, and the language he used when she was declared an infected ship may be imagined. As Adelaide and Albany [in Western Australia] had passed the small pox [thinking it chicken pox], he concluded to go on to Sydney on the chance that the doctors there might differ from those of Melbourne (which of course they would have been only too willing to do) and let the passengers loose. But the Sydney doctors found three more cases instead; and Mr Smythe was condemned to a week or two's extra term. All he has left to congratulate himself about is that his lecturer did not travel by the Cuzco too. ["Our

Australian Letter," Melbourne, 30 October, *Otago Daily Times*, (Dunedin), 9 Nov., p. 2.]

Twain became fully aware of Smythe's detention by the twentieth when Smythe's son and business partner, Carlyle G. Smythe, brought letters from home to them at Ballarat, Victoria. Young Smythe must have told him that the sailor who was infected "didn't have it bad, & has now had it 20 days." Twain expressed dismay that "enlightened communities [were] quarantining for small pox in *this* day" (MTP:NB34).

Many passengers on the *Cuzco* intended to see the Caulfield and Melbourne Cup races, but the disappointment "of a young lady whose marriage had been fixed for next Wednesday" was far greater.

> This is the second occasion on which the lady in question has been quarantined within a year, but she has ascertained with joy that her former misfortune will now prove her salvation, for, as she was previously vaccinated with success . . . , her reception into quarantine will be a mere matter of form, and . . . she will be free to join her friends as soon as her trousseau is disinfected. [*Courier* (Ballarat), 22 Oct., p. 4, reprinted from the *Age* (Melbourne).]

Twain was aware of this bride and joked that "as the new & powerful fumigation is to be used, we shall smell her in Ballarat" (MTP:NB34).

CHAPTER FIVE

The Country Tour

"Even More Operative in the Country"

A very successful part of the five weeks in Australia was the tour of five Victorian country towns and two towns near Melbourne. Yet students of Twain's visit have generally relied only on the capital city newspaper accounts, neglecting the less accessible country papers. Hence they have occasionally referred to Twain's having "a green-horn from the Ballarat *Star* at his mercy" or alluded to "goldmining and agricultural towns which monotonously insisted on official welcomes."[1] Because scholars have restricted their interest to what Twain said on the stage and in interviews, disregarding the response of literate Australians, some material has been dismissed as "unimportant because highly fanciful" or because the "reporter gushes obtrusively."[2] And while what "Mark Twain" had to say may be of intrinsically greater interest than what "Asmodeus" of Sydney, or "Aubrey" of Melbourne, or "Tom Touchstone" of Ballarat had to say, their remarks are not devoid of interest. Twain's visit required his cooperation with Australians and with the press: without a receptive audience and congenial press it would not have been a successful tour, and Twain demonstrated mastery in promoting his own cause, largely through the free publicity that an official welcome or interview afforded.

Vance Palmer has lamented that Australia did not have an observer of

---

1. Parsons, "Mark Twain in Australia," p. 456.

2. Louis Budd, "A Listing of and Selection from the Newspaper and Magazine Interviews with Samuel L. Clemens," *American Literary Realism* 10 (1977), 1–100, quotations on p. 10.

the quality of Tocqueville in America. Yet he overlooked, in *The Legend of the Nineties*, Twain's observations about Australia, thinking perhaps that *More Tramps Abroad* was equivalent to the whimsical satire found in *Innocents Abroad*. However, the newspaper record of Twain's visit to Victoria and his recollections in his Australian book provide glimpses of Clemens as traveler not available in the earlier books and affirm the wide familiarity Australians had with Twain's writings. The newspapers reveal a man known to be physically ill, bankrupt, and growing progressively fatigued, who nevertheless maintained his grace, good humor, and ready wit during impromptu remarks, official welcomes, and interviews with country editors. And when the natives join in the fun themselves with their exaggerations and send-ups, the similarities between the Australians and Americans of the nineties, on which Twain himself so often remarked, become clearer.

The fact is that, wherever Twain went in Australia, newspapermen—and politicians—were likely to try to get into the act themselves or, at the very least, to extract from him either printable or spoofable material. That was, after all, their job. This was true not only in the cities but also in the country, and nowhere were Australians more successful in getting Twain to say something clever than in the Victorian towns of Ballarat, Bendigo, and Maryborough. Examination of his week in these three important gold-mining areas yields several previously unknown Twain anecdotes and reveals the rapport and mutual enjoyment that developed between the famous American and the provincial towns he visited. The record in the agricultural villages of Horsham and Stawell demonstrates the fascination with which country people—whether Australian, English, or American—attend to famous people who honor them with a visit. And Twain was widely considered the most famous American and the most loved literary person to have visited Australia in the nineteenth century. Twain's country tour shows an enthusiastic response from the ordinary people who were his audience for both the written and spoken word. In fact, the Victorians' universal love of Twain's stories led the editor at Stawell to surmise that "this is one cause of the fervor of Mr. Clemens' reception in the cities of the colonies, and it should be even more operative in the country" (*Stawell News and ... Chronicle*, 12 Oct., p. 2).

The newspaper record of the country tour reveals some interesting information both about Twain and about the towns themselves. First,

all of the towns that Twain visited in Victoria had more than one newspaper, indicating a relatively keen interest in keeping abreast of current
events, and in several instances it is clear that the editors of the papers
were concerned with literature and other arts as well as with the agricultural and mining matters that directly affected the economic well-being
of the country people. Moreover, there was quite an active entertainment season that spring, ranging from talks on better farming methods
by J. L. Dow, the agricultural editor of the *Leader* in Melbourne, to
Christmas choral groups, to Professor T. A. Kennedy, a mesmerist on
tour from Europe.

At first Twain's country tour was to include only Bendigo, Geelong,
and Ballarat on his leisurely trip from Melbourne to Adelaide. He
would stop at Stawell and Maryborough, taking in some sightseeing
of vineyards, mines, and public gardens on his return to Melbourne,
whence he would depart for New Zealand. However, his carbuncle
forced a rearrangement of these plans; performances were added in the
major cities, giving additional time for increased publicity in the country. One could almost say that the detested carbuncle improved his
success in Victoria and added at least three new engagements for the
lecturer in the provincial towns.

"Lay Back ... and ... Risk ... Apoplexy"

Twain's first country stop was to Horsham, evidently not
on his original itinerary. The town is on the direct rail line between
Melbourne and Adelaide, about eighty miles from the South Australia
border. The smallest town Twain spoke in, its population was only
about 3,000, but it had an active Mechanics' Hall, three newspapers including the district weekly, and an agricultural college nearby. Twain's
appearance at Horsham was unusual in that the citizens, led by Herbert
Cooke, secretary of the Mechanics' Institute, advertised a "meeting of
Gentlemen interested in Mark Twain's proposed Lecture" and invited
"Country correspondence" for the purpose of underwriting the costs
of Twain's appearance, tentatively scheduled for Thursday, 10 October. R. S. Smythe "required a guarantee of £35 before he would accept
a Horsham engagement"; by 3 October, the officers of the Mechanics'
Institute "had received definite promises of support to the amount of
over £30." Guarantors included visitors from Natimuk, Warracknabeal,
Murtoa, and Dimboola (*Horsham Times*, 4 Oct., p. 2). The lecture was

advertised in the twice-weekly paper on 4 October over Cooke's name. But with Twain's failure to appear in Bendigo on the third, a "Lecture Postponed" announcement appeared on the eighth. The editor explained that "Mr Cooke, who has the matter in hand, was yesterday informed by wire that Mr. Clemens (Mark Twain) ... had been compelled to postpone his visit in consequence of illness" (*Horsham Times*, 8 Oct., p. 2).

However, the short delay of Twain's arrival allowed continuous free advertisement in the editor's announcements about the impending visit. At one point the visitor had

> so far recovered ... as to justify him in arranging to lecture in Horsham on Thursday next, 17th inst. The lecture is likely to be very largely attended by people from the neighboring towns, and indeed so great is the rush for tickets that those desirous of occupying good seats on the occasion will do well to secure them without delay. It is unnecessary to say anything in recommendation of the lecturer, for the magic of his name may be depended upon to command such an audience as has seldom assembled in Horsham. [*Horsham Times*, 11 Oct., p. 2.]

Smythe's prepared publicity about the world tour, including the proposed £2,000 engagement in London, appeared to whet Horsham's appetite for fun and showmanship (*Wimmera Star*, 15 Oct., p. 2).

Two days before the scheduled lecture, so many tickets had been sold at three shillings that "those who have accepted the responsibility of Mr. Clemens' visit ... have decided to make a limited number of back seat tickets available at 2s" (*Horsham Times*, 15 Oct., p. 2). Twain's visit was considered so important that the ladies' committee of the annual Charities' Carnival postponed a meeting to be able to hear the lecturer (*Horsham Times*, 18 Oct., p. 2). Although a special train could not be arranged, additional cabs were run from the Nhill showgrounds "in time to catch the 3 p.m. train"—necessitated by the postponement of Twain's visit, which now conflicted with the annual spring show (*Wimmera Star*, 15 Oct., p. 2); about thirty-five "ladies and gentlemen" drove their carriages over from Natimuk, Vectis, and Quantong (*West Wimmera Mail*, 25 Oct., p. 5).

The Clemenses were greeted at 2:30 on Thursday morning by Cooke and another young man, who took them to Lucas's White Hart Hotel. Around noon they were driven in an open carriage by T. K. Dow "with several townspeople, ladies and gentlemen, to the Longerenong College" to be entertained at afternoon tea by the principal and Mrs.

Dow. The Clemens ladies also received flowers and candy.[3] They examined dozens of kinds of "vigorous and flourishing" fruit trees and watched the sophomores "shear a dozen sheep ... [which] looked like the fat woman in the circus" (*More Tramps*, p. 150; this information is taken closely from MTP:NB34). Twain was greatly impressed with the college. About eight miles from Horsham, it had around forty students who were studying the newest techniques in sheep and orchard management, alternating with the study of chemistry and other sciences.[4]

Reviews of Horsham's "At Home" were universally ecstatic. The *Horsham Times* reported that "the lecture, or address, or friendly chat, or whatever it was, was simply unreportable .... If to read Mark Twain is delightful, to listen to him is to reach a height of enjoyment attainable only once or twice in a lifetime .... Were Mr. Clemens able to pay a second visit to Horsham his audience would certainly not be smaller than that of last night" (*Horsham Times*, 18 Oct., p. 3). The *Wimmera Star* concurred: "The audience simply packed the building ... [and] by the time the 'At Home' commenced there was only standing room available ..." (18 Oct., p. 3). The weekly *West Wimmera Mail* provided a description of Twain—now well known both verbally and pictorially: "everyone is quite familiar with his tall spare figure, thick bushy hair, thin beaky nose, merry twinkling eyes and heavy over-hanging eyebrows and moustaches." The popularity of his writing was obvious: "There were no new jokes or fresh stories, all of them may be found in his celebrated books, and fully two-thirds of his large audience must have known them by heart. But yet one was obliged to lay back on the seat, hold one's sides, and run the risk of an attack of apoplexy at the inimitable manner the humorist related his stories." The stories were told "in a hesitating, yet confidential, manner. His voice is rarely raised above an ordinary conversational tone, and has a strong nasal twang, yet he is distinctly heard all over the building, and not a single atom of his dry humor misses fire." The reviewer noted Twain's alternating humor and pathos—as had been remarked in the cities—when the story begins "in so serious a vein" and then "he drops out

---

3. Olivia L. Clemens to Susy Clemens, 20 Oct., Caroline T. Harnsberger, *Mark Twain, Family Man* (New York: Citadel Press, 1960), p. 155. This book must be used with extreme care; it contains many errors of fact.

4. *Notebook*, ed. Paine, p. 254.

such an irresistible humorous turn ... that your hands are once more jammed to your sides and the tears flow freely" (*West Wimmera Mail*, 25 Oct., p. 5). Among the stories told in Horsham were the fishing excursion that ended with a dead body, Twain's Nevada experiences, and the German language story, which became the usual close for the country "At Homes." Huck Finn's "struggling against the voice of conscience advising him to inform the authorities of the attempted escape of the slave Jim, and the tugging of friendship on the other hand compelling him to endeavor to save him from capture" were "graphically pourtrayed" (*Wimmera Star*, 18 Oct., p. 3). Twain introduced the punch brothers jingle in Horsham, and it became a staple for the remainder of his Australasian tour (*Horsham Times*, 18 Oct., p. 3).[5]

The performance in Horsham seems to have been one of the best of the Australian tour, probably because Twain was in good health and good spirits, and because he spoke there on the genuine invitation of the townspeople. The Mechanics' Hall was "packed," and "about five minutes after the doors were opened [at 7:30] scarcely a seat was unoccupied, and fresh accommodation was provided" (*Wimmera Star*, 18 Oct., p. 3). Twain noted in his journal that the institute was "crammed" with a "delightful audience" (MTP:NB34). Not even "the most sanguine" expectation was disappointed, the *Horsham Times* reported. Livy wrote to their daughter Susy, "I think that Papa never talked to a more enthusiastic audience .... They were entirely uproarious, taking a point almost before he reached it." People were "sitting on the stage and standing around the sides of the hall .... Well it was a most jolly house." The young man who sat next to her "began to pound his sides as if troubled with stitches," so great was his mirth. He brought Clara a bunch of roses the next day.[6] After the lecture "a number of townsmen [spent] a pleasant half hour over a glass of wine" with the Clemenses at their hotel. Toasted by T. K. Dow, Twain "responded in a sympathetic, appreciative and highly characteristic speech ... deeply grateful for the magnificent reception accorded him at Horsham." He enjoyed the visit "more particularly ... because whilst [in Horsham] he had been in perfect health—for the first time since he

---

5. This information is corroborated in MTP:NB34, and other newspapers. See chapter 6 below for the jingle.

6. Olivia L. Clemens to Susy Clemens, 20 Oct., Harnsberger, *Mark Twain, Family Man*, p. 155.

landed in Australia. He felt he was undeserving of all the kindness he was everywhere receiving, but appreciated and enjoyed it all the same, as did also his wife and daughter" (*Horsham Times*, 18 Oct., p. 3). Livy recorded that one person drove 150 miles round trip, and several who stayed for the toasts drove home 8 miles after midnight.

"Dry Mellow Fun Suits ... the 'Bush' "

The train to Stawell, a railway changing station between Adelaide and Melbourne, about forty miles east of Horsham, arrived thirty minutes late on the afternoon of Friday 18 October. The Clemenses were met by Mayor H. Menzies and other dignitaries, and Olivia and Clara were taken immediately to the Commercial Hotel. Twain was welcomed at the Town Hall by Harry Foster, minister of mines for the colony, and Mr. Burton, district member of Parliament, who had come up from Melbourne on colony business. After the mayoral welcome, a toast to Twain and Foster "was drunk most heartily and with the vocal welcome of 'They are jolly good fellows.'" Twain responded "with much feeling" that he "thought he had been coming to a nation of strangers, but found himself among a nation of comrades." He said "many good things in his inimitable way ... giving those present a hint of what to expect in the evening" (*Stawell News and ... Chronicle*, 19 Oct., p. 2).

Despite the already hectic day, Twain was able to crack jokes apparently unrehearsed. Twain had met Foster at least twice in Melbourne, once when he offered a toast at the Yorick Club and once after Twain's third performance. In Stawell on Saturday, he would accompany the Clemens party to the Great Western Vineyards. In complimenting the minister of mines, Twain quipped that "in his opinion, Mr. Foster was deserving of their hospitality, because he was producing wealth in various ways, while he himself (Mark Twain) was simply in the colony for the purpose of taking a little of the wealth produced from the mines with him back to the United States." It was well known that the purpose of his "talking tour round the world" was to earn enough money from the lectures and the resulting book to repay the losses incurred by his defunct publishing company and his speculation in the Paige typesetting device, though this was less publicized.

Twain also joked that "it was astonishing how old superstitions still lingered. The one referring to the impossibility of getting a joke into a Scotchman's head save by a surgical operation," Twain said, "was absurd" (*Stawell Times*, 21 Oct., pp. 2–3). This joke was sometimes introductory to his performances, but since there would be only one show in Stawell, it was well used at the welcoming ceremony. Twain then explained that, although "it was popularly accepted as true that the French were the politest people of the world ..., they were not" (*Stawell Times*, 21 Oct., pp. 2–3). This joke may have been intended as a compliment to Australians, or it may have been an allusion to Max O'Rell, with whom Twain differed on literary matters, but whose visit to Australia was a tremendous success. This difference had been widely published by interviewers in Sydney, and it had been reprinted from Brisbane to Adelaide.

It was probably while her father was joking with the city officials that Clara took a walk out into the country. In a field she saw a sheep she believed to be dying of heat prostration. Going back to the drugstore, she got some ether and was on her way to "put the poor animal out of his misery" when the owner found her. Seeing the sheep, the farmer explained, "at this time of the year, when their wool is very thick, they cannot get up alone if once they fall down." When he lifted the animal, it "toddled off, contented with the world."[7]

Stawell had been well prepared for Twain's visit for, since 4 October, periodic notices of his appearances in the cities including a reprint of his interview with the *Sydney Daily Telegraph* had appeared in the town's two newspapers. And on 12 October, the *Stawell News and ... Chronicle*, a semi-weekly, had announced that the town "has been paid the high compliment of being chosen as one of the few inland centres" the humorist would visit. The gracious editor of the *Stawell News and ... Chronicle* described Clemens as "in the front rank of notable men" for he "has made the world laugh more heartily and more innocently than any other man." He said Twain's "humour is neither that of the cynic nor the clown, so there is neither bitterness nor folly in its enjoyment. It is rather that of the genial philosopher who is quick to see humanity's weaknesses and eccentricities, and to laugh at rather than gird at them." He stated an important component of Twain's success in Australia: "We question if Mr. Clemens' books are better understood

---

7. *My Father, Mark Twain*, pp. 146–148. Although Clara is not always accurate in her recollections, she explained that they were in town only twenty-four hours and she was late for an early supper. Some scholars have misplaced this episode in Adelaide.

or more enjoyed anywhere than in Australia. The dry mellow fun suits the Australian temperament and environment especially of those living in the 'bush' and there are few homesteads or huts in which Mark Twain's creations are not an ever available source of pleasure and relief" (*Stawell News and ... Chronicle*, 12 Oct., p. 2).

The *Stawell Times* printed a factual account of the world tour provided by agent Smythe. Even if some of the preliminary newspaper comments were not original, the appreciation for his humor was genuine. "Mr Foster was delighted to make the acquaintance of Mark Twain, with whose works he had been intimately acquainted from boyhood. As minister of mines of Victoria, he would in a few years be forgotten, but Mark Twain's works would live after him, and would cheer the hearts of men wherever the English language was spoken" (*Stawell Times*, 21 Oct., p. 2).

A "large attendance" from Stawell's 5,300 residents greeted Twain at the Town Hall that evening. Forty people traveled eighteen miles (perhaps from Ararat, which was a well-established center), and with the fortnight's notice others came seventy-five miles to hear the humorist (MTP:NB34). The "At Home" itself had no formal introduction—by now a Twain trademark. The audience was described as large, and, judging by the newspapers, even at 4s for a reserved seat, the people felt they got their money's worth. Twain told the stories of the Mexican plug horse, Huck's conscience and the difficulty in inventing a lie, and the green watermelon. "The audience was convulsed with laughter when with his characteristic way-down-in-the-Mississippi-Valley-drawl, he described the uncertainty of a cat's sex in Germany." "The lecture was as caviare to a few, but to those who have read Mark Twain, and were acquainted with American humor the 'talk' was a rare treat. It was not the matter of the lecture, but the inimitable drollery of expression, the joke which came as an afterthought which caused the enjoyment" (*Stawell Times*, 21 Oct., p. 3).

On Saturday morning, the mayor, the minister of mines, the district parliamentarians, and others showed the Clemenses the countryside, and they were entertained at the Great Western Vineyards by Mr. and Mrs. Hans Irvine, the proprietors. There they saw "120,000 bottles of champagne" stored in the under-granite cellars (*More Tramps*, p. 151; MTP:NB34). Twain was also impressed with "half a peck of surface-gold," "a couple of gold bricks ... worth £7,500 apiece," and a lady who "has an income of £75,000 a month" from her gold mine (*More Tramps*, p. 151; MTP:NB34). In his journal Twain recorded highly favorable impressions of the cloud-flecked brilliant sunshine, dry heat, coppery gum trees, wattle bushes and trees, and rock formations near Stawell (MTP:NB34). They left Stawell on the afternoon train, twenty-four hours after arriving (*Stawell News and ... Chronicle*, 22 Oct., p. 2).

"Purely Australians ...
But More American than English"

The Clemenses arrived in Ballarat, a town of about 40,000, some seventy-five miles from Stawell, at seven o'clock on Saturday evening, 19 October. As soon as they arrived, they received a telegram from R. S. Smythe's son and business partner, the "more travelled" Carlyle Greenwood Smythe. It announced that he was bringing a "portmanteau of letters for Mrs. Clemens," the first news from home since they had left North America in mid-August. When he arrived in Ballarat on Sunday, 20 October, he also brought with him from Melbourne the unwelcome news that his "much-travelled" father was under smallpox quarantine aboard the *Cuzco* at Queenscliff, near Melbourne (MTP:NB34). Therefore, Carlyle Smythe became Twain's guide somewhat sooner than planned and continued as his escort for the remainder of the world tour (except for a few days at Bendigo and Maryborough).

The younger Smythe had been born in 1865 at the foot of the Himalayas while his parents were touring the Punjab. His mother was a popular soprano with a musical company, and his father was their manager. Young Smythe had grown up in Melbourne where he was educated at Hawthorn Grammar School, capturing the Shakespeare scholarship. An excellent student of literature, he earned the bachelor of arts degree in Trinity College of the University of Melbourne. He had a brief career as a journalist both in Australia and in Europe before becoming his father's partner in tour management. Carlyle G. Smythe would continue conducting lecturers around the world even after his father retired, with Sir Arthur Conan Doyle, Max O'Rell, Captain Amundsen, and Annie Besant as clients. After suffering a mysterious accident abroad, he resided at Highgate, Burke Road, Camberwell, in Melbourne acting as music and drama critic and writer on international policy for the *Argus* and other papers.[8]

---

8. *Argus*, 18 Dec. 1925, p. 21; *Australasian* (Melbourne), 26 Dec. 1925, p. 1665.

Twain had intended to visit Bendigo on Thursday and Friday, 3 and 4 October, going south to Geelong on Monday the seventh, then westward to Ballarat for the eighth and ninth. According to Smythe's usual practice, advertisements appeared in Ballarat four times prior to the first scheduled engagement beginning on 3 October. On the fifth, the *Courier* reprinted from the *Australasian* Twain's remarks to Melbourne's Yorick Club in which he had complimented the Australians and English-speaking peoples and had told some of his Mississippi River experiences (*Australasian*, [Melbourne] 5 Oct., p. 615).[9] The delay in his appearing in Ballarat allowed for additional free publicity from the editors and from telegram releases. It was reported, for example, that he had passed through Ballarat by the express train in the middle of the night on his way to Adelaide and that he was experiencing huge successes there. Readers of the *Star*, the *Evening Echo*, and the *Courier* knew that Smythe came to town to book accommodations and, presumably, advertisements, that Twain left Adelaide, where he had given four lectures instead of the planned two, that he reached Horsham at 2:30 a.m., and that he had arrived in Ballarat on Saturday afternoon. On the tenth, the *Suburban Advertiser* reprinted his interview from the *Sydney Daily Telegraph* in which he discussed wit and humor. Certainly this kind of editorial "hype," supplementing Smythe's five well-placed advertisements in each paper, helped insure the two successful nights in Ballarat.

Of all the country towns, perhaps Ballarat felt most kinship with Twain, and he with it. It had been a boom town in 1851–56 when surface gold was first discovered. Miners and other adventurers had come out from California for a second gold rush. In 1895, when Twain visited the city, he professed "surprise" at its sophistication. He wrote, borrowing from the city guide *Ballarat the Beautiful*, that it had a park of 326 acres; a flower garden of 83 acres including an elaborate fernery and unusually fine statuary; and a man-made lake of 600 acres equipped with some 200 boats.[10] Twain's affinity with Ballarat, however, was probably less for its "advanced and enlightened big city" attributes than for its impetuous, upstart, rough-and-tumble history, so like the Califor-

---

9. The text, but not the audience responses, is reprinted in *Mark Twain Speaking*, ed. Paul Fatout (Iowa City: Univ. of Iowa Press, 1976), pp. 292–298.

10. Twain claims the city guidebook was written by Mayor William Little; the earliest edition I have seen is the 1907 edition.

nia and Nevada and Mississippi Valley of Twain's young manhood. In
More Tramps Abroad these characteristics are symbolized for Twain by
the incredible richness of the gold deposits, including—he said—two
nuggets of 180 pounds each, and the fact that Ballarat alone had produced one-fourth the gold that the whole of California had produced
in the same time since 1850.

Yet it was not just the wealth of the mines that Twain admired but
also the brashness of the people, epitomized by the revolt at Eureka
Stockade in which perhaps thirty miners were killed. He was quick to
see the spiritual affinity of the miners with the democratic Americans
instead of with the monarchist Europeans.[11] The British government's
tax on frontier initiative and the response of the miners touched Twain's
own pioneering spirit. Appalled by the "license-tax—license to work
his claim—and it had to be paid before he could begin digging," the
humorist sounded like the true American capitalist he had tried to be
with his various business speculations. He wrote, "It might be wise policy to advance the miner a monthly sum to encourage him to develop
the country's riches; but to tax him monthly in advance instead—why,
such a thing was never dreamed of in America. There, neither the claim
itself nor its product, howsoever rich or poor, was taxed."

"The Ballarat miners," he continued,

protested, petitioned, complained—it was of no use . . . .

By and by there was a result; and I think it may be called the finest thing
in Australasian history. It was a revolution—small in size, but great polit-
ically; it was a strike for liberty, a struggle for a principle, a stand against
injustice and oppression. It was the Barons and John over again; . . . it was
Concord and Lexington; small beginnings . . . [but] great in political results,
all of them epoch-making.

It is another instance of a victory won by a lost battle. It adds an hon-
ourable page to history; the people know it and are proud of it. They keep
green the memory of the men who fell at Eureka Stockade, and Peter Lalor
has his monument. [*More Tramps*, p. 155.]

In 1895, though the gold boom was over, Ballarat must have still had
the same spirit. The columnist "Tom Touchstone" said he had long ago

---

11. Potts and Potts, pp. 46–50, comment on Twain's views about Australian indepen-
dence from Britain. The real kinship between the American and Ballarat, emblemized
in Eureka Stockade, is not a political one, but a spiritual one. Twain had gotten into
enough trouble over free trade and protection while he was in Sydney to avoid stating
any more political opinions.

read the "Jumping Frog" story "to my mates in the bush, for I was earning an honest living then. I remember how we laughed, and wondered what sort of a fellow was the fellow who wrote it" (*Courier* [Ballarat], 19 Oct., p. 4). On 18 October, the Pioneers of California society met with the Pioneers of Ballarat in the Old Colonists' Hall to arrange a welcome to the "pioneer" Twain. They were correct in believing that "this was the initial welcome in the colony proposed by pioneers," although when Twain returned to Adelaide on New Year's Eve, he met several South Australian pioneers on Commemoration Day. After a "graceful tribute to the humorous author" by Mr. Nivens, Ballarat's pioneers elected Graham and the former Californians Purdue and Vallins to arrange an afternoon social hour at the Old Colonists' Hall (*Star* [Ballarat], 19 Oct., p. 2; *Evening Echo* [Ballarat], 19 Oct., p. 2).

On Sunday evening, 20 October, these gentlemen "were accorded an interview" at Craig's Hotel for about an hour. It was probably during this interview that Twain was told about the "Indicator" and the "Pencil Mark," thin black streaks running through the slate around Ballarat, which, when they crossed a quartz reef, pointed the way to a fortune in gold (*More Tramps*, p. 156; MTP:NB34). Other than this visit, Twain said he was unable to accept their hospitality because of his full schedule (*Courier*, 21 Oct., p. 2). He also was in poor health and needed to rest.

The interviewers found Twain suffering from a third boil, "stretched out at full length on a comfortable couch, his head propped up with a pillow," alternately smoking a cigar and a pipe (*Courier* [Ballarat], 21 Oct., p. 4). In spite of his ill health, Twain kept up a good-humored banter, commenting on the Australian colonies and their people, telling amusing yarns, and quipping about his local experiences. Twain complimented the distinctiveness of Sydney and its harbor (which he did think extraordinarily beautiful), praised the "superb" drives and "exceptionally picturesque" views in Adelaide, and called the buildings in Melbourne's Collins Street "worthy of a place in Regent Street" (*Star* [Ballarat], 21 Oct., p. 3). The reporters said that Twain spoke of Australians "almost affectionately," calling them "a warm-hearted, genial, sympathetic, and appreciative people." They are "purely Australians—not English, not American, but more American than English." He praised their frankness, energy, manners, and customs, and said their country was "a place in which he would like to live" (*Star* [Ballarat], 21 Oct., p. 8). Twain "rambled on from one subject to another, incidentally expressing a disbelief in faith healing, giving a disquisition on ghosts, early associations, and a host of other subjects." But he could not be induced—even by Californians themselves— to tell about his California mining adventures. "All my mining experiences worth giving to the world have been published in my books. There are not many things that happen to human beings in this life— whether life be long or short—that are capable of being worked up into good printable material outside autobiography," Twain said, "and then no incident is too trivial to be set down" (*Courier* [Ballarat], 21 Oct., p. 4).[12]

When, during the interview, the firebell rang, Twain told a yarn about

speaking in New York, when a full brass band outside opened fire . . . . when I found I could not make myself well heard I had a good time, too, by giving them an unspoken speech—throwing in the gestures in a way that would have done for a deaf and dumb asylum. [*Courier* (Ballarat), 21 Oct., p. 4.]

Commenting on Ballarat's famed statuary, Twain claimed to be "not accustomed to see good statuary in the public gardens in America." New York City was "disfigured by a number of statues disgraceful in art; in fact, there is nothing suggestive of art about them. They have a statue of Garibaldi in Washington Park. It would be no crime to hang the man who made that statue; and it would be a most meritorious thing also to hang the committee who selected it" (*Courier* [Ballarat], 21 Oct., p. 4). Finally, he declared his intention not to be "swindled out of everything by a carbuncle." He had not seen any of Ballarat's mines because "I've been down on the blankets pretty well ever since I arrived, and have done little else—outside lecturing—but study wall-papers. Every kind of wall-paper you possess in Australia has come under my purview, and if I fail as a lecturer, I shall write a book on Australian wall-papers" (*Courier* [Ballarat], 21 Oct., p. 4).

Such publicity perhaps contributed to the nearly full auditorium the next two evenings in spite of the rather steep two-, three-, and four-

12. In a letter to their oldest daughter Susy, Olivia Clemens wrote that Twain gave two separate interviews to reporters on this Sunday instead of only one "group" interview (transcription in Mark Twain Papers). This would account for the great difference in the newspaper reports. Harnsberger quotes most of this letter, omitting the paragraph about the interview (p. 155).

shilling tickets. Smythe's judgment had already been questioned by "A Countryman," who had written the *Courier* editor immediately after the cancellation: "I wish the agent of 'Mark Twain's' lectures would reduce the price of admission. I believe numbers will be prevented from attending if the present prices are maintained. I think three persons would attend if the lowest price were 1s where only one will attend if the price is 2s" (11 Oct., p. 1). Columnist "Tom Touchstone" echoed the sentiment, adding,

> It seems to me that his much travelled agent, Mr Smythe, should have engaged the largest hall in Ballarat, and have charged more popular prices to suit the times, for hundreds of Mark Twain's admirers would manage to pay the "splendid shilling" who cannot manage to pay 2s. Still Mr Smythe may be credited with knowing his own business best; but at the same time it is no harm to remind him that two shillings is a lot of money nowadays, and the bulk of people when they pay that, for even a Mark Twain lecture, expect a gold watch or a suite of furniture to be thrown in. [*Courier* (Ballarat), 19 Oct., p. 4.]

Despite the "dulness of the times"—the result of the longest drought Australians could remember—"and the fact that the tariff for admission is above what are known as 'popular prices,'" the Mechanics' Institute was crowded for the first "At Home": "But none who went last night would say they did not get full value for their money," the *Star* reported (22 Oct., p. 4). The *Courier* claimed that some went "with the avowed intention of refusing to be inveigled into laughter, but if any man in the gathering failed to be moved by the almost irresistible flow of humor . . . then he lives centuries behind his times, and should have sat with the Greek philosopher Zeno, under the Stoic's porch at Athens" (22 Oct., p. 4). With more time for reflection, perhaps, the evening paper described the audience, "varied as is the population of Ballarat." Among them was "an old, hard-featured man . . . who after many struggles wholly gave himself up to laughter." Nearby were "an ancient, sharp featured dame," "an emotional girl abandoned . . . to merriment," a "merchant . . . with iron jaws . . . struggling against the mirth," a "fair lady, apparently quite devoid of humor," "the inevitable dull man," uncouth "hobbledayhoys," and a "few devoted couples" who heard none of the jokes (*Evening Echo* [Ballarat], 22 Oct., p. 2).

Upon appearing on the stage, the papers reported, Twain acknowledged "round after round of applause" for "two or three minutes" (*Star* [Ballarat], 22 Oct., p. 4). He then apologized for postponing his engagement "because he had a carbuncle staying with him at the time, and was constrained on the advice of his physician to stay in Melbourne and entertain his guest" (*Courier* [Ballarat], 22 Oct., p. 4). His carbuncle was, of course, familiar to the audience, having been reported in the city newspapers and reprinted in the country ones. But the fact that both Ballarat papers printed the opening joke indicates the pleasure the audience must have taken from this bit of self-satire. Occasionally, a "slight twitch of the mouth, or the raising of the eyebrows" warned the audience of an impending joke; "others were fired point blank, without any warning but the result was the same" (*Star* [Ballarat], 22 Oct., p. 4).

Twain repeated the stories he had used in the capital cities—first the fishing excursion, then the buck-jumping horse, followed by the punch brothers routine (first used in Horsham), Artemus Ward's whiskey cocktail, Huck's helping Jim to escape—mostly taken from his books. Giving some hints of the next night's lecture on morality, he concluded the first "At Home" by reading his discourse on the German language and the tale of the mixed-up genders of the fishwife. The lecture "bristled with the humor Americans have made so peculiarly their own, thanks in no small measure to the writings of Mark Twain" (*Star* [Ballarat], 22 Oct., p. 4). The auditors had varying responses: a few left at the intermission; others leaving the theatre said it was not "worth listening to"; but no doubt most agreed that they had not "laughed so much for a long time" (*Evening Echo* [Ballarat], 22 Oct., p. 2).

The second evening began with Twain's admiration of the Australian custom of not introducing the speaker: A Nevada miner had once introduced him by saying, "I don't know anything about this man. At least, I only know two things about him. He has never been in gaol; and the other is I don't know why" (*Courier* [Ballarat], 23 Oct., p. 4; this seems to be first time he had used the jail introduction). This talk was on "the moral rejuvenation of the human race," beginning with the stolen green watermelon story. Twain warned against jumping to conclusions on circumstantial evidence, citing the woman with a sharpened pencil, apparently used only this once. Twain claimed that even if a person were told that the woman had used a knife to sharpen the pencil, to look at the evidence "you would swear she had used her teeth" (*Star* [Ballarat], 23 Oct., p. 4). He told of the champion liar of the Sandwich Islands; Jim, Tom, and Huck on the Holy Land; the jumping frog; the whistling stammerer; and the ship captain's yarn (*Courier* [Ballarat], 23 Oct., p. 4). He told about the slave woman's dead son, and about christening a boy who turned out to be a girl (*Star* [Ballarat], 23 Oct., p. 4). Making his usual remarks about the poem on the exotic Australian animals, he gave it a try. The Australian poem had become a favorite—along with the German language lesson—for, as the Ballarat *Star* put it, "it is new and touches our own land" (23 Oct., p. 4). He concluded the night's entertainment with the editorial rivalry in Nevada and Uncle Dan'l's ghost story (*Courier* [Ballarat], 23 Oct., p. 4).

"A Feast of Intellectual Fun"

The Clemenses traveled approximately seventy-five miles the next day from Ballarat to a Bendigo that had already been prepared for their visit by quotations from the Melbourne papers, reprints of the interview in Ballarat, and Smythe's advertising. The visit had been announced from 30 September through 3 October, when the original show was to have been given at the Masonic Hall. Who could resist a performer who kept the "archdeacon, and close to him ... a rural dean, backed by a number of the minor clergy, all cackling like school-boys"? Twain had appealed to everyone: An "aged senator[,] ... a bookmaker[,] ... the Church of England Assembly[, which] had evidently adjourned to the theatre in a body[,] ... the Catholic priests ..., several Presbyterians laughing really hard ..., one burly Wesleyan, even some particular Baptists ... seemed more convinced that [they] had got the worth of [their] money" (*Advertiser* [Bendigo], 19 Oct., p. 5; reprinted from *Argus* [Melbourne], 28 Sept., p. 7). An article in the same paper, however, had given some indication of Twain's earnings from his writings and had accused Twain of not being "content with his profits as one of the most successful authors of the world"; it said that he had "nobody but himself to blame" for the poverty that sent him talking round the world. Even though "all the world wishes him well out of it," it seems possible that the imputed greed might have affected attendance.

Bendigo was a thriving country town in 1895 with a score of factories and industries, 144 square miles of mining operations including a thousand quartz leases, and ample municipal services. It had five parks, at least seven auditoriums, nineteen churches, and various galleries and libraries. It was served by rail connections, a tram, and a hundred miles of streets, much of them electrically or gas-lighted. There were at least three buildings with chimes worthy of Twain's attention—the Post Office, an Anglican church, and a Catholic church. It was one of the larger provincial centers with a population of 27,500; yet the first night was the most poorly attended of all Twain's performances. Although Ballarat's patrons had complained of the high prices, Smythe did not reduce tickets at Bendigo; consequently, "the prices of admission were not so popular as 'Mark Twain,' and the result was but a moderate attendance" (*Advertiser* [Bendigo], 24 Oct., p. 3). Nevertheless, the audience gave him a "hearty welcome" and responded "in roars of laughter." Twain was in Bendigo—one of only four inland towns originally scheduled—probably because of the efforts of John Gregory Edwards, editor of the *Independent*. Edwards had chanced to be in New York when the itinerary for the world tour was being drawn up; when he returned to Bendigo, Edwards made various arrangements, and the Clemenses spent much of their free time with the family.[13]

The Bendigo *Advertiser* reviewer described Twain's stage mannerisms and appearance: His

> drawl, which all have heard of ... with the solemnity of his features ..., a merry twinkle of the eye ..., together with the general quietness of his attitude, centred attention, and gave point to his fun, which was further emphasised by happy elocutionary working of the voice, frequent shakes of his head of frizzy whitish hair, smoothed down only round the crown .... He spoke just like his books; drollery and quaintness crawled out of him. Ideas, comparisons, expressions and facts were twisted and turned upside down and inside out, and mixed up in apparently the most incongruous fashion; yet there was a method in the madness that tickled the fancy, touched the feelings and delighted the soul. [24 Oct., p. 3.]

He gave many of the same "moral lessons" reported in Ballarat; reviewers often noted both the "pathetic and rollicking chapters" from his books; and the German language discourse, used again at Bendigo, was evidently a crowd-pleaser. His "illustrative story in English set in the German idiom ..., one of the happiest efforts," probably referred to the fishwife tale. His "explanation of the inconvenience he was put to by the detention of his manager, Mr Smythe, in quarantine" on the *Cuzco* was appreciated by his audience, who had by now read about

---

13. From statements by Edwards's daughter to Mrs. Lucy Hill, Bendigo Branch of the Royal Historical Society, *News Letter*, May 1974 (photocopy provided by Alex Stone).

the episode in the newspapers. He would continue to joke about poor Smythe off and on until he was released from the quarantine station.

On Thursday morning, 24 October, Edwards himself drove the Clemenses and Mrs. Edwards "in a Victoria drawn by spanking horses" around the city. At Lone Tree Hill they walked "to the summit of the stone look-out, and Mark Twain said it was one of the finest panoramas he had ever seen, and it was typically American in its distance."[14] In *More Tramps Abroad* he spoke fondly, although somewhat ironically, about "the dean of the editorial fraternity" who showed him "105 miles of shade-trees" in the city, Weeroona lake and park, the Pall Mall, and other sites (*More Tramps*, pp. 159-161; MTP:NB34). He also may have visited the hospital.

On the afternoon of Thursday, 24 October, Twain was entertained by the Mayor and city fathers. At the ceremony he was presented with a keepsake letter by Mr. Frank Fearn, a scenic artist and sign painter who was "possessed of considerable literary ability."[15] The artist had arranged the letter in a "handsomely illuminated" booklet with "appropriate embellishments ... [of] the Australian and American flags, while Jim Smiley's famous jumping frog was not forgotten." Inside were numerous jokes and puns about the city fathers, which concluded by telling about "a profound worker. He founded a foundry, and thereby laid the foundation of a business which is not likely to founder. But, confound it," Fearn had run out of space. Twain wrote him a note the same day thanking him for the artwork and kind words. "It is kindnesses and courtesies like these from unknown Australian friends that convince me that I am not held as a stranger in this land" (*Bendigonian*, 31 Oct., p. 10).

On the second night, the Royal Princess Theatre was filled due to the reduction in prices. Twain told his watermelon story and about his first interview with Artemus Ward. The "illustrations of picturesque lying, in which exaggeration forms a conspicuous part ... gave opportunity for telling some marvellous yarns" including the troubles of a guide for some tourists across Europe. The tales "stirred the cachinnatory nerves till they tired, and it was a sort of relief to get away from the flood

---

14. Ibid.

15. George McKay, *Annals of Bendigo*. Particular thanks are extended to Alex Stone and Frank Cusack of Bendigo for providing me with information on the city officials, Frank Fearn and J. G. Edwards.

of humor, wit, and drollery, which the lecturer slowly poured forth."
The full house, the reviewer opined, would long remember the visit
"as providing a feast of intellectual fun" (*Advertiser* [Bendigo], 25 Oct.,
p. 3).

"Upon his entrance," the reviewer for the *Advertiser* said, "according
to his habit, slowly on the stage, he was at once recognised. There
could be no mistaking the likeness to his portraits which flooded the
city." Evidently, Smythe had provided posters as he had in the capital
cities, and the *Bendigonian*, the local weekly, carried a photograph, as
had the Melbourne papers, which must surely have been available only
ninety-five miles away in Bendigo.

Twain tells a long yarn in *More Tramps Abroad* about his photographs,
explaining that he met an Irishman in Bendigo, "an educated gentleman; grave, and kindly and courteous; a bachelor, and about forty-five
or possibly fifty years old." The Irishman claimed to have been president of the Mark Twain Club some fifteen years earlier. In Bendigo,
he had a remarkable collection of Twain's books and knew them thoroughly; "he showed [Twain] an album with twenty-three photographs
of [him] in it. Five of them were of old dates [sent by Twain himself],
the others of various later crops; the list closed with a picture taken
at Falk's in Sydney a month before" (*More Tramps*, pp. 160–162). Although ninety years later it is hard to know if Twain was telling the
truth, there is enough verifiable information in *More Tramps Abroad* to
believe the outline of the story is true.

In later years, J. G. Edwards's daughter recalled that

> just before the visitors were leaving, Mr. Edwards said that he would like a
> momento to their stay in Bendigo, and Mark Twain looked at them whim-
> sically, took a slip of paper from his pocket, wrote some words on it, signed
> it, then passed it to his host. It read:—"Let us endeavor to so live, that
> when we die, even the undertaker will be sorry. Yours truly, Mark Twain,
> October 24 1895."

"The Bell Clock Is the Vilest"

From Bendigo the Clemenses took the five o'clock train
to Maryborough (where Twain actually followed his original itinerary),
arriving in the afternoon of 25 October. It was a town of only 5,200 people, but in the gold district surrounding it lived another 12,000 souls.
Only about fifty miles from Bendigo via Castlemaine (or forty from Bal-

larat on a direct spur), Maryborough had an impressive new station. The Clemenses were met there by leading residents, who drove Twain to Town Hall, "where he was accorded a hearty welcome" by Mayor F. J. Field and a "representative gathering of the townspeople." The mayor made a brief complimentary welcoming speech expressing the belief that a "gentleman of the character of Mr. Clemens coming amongst us helped very much to remove the erroneous impressions formed about the Australian colonies, which to many were an unknown world." The mayor voiced some insecurity about an Australian identity or at least its "image" to the world, when he said

> he had no doubt Mr. Clemens, when he returned to America, would give to the world some racily-written account of his trip, showing that the people were not altogether black, but were in the enjoyment of enlightened civilisation—a people loyal to their Queen, striving to make their own little world better than they found it, with happy homes and a contented people. [*Maryborough and Dunolly Advertiser*, 28 Oct., p. 5.]

Wishing Twain a pleasant trip through Australia, the mayor toasted the guests. Twain addressed the Maryboroughans as "friends," saying in his "quiet drawl that since his arrival on these shores five weeks ago he had took to considering himself not as a stranger, but as a friend." He joked that not only had officers of dignity applied the term, but so also had the larrikin, and he expressed Mrs. Clemens' thanks for the hospitality. To the mayor's "inevitable" lament about the lack of a clock on the railway tower—owing to a change of government—and the request that Twain use his influence to obtain one, the humorist "sympathised with the Mayor .... But he had no vote, no influence in the land, otherwise he would pray, he would beseech, that a clock be provided—but let it be a blank silent clock. (Laughter) Of all the nuisances in the world, the bell clock is the vilest. It strikes the hours, it strikes the quarters, the half, the three quarters." Twain told about being wakened by the Bendigo clock at six a.m.

> It struck a lot of things, and then the hour of six. . . . at the quarter three or four discordant notes rang out, then at the half-hour eight more discordant notes, at three-quarter 16 discordant notes, and when it began the hour of seven we had 150 discordant notes. . . . Mr. Mayor, I am willing to glorify your station as much as you desire, but I would like to see that station clock remain deaf and dumb for one thousand years. [*Maryborough and Dunolly Advertiser*, 28 Oct., p. 5.]

The Bendigo clock does in fact strike "a lot of things"—so many things that legend has it, when the singer Madame Melba stayed in the same hotel, she had the clock disconnected. The Maryborough newspaper contains the only record of this tale about the Bendigo clock. After Twain's response, an official photograph of the welcoming party was made, which Twain professed to have liked so much "that he would have favored Mr. [Charlie] Farr with a special sitting had time permitted—no small compliment to our photo artist."

That very morning area readers had been warned to "keep your Clothes Loose, so that you will not burst them or hurt yourself whilst laughing" (*Dunolly and Betbetshire Express*, 25 Oct., p. 2); evidently, Maryboroughans were genuinely in danger of excessive laughing. The thrice-weekly *Advertiser* reported in detail on Twain's "At Home" at the Town Hall. The reviewer said the prologue was "a delightful piece of dry humor, smart and complete in itself, and one of the smartest and neatest of his inventions in that particular class. He had a little scheme to offer, but he did it with some difficulty, because it was a large scheme for a person of his size" (28 Oct., p. 5).

The moral lessons included the watermelon story, which taught the farmer not to "sell" green watermelons and the boy not to steal melons "like that." He followed this with the story of being a Nevada editor, the lost dime, an "illustration of the disposition to jump at conclusions on circumstantial or insufficient evidence" (the christening of the boy who turned out to be a girl) and finally his trouble as a continental courier. Twain then gave his Australian poem, explaining that "everyone knew the trouble about poetry was writing the last line—any one can write the first line; but nothing would really rhyme with ornithorhynchus." So he tried again: "Land of the fruitful rabbit, Land of the boomerang." The reporter paraphrased the humorist: It was "kind of hard to make anything rhyme with long three syllable words. Finally he hit on the golden secret of making all the ends of the lines words of one sylla-ble, and he succeeded in sketching out a few more lines, the reading of which provoked hearty and continuous laughter." He concluded with what had by now become the apparent favorite—the exposition of the German language (MTP:NB34, corroborates the list of stories given in Maryborough).

The first six inches of this review were reprinted almost verbatim from the Bendigo *Advertiser* of 24 October. Tickets were advertised at one, two, and three shillings—the popular prices—and, "in anticipation of [being filled,] the 'syndicate' who brought him to Maryborough entirely suspended the free list, not even excepting the press. ... The result was that while the chairs and body of the hall were filled, there was an array of empty benches in the balcony."

Twain had complimented the energy of the Australians, finding them more like Americans than like Britons, but above all "purely Australians." Clearly the iconoclast Twain felt a kinship with Ballarat, Bendigo, and Maryborough that – except for gatherings of journalists only—was special in his Australian tour. The frontier spirit of these towns lingered far into the century, and, confronted with a notorious liar, they joined in the fun with some pranks of their own.[16]

"As Popular as His Books"

After Maryborough, Twain gave only four more public appearances before sailing for New Zealand on 31 October. It was with unrestrained good humor that these towns responded to Twain and he to them. He was obviously impressed by their history of gold— he wrote in *More Tramps Abroad* that Bendigo was even richer than Ballarat and that between them they had produced in even less time half as much gold as all of California had produced. Evidently he found out very quickly that he could spin a tall tale about these miners and their towns and they would not take offense—in fact they seemed to egg him on. In his travel book Twain told an elaborate story about the Irishman in Bendigo who had for nearly a decade carried on "altogether the most ingenious and laborious and cheerful and pains-taking practical joke I have ever heard of .... Finally [the Irishman] said: 'Do you remember a note from Melbourne fourteen or fifteen years ago, telling about your lecture tour in Australia and your death and burial in Melbourne? ...I wrote it.... Yes, I did it'" (*More Tramps*, p. 165).

Long after Twain left Victoria, he claimed that on the train from Bendigo to Maryborough he had met a gentleman in the smoking car who warned him just how poor he would find the accommodations: sandbags to sleep on, pillows filled with rocks, tiny rooms with icy floors, stinking coal-oil lamps, clothing nails, and "there isn't any slop-

---

16. Some of the information in these three sections appeared in Miriam J. Shillingsburg, "From Ballarat to Bendigo with Mark Twain," *Australian Literary Studies* 12 (May, 1985), 116-119.

jar. The hotels don't keep them. That is, outside of Sydney and Melbourne" (*More Tramps*, p. 202). While the foregoing sounds like a whole-cloth lie, the jokes about the Victorian railroads were "factual" and the subject of much satire in the colony. The government ran them: "In the beginning they tried idiots; then they imported the French— which was going backwards ... now it runs the roads itself—which is going backwards again.... the Government puts down a road wher- ever anybody wants it ... and by consequence," Twain's informant told him, "we've got, in the colony of Victoria, 800 railway stations" (*More Tramps*, p. 204). By the time he wrote this in his book, he had appar- ently forgotten that there was no clock on the Maryborough station, merging it with the one in Bendigo. He claimed that the man in the train said:

> And the clock! Everybody will show you the clock. There isn't a station in Europe that's got such a clock. It doesn't strike—and that's one mercy. It hasn't any bell; and, as you'll have cause to remember, if you keep your reason, all Australia is simply bedamned with bells. On every quarter-hour, night and day, they jingle a tiresome chime of half a dozen notes—all the clocks in town at once, all the clocks in Australasia at once, and all the very same notes! [*More Tramps*, p. 204.]

But Twain's irreverence about "Ballarat English" best demonstrates the rapport between the American and the Australians. In *More Tramps Abroad* he wrote that "as in the German Empire all cultivated people claim to speak Hanoverian German, so in Australia all cultivated people claim to speak Ballarat English." He continued,

> Even in England this cult has made considerable progress, and now that it is favoured by the two great Universities, the time is not far away when Ballarat English will come into general use among the educated classes of Great Britain at large. Its great merit is, that it is shorter than ordinary English—that is, it is more compressed. ... An illustration will show what I mean. When [Mayor Little] called and I handed him a chair, he bowed and said:
> "Q."
> Presently, when we were lighting our cigars, he held a match to mine, and I said:
> "Thank you;" and he said:
> "Km."
> Then I saw. "Q" is the end of the phrase "I thank you"; "Km" is the end of the phrase "You are welcome." [*More Tramps*, pp. 157–158.]

A few points worth noting from the country reports modify somewhat the present understanding of the season's lectures. First, Twain seems not to have used a firmly set routine. The stories were discrete, the transitions between them various, and several stories, among which he chose, illustrated the same "moral." By the time he had given some thirteen performances and half a dozen "impromptu" talks to journalists and private gatherings, Twain had discovered the "humor provocative of innocent laughter" (*Advertiser* [Bendigo], 24 Oct., p. 3) that tickled the Australian imagination. This can be seen more easily in the provincial phase of the tour than in the cities, because in the country Twain gave lectures to a different town—not just a different audience—every night but two. And whereas in the cities the "At Homes" were advertised as being three different performances, this was not necessary in the country. Therefore, one would expect Twain to rely on crowd-pleasers; if he did, the Australian favorites must have been the Australian poem, the stolen watermelon, the christening of a boy who turned out to be a girl, and—most of all—the vagaries of gender in the German language. Finally, it seems clear that Twain used comparatively few—if any—notes. However, wherever he went, the humorist "lived up to his reputation as a writer [and] his 'At Homes' [were] as popular as his books" (*Maryborough and Dunolly Advertiser*, 25 Oct., p. 2).

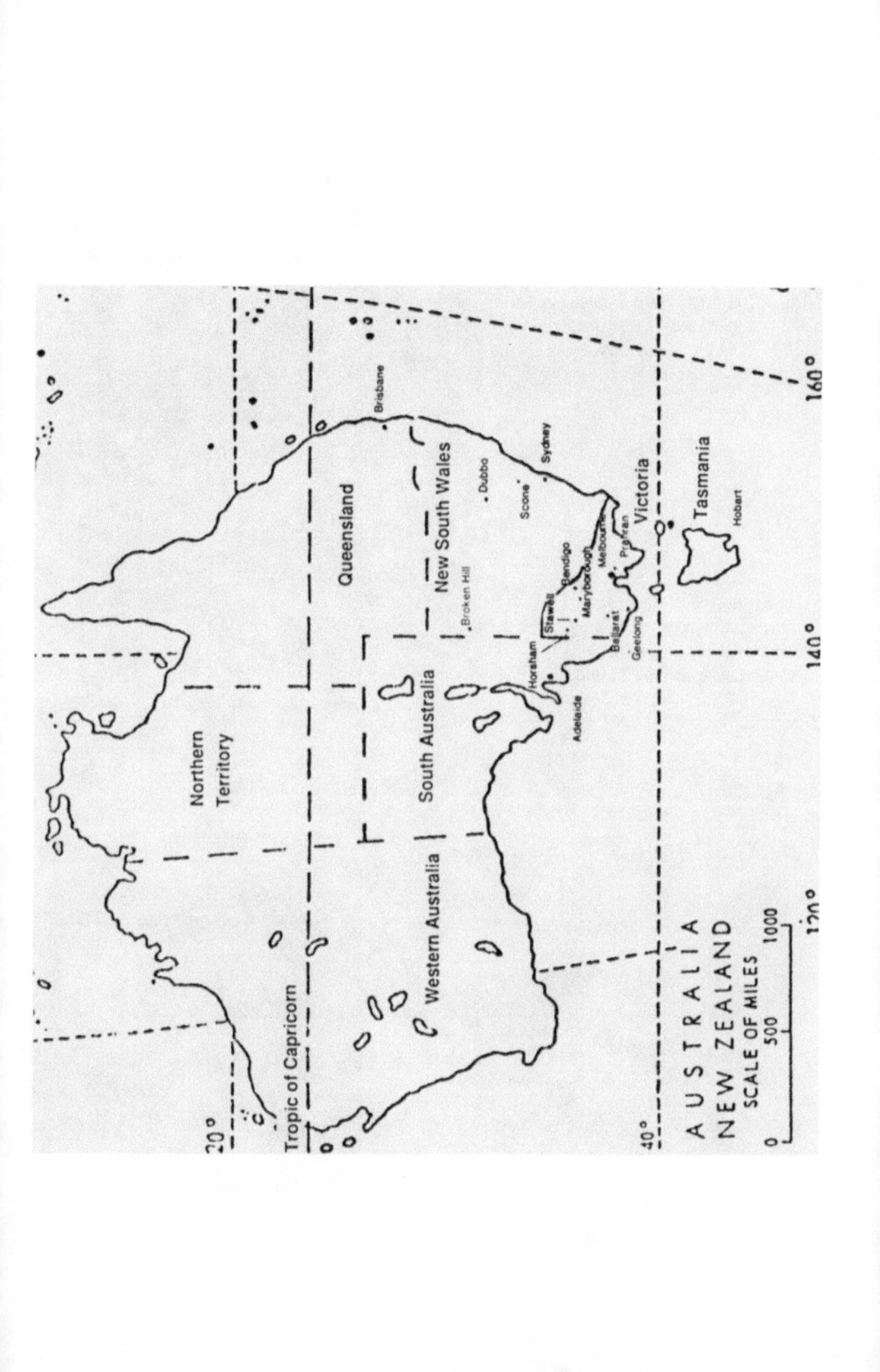

Twain and manager, Carlyle
Smythe. Photo almost surely
made by Joseph Kinsey,
Christchurch, New Zealand,
November 1895. From Arthur
Scott, *Mark Twain At Large*,
1969. (Part of this photograph is
in the Alexander Turnbull Library
Picture Collection, Wellington,
New Zealand)

Warrimoo and *Mararoa* in
Dunedin Harbor. Sketch by
W. Hodgkins (Field-Hodgkins
Collection, Alexander Turnbull
Library, Wellington, New Zealand)

Sketch of Mark Twain at the
City Hall, Dunedin. *A Sketch
from the Stalls* by W. Hodgkins
(Field-Hodgkins Collection,
Alexander Turnbull Library,
Wellington, New Zealand)

Twain's manager, Robert
Sparrow Smythe. Photo by
Talma, Sydney, *The Referee*,
May 1917. (Courtesy, State
Library of New South Wales)

NOT A REPRESENTATIVE BIRD.

"I did see one of your native creatures while I was in New South Wales. That was the laughing jackass. It sat on a tree and I stood looking at it. But it wouldn't laugh for me. I tried to make it laugh, indeed I did; but it respectfully declined."—Mark Twain *interviewed by the "Herald."*

Mark Twain (later)—"GREAT SCOT! THAT FIRST BIRD MUST HAVE BEEN STUFFED. I NEVER HAD SO APPRECIATIVE AN AUDIENCE IN MY LIFE BEFORE."

Melbourne Punch, October 1895. (Courtesy, State Library of Victoria)

Mark Twain—"Alas! that I should envy you!" Parkes—"What do you envy? My politics, my poems, or my brains?" Mark T—"Alas! neither, 'Tis your hair consumes me with envy!" *The Bulletin*, September 1895. (Courtesy, State Library of New South Wales)

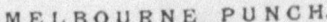

MELBOURNE PUNCH.

PREPARING FOR MARK TWAIN.

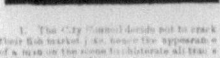

1. The City Council decide not to crack
their fish market; &c. hence the appearance
of a man on the scene to obliterate all trace
of the recent subsidence.

3. The citizens are now signing a
petition to send Mr. Zox on an aerial excursion to the moon. Two jokers in the place at
once might bring about a national calamity.

2. The Ministry have taken precautions,
in order to save the city from utter destruction, to gag Ha ! Ha ! Peacock.

4. Patterson prepares to break Mark all
up with his big joke.

Melbourne Punch, September 1895. (Courtesy, State Library of Victoria)

Olivia and Clara Clemens. Photo by Mr. Barnett, Falk's Studio, Sydney. *Melbourne Punch*, September 1895. (Courtesy, State Library of Victoria)

The Dean Case. *Quiz and Lantern*, October 1895.
(Courtesy, State Library of South Australia)

QUIZ.   JUDGE, GOVERNOR AND PARSONS.   QUIZ.

Appearance cancelled, Bendigo, October 1895.
(Courtesy, State Library of Victoria)

MARK TWAIN.

THE appearance in Bendigo of the Celebrated Humorist has been unavoidably postponed. Due notice will be given of the dates of his lectures. Ticket holders can have their money returned on application at Suttons' to-day.

R. S. SMYTHE.

MARK TWAIN,
MARK TWAIN,
THE   ONLY.
THE   ONLY.
THE   ONLY.
THE   ONLY.

BIJOU THEATRE—TO-NIGHT.

Fifth Appearance of
THE INIMITABLE ENTERTAINER
On his
TALKING TOUR ROUND the WORLD.

OVERFLOWING AUDIENCES.

Positively No Free List.

LAST APPEARANCE in MELBOURNE
LAST APPEARANCE in MELBOURNE
LAST APPEARANCE in MELBOURNE
Of the
AUTHOR of "THE INNOCENTS ABROAD."

THIS (WEDNESDAY) EVENING,
At 8 o'clock,
The
SECOND MARK TWAIN "AT HOME."
SECOND MARK TWAIN "AT HOME."
SECOND MARK TWAIN "AT HOME."
SECOND MARK TWAIN "AT HOME."
Introducing "The Boy and the Corpse," &c.
HUMOROUS LIFE and CHARACTER SKETCHES.

Dress Circle and Reserved Stalls, 5s.; Unreserved
Stalls, 3s.; Family Circle, 2s.; Gallery, 1s.
Seats may be secured at Glen's, where Stalls and
Family Circle Tickets may also be purchased in ad-
vance, and at Mullen's.
R. S. SMYTHE.

BENDIGO—THURSDAY and FRIDAY.
GEELONG MONDAY.
BALLARAT TUESDAY.

Melbourne, October 1895.
Parts of two performances
advertised as one. (Courtesy,
State Library of Victoria)

Bendigo, October 1895. Only
two towns were not sold out.
(Courtesy, State Library of
Victoria)

REDUCED PRICES

MARK TWAIN,
MARK TWAIN,
Who last evening kept a thronged and enthusiastic
audience in a ripple of laughter from the beginning
to the end of the entertainment,
THE GREATEST HUMORIST OF THE AGE,
Will
TO-NIGHT, IN THE PRINCESS THEATRE,
Give his positively
LAST MARK TWAIN "AT HOME"
IN BENDIGO,
Illustrated with Humorous and
NEW LIFE AND CHARACTER SKETCHES.
An
ENTIRELY DIFFERENT ENTERTAINMENT.
Circle, 3s ; Stalls, 2s ; Pit and Gallery, 1s.
Box plan at Suttons'.

Sir Henry Parkes and twenty-three-year-old bride. (Courtesy, State Library of New South Wales)

Sydney School of Arts, ca. 1895. (Courtesy, State Library of New South Wales)

CHAPTER SIX

Farewell
to Australia

"I Have Been Young Again"

When the Clemenses returned to Spencer Street Station on Saturday morning, 26 October, Twain was fatigued. In the last fourteen days he had "lectured" eleven times in six different towns, attended at least five public welcomes, granted three interviews, and ridden in trains or sat in train stations countless hours. In his spare time he nursed his carbuncle. They left Maryborough that morning on the 5:00 train, and in his notebook he made rather frank judgments about the inefficiencies in the Victorian railroad system. He confided, "The railroad is the only thoroughly European thing here. That is, they build fine stations and then have all the idiotic European railway system in perfection—slow trains, no drinking-water, no sanitary arrangements, every conceivable inconvenience; an utterly insane system—the jackass system."[1] Most of his complaints later turned up in *More Tramps Abroad* in the guise of a yarn told to him on the train between Castlemaine and Maryborough (*More Tramps*, pp. 201–207).

Between Bendigo and Maryborough Twain went by Castlemaine (so he said) in order to save some time "fooling along the road." But a passenger on the train explained that his round-trip Sydney-Adelaide-Sydney ticket was not good "over that twelve miles"; he should have gone by Ballarat instead. Although "if you shake a rag the train will

---

1. *Notebook*, ed. Paine, p. 254.

stop in the midst of the wilderness to pick you up," the Victorian railways "repudiate their own tickets, and collect a poor little illegitimate extra shilling out of you for that twelve miles." Moreover, "there's nobody on hand to examine your ticket" at the station, and when the conductor examines it, "he is not authorised to receive the money, and he won't. You must climb out" (*More Tramps*, pp. 201-205). Although this must surely be a comic exaggeration, corruption and strife in the system were in the newspapers nearly every day while Twain was in Australia, and while in Melbourne, he noted a court decision against transferring return tickets (MTP:NB35).

Before they would leave for the five-day cruise to New Zealand, Twain would give a lecture and a "smoker" in Melbourne, and lectures in the nearby towns Geelong and Prahran. Three fourths of these were, apparently, unqualified successes. Twain gave a farewell matinee at 3:00 on Saturday at a crowded Athenaeum Hall (Twain pronounced this word Athee-neum, according to *Melbourne Punch*, [26 Sept., p. 203]). His "new Life and Character Sketches were remarkably funny .... the matinee was an undoubted success in every particular" (*Evening News* [Melbourne], 26 Oct., p. 1). In the early evening Twain attended one of the last Melbourne performances of Russian pianist, Mark Hambourg. No doubt the humorist hoped to be unobtrusive, but his entry into Town Hall "was the signal for a round of hearty cheers, which were continued until Mr. Clemens bowed his acknowledgement," reported the *Age*, (28 Oct., p. 3). The program included selections from Bach, Liszt, Chopin, Schubert, and Tschaikowsky, among others, but Twain must have left at the intermission, for he had an engagement with the Institute of Journalists at the Cathedral Hotel on Swanston Street.

The Institute gave Twain a dinner at which they made him "a life honorary member of the Australian Institute of Journalists." The "gathering was thoroughly representative of Victorian art and literature," and included pressmen from other towns in the colony. During the proceedings Twain gave five short speeches, four of which were reported by the newspapers. Mr. W. P. Lambie of the *Age* gave Twain a basket of home-grown flowers for his wife Olivia and daughter Clara, who, Twain said, were "thoroughly well qualified to appreciate" them. In accepting, Twain explained that at first he had intended to travel the world alone, but "for reasons which those who are married ... will understand," the ladies came with him.

I am technically "boss" of the family which I am carrying along—(laughter)—but I am grateful to know that it is only technically—that the real authority rests on the other side of the house. (Hear, Hear.) It is placed there by a beneficent Providence, who foresaw before I was born, or, if he did not, he has found it out since—(laughter)—that I am not in any way qualified to travel alone. [*Age* (Melbourne), 28 Oct., p. 7.]

Twain was perhaps alluding to his recent panic when, arriving at the railway station to leave Adelaide, Olivia, Clara and the luggage were not there waiting. The ladies had gone carriage riding with the Lieutenant Governor Mr. Samuel James Way! Twain expressed his "good fortune" in having a wife who for twenty-five years was "always capable, both by brain and by heart, to make up all shortcomings which exist in me." While Twain attributed this "to an over-ruling Providence," he said, "my experience with Providence has not been of a nature to give me great confidence in his judgment, and I consider that my wife crept in while his attention was occupied elsewhere" (*Age*, 28 Oct., p. 7). Through the humor, his profound admiration for his petite wife and her quiet discipline is clear. Of Olivia during this period of Twain's life, his friend steel magnate Andrew Carnegie said, "He had a heroine in his wife. She it was who sustained him and traveled the world round with him as his guardian angel, and enabled him to conquer . . . . This he never failed to tell his intimates."[2]

In proposing the toast to "Our Guest," John Lamont Dow, formerly Parliamentarian, but presently on the *Age* staff, announced that he "had the extreme pleasure some years ago of meeting Mark Twain in the United States of America, and told then that he would find an appreciative people here" (*Age*, 28 Oct., p. 7). Dow must therefore have been the "eminent Melbourne journalist" who had attempted in 1886 to bring the American to "the fifth quarter" of the globe. Responding to the honorary membership into the Institute, Twain alluded to his birthday which was coming within a month: "I shall be sixty years of age. I have detested old age from my infancy, and anything that removes from me even for a few moments the consciousness that I am old is gratifying to me. For the two or three hours that I have been here tonight . . . I have been young again" (*Age*, 28 Oct., p. 7).

The last toast of the evening was proposed to Clara by Ephraim Zox, M. L. A., who had been satirized in a cartoon celebrating Twain's ar-

---

2. *Autobiography of Andrew Carnegie*, p. 284.

rival earlier in the month. The free trade member for East Melbourne, he was a feisty Parliamentarian with a reputation as a joker. Recently the newspapers had reported that although he was very sick with a bronchial ailment, he still had gone to Parliament. When his opponent told him he looked terrible and ought to be in bed, Zox had answered, "you ought never to be out of it" (*Age*, 10 Oct., p. 4). It is not clear whether Twain knew Zox except in the context of the Institute of Journalists' roast.

Twain stayed after the smoke-night until the wee hours chatting with friends, including, most likely, Herbert Low. It was probably this same evening that Twain, after five toasts, craved "saveloys, hot, bought from street vendors late at night. 'Say,' he remarked to a party of convivial friends who were seeing him home a few evenings ago, 'can you point out where we can see a saveloy man? I reckon hot saveloys are the most sobering things on earth.'" A cart could not be found, but *Punch* analyzed: "Success has not spoiled him in the least degree. He confesses that he would rather meet a company of convivial friends—penmen for preference—and finish with a saveloy impromptu supper on the kerbstone, than dine with the great off silver dishes!" (*Melbourne Punch*, 31 Oct., p. 278).[3] Twain had certainly had his share of dining off silver dishes on two continents before even coming to Australia. And in Sydney and Melbourne he was often a guest along with the great.

The family were overnight guests, probably on Sunday, of Mr. John Wagner at his "superb house looking on a most beautiful view." This was a new house, built in 1892 in Malvern, now belonging to the State College of Victoria. "We had a very large bedroom," Livy wrote, "with six windows in it, three of them leading onto a very extensive porch. Our bedroom was about thirty feet square ...[and] the lower hall of the house ... is twice the size of our Hartford Hall" back home in Connecticut.[4] No doubt it was Mrs. Wagner or her daughter Mrs. Mc-Cullough who "asked him to include in his programme the story of the yellow dog. For the life of him he could not recall the faintest outline of that story, and it was only after mentioning the request to his wife that he was reminded of the incident in 'Pudd'nhead Wilson,' the latest book he had published."[5] While they were in Melbourne "the

---

3. See also *Herald*, 28 Oct., p. 2.

4. Potts and Potts, "The Mark Twain Family in Australia," *Overland*, 70 (1978), 47.

5. Carlyle Smythe, "The 'Real' Mark Twain," *Pall Mall Magazine*, 16 (September

journals contended one against the other in making alluring offers to write a description of the 'Melbourne Cup,'"[6] which is run annually on 5 November. Frederick W. Haddon, who had in 1868 been a founder of the Yorick Club which had honored Twain during his first visit to Melbourne, wrote a letter on 30 October inviting him to contribute an article, presumably for the *Argus*, the newspaper which Twain had complimented and which Haddon had edited since 1867.[7]

On Monday evening Clara and Olivia were guests of the vice-regal party—part of what the *Age* called a "large and brilliant assemblage"— at the Royal Metropolitan Leidertafel concert in Town Hall. They quite enjoyed sitting "about two seats from Lord and Lady Brassey," who had arrived just that Saturday from London to take up the Governorship of Victoria. When the Clemenses had been in Adelaide his arrival there was imminent, and the papers were full of the plans being made to welcome him. His yacht, the *Sunbeam*, reached Adelaide on Sunday 19 October, after Twain had begun his country tour. Lord and Lady Brassey arrived at Port Phillip on the twenty-fourth; the reception and swearing in were on Friday. And on Monday the Clemens women met them. Livy wrote her sister Sue, "It was all very interesting to see and be in. We were with a gentleman and lady who have been very kind to us since we arrived in Melbourne."[8]

"The Expectancy of Something Better"

Geelong, with a population of nearly 23,000 and another 10,000 in the suburbs, was located about forty-five miles southwest of Melbourne. It had a good harbor, excellent location, and salubrious climate. Settled as early as the forties, the present suburb of Grovedale was known until 1915 as "Germantown" from the original ten families who moved there. For a century from the 1840's the city called itself the "pivot" of the Victorian colony because of its active commerce. Geelong gave the Twain visit excellent press coverage, partly because it had five newspapers, including the *Geelong Advertiser*, the oldest in Victoria. The papers, like those in Ballarat and Stawell, had promoted the visit with reports from both Adelaide and Melbourne for

---

1898), 32.

6. Smythe, p. 34.

7. Samuel L. Clemens to Fred. W. Haddon, 14 November 1895, Victoria State Library.

8. Potts and Potts, p. 48.

nearly a month before Twain actually came to Geelong. The original plan was for all three Clemenses to visit Geelong on Monday 7 October, squeezed in between Bendigo and Ballarat on the way west to Adelaide. Geelong had planned for the party to be welcomed in the morning by Mayor Richardson and the town councillors and then taken for a drive "through the neighborhood." He was to speak at the Exhibition Theatre in the evening (*Evening Star* [Geelong], 3 Oct., p. 3).

Smythe had seen to the early press releases describing the complete world tour, using expressions like "the most comprehensive lecture tour ever organised" and announcing a prospective "10 lectures in London, for which he is to receive £2000, the highest price ever paid to a one-man entertainer" (*Geelong Advertiser*, 5 Oct., p. 2). Carlyle Smythe, younger member of Twain's managerial team, was in Geelong on 4 October making final arrangements for what promised to be "something for the Pivotonians to congratulate themselves upon that their city is included" in the proposed fifteen-month world tour (*Evening Star* [Geelong], 5 Oct., p. 3).

Twain's imminent arrival was announced in the morning's papers, and it was not until the afternoon of the scheduled performance that an announcement appeared of Twain's illness in Melbourne and the consequent cancellation of his visit to Geelong for that evening. Dr. FitzGerald had wired young Smythe that Twain was "quite unfit to leave to-day. Not able for professional work until after Saturday." Smythe immediately announced a tentative rescheduling for the week of the seventeenth at which time tickets already purchased would be honored (*Evening Star*, 7 Oct., p. 3). Handbills were distributed "to that effect," but even so, "much disappointment was expressed by a number of persons who visited the Exhibition Theatre"—some from long distances—who hoped to see and hear Twain (*Geelong Advertiser*, 8 Oct., p. 2).

The free publicity continued, especially as Twain, nearing Geelong, spoke in the nearby country towns. It was deemed newsworthy that "now, when everything promised to run smoothly, his 'much travelled' impressario manages to get into quarantine. Mr R. S. Smythe is a passenger from Adelaide by the Cuzco. Until last week there were two places on this globe which Mr Smythe had not visited—quarantine and the North Pole—both considered unsuitable for lectures. Now there is only one" (*Evening Star*, 22 Oct., p. 3). Twain's success in Adelaide—

both professional and social—which "surpassed that of Sydney and Melbourne," as well as the success in the Victorian towns, was touted to justify "the enterprise and prescience of the much-travelled impressarios" Smythe and Smythe (*Evening Star*, 25 Oct., p. 2; *Geelong Advertiser*, 24 Oct., p. 2). It was expected that his wife and daughter would accompany Twain to Geelong, but, apparently at the last moment, they decided to stay behind in Melbourne to attend the Leidertafel as guests of the Lieutenant Governor's party. This performance was one of only three which they are known to have missed in Australia.

When Twain finally did arrive, the Exhibition Theatre was well filled, even at prices from 4 shillings to 2 shillings, and Twain "received a most friendly welcome" (*Advertiser*, 29 Oct., p. 3). But for the first time on his Australian trip, Twain offended his audience.

In three separate reviews, all four dailies panned the tale which had become his most often repeated one—the disquisition on the German language. The morning *Times* and the *Evening Star* both printed the same review (29 Oct., p. 2) which was generally unfavorable:

> He simply stood before the audience in a careless attitude ... [and] told the people all he had to say to them. He spoke with a pronounced American accent, and [when he had finished] the network of stories, ... there were few who could sincerely say more than that they heard "Mark Twain." ... [It] was the expectancy of something better that caused the people to follow the most frivolous utterance that the American thought worthy to breathe. Some of the stories were old, though possibly original; others were apparently unfinished .... But in any case his style of oral narration is too protracted a fault that should not be found in a good story-teller. But that is not "Mark Twain's" business. He is a humorous writer. [*Evening Star*, 29 Oct., p. 2.]

All reviewers agreed that the first half of the moral lesson—about the watermelon, the Nevada "duel," the lost dime, and the christening—was acceptable, but Twain's continental courier story about leading four ladies through Switzerland and Bavaria "was not so effective as his previous efforts" (*Advertiser*, 29 Oct., p. 3).

The best that could be said about it was that it "put the audience in a laughable mood." The christening "was perhaps the best number" (*Advertiser*, 29 Oct., p. 3). The reviewers did not even like his Australian poem, which had brought down the house in previous tellings. The entire performance was spoiled for the reviewers by "his concluding subject, the alleged complexities of the gender in the German language [which] would have been amusing enough had it not been based upon an entirely erroneous hypothesis, which an intimate acquaintance with the German grammar would have removed" (*Evening News* [Geelong], 30 Oct., p. 1). Any performer can have a bad night and Twain certainly had reason to be off his stride. But it is the *Advertiser* which revealed the real reason Geelong took such offense: It was not merely the "expectancy of something better"; rather "the concluding story, regarding the German grammar, and the confusion of the genders, although somewhat mirth provoking, was not taken with that feeling by several gentlemen present" (*Advertiser* [Geelong], 29 Oct., p. 3). "It served its purpose however in giving the lecturer an effective sentence by way of peroration, in which he expressed the hope that a deceased fishwife would be rewarded for the uncertainty of gender during her life in Germany by having in her eternal home 'only one good square sex and have it all to herself'" (*Evening News*, [Geelong] 30 Oct., p. 1).

Perhaps Twain saw the review in either the *Times* or the *Advertiser*, for he stayed in Geelong until the "forenoon" on Tuesday when he left for Prahran. To Mayor Richardson, "who was engaged at the police court in giving evidence," Twain sent the following letter, thanking him for the planned ceremonies attending his aborted earlier visit:

> October 28th, 1895. Dear Sir:—I wish to thank your worship heartily for remembering me, and I very much regret that you had to be away, for I should have been glad to say by word of mouth my appreciation of the honor which you lately intended me, but which my illness, unfortunately for me, forestalled and defeated. With great respect from very truly yours (signed), S. L. Clemens. [*News of the Week* (Geelong), 2 Nov., p. 9.]

Although it is clearly a compliment to the mayor and other aldermen, Twain may also have hoped to placate those whom he had unintentionally offended. Despite the fact that the Australian part of his tour was almost over, Clemens—quite apart from Mark Twain—would not have wanted to leave unpleasant memories. If asked, he likely would have echoed his comments to the *Sunday Times* in Sydney that he wished to commit no offense against the reader.

"Compelled to Relinquish the Attempt"

Twain's last talk was on Tuesday 29 October in Prahran, which, though now a Melbourne suburb, was then a town with a population of 37,000. While Twain was still at Maryborough the Melbourne *Herald* reported that "efforts are being made to induce" Twain to speak in Prahran, but whether they were agent Smythe's efforts or the citizens' as in Horsham is not absolutely certain, though the advertisement appeared over Smythe's name. The visit was advertised as "the last appearance in Victoria" of the man who was still "en route to Queensland and India." Of all Smythe's celebrities, "none have approached in popularity or fame Mark Twain," the papers declared. Melbourne's *Argus* noted that the "At Home" was to be in Prahran because the "Melbourne Town Hall [was] otherwise engaged" with a benefit ball for the Nursing Society. Notice of Twain's accepting the engagement was given in the weekly paper on the twenty-sixth, but Prahranians had read enough of Melbourne papers not to require much advance publicity locally. The town was prepared for a "great influx of visitors" to hear Twain, who was rumored to be "composing a native Australian song ... to be recited" in Prahran (*Herald* [Melbourne], 28 Oct., p. 2).

In Town Hall, which seated 1,000 persons, a vast audience paid the popular prices and "filled the building in every part." They listened to his "inimitable drollery." He thanked the audience for the "kindly treatment which had so uniformly been his lot to enjoy." That night he read an up-to-date version of the Australian poem, "which he explained took him an immense amount of time to perfect." It "was received with bursts of laughter." However, Saturday's *Prahran Telegraph* continued, "Our reporter says he has been compelled to relinquish the attempt to write a full account of the evening's amusement, because ever since Tuesday evening he has had 'Mark's' tram yarn running in his head, and everything seems to be going in a swing to the rhythm of

'A green slip for a five cent fare,
To be punched in the presence of the passengare.'"

Of course this was the punch brothers routine which Twain had used to good effect since Horsham.

One day this week (probably Wednesday 30 October),[9] "Mark Twain turned up at the big Melbourne wool-sales ... [and] remained an interested spectator for half-an-hour." The Sydney *Bulletin* claimed he was "feeling the market before visiting a barber" (9 Nov., p. 13). Ac-

---

9. His notebook is dated 31 October for this event, but the end of the entry says they are leaving Melbourne "tomorrow"; they actually left on 31 October, and it seems unlikely that he would go to the sale the same day he was to leave the country.

companying his new friend John H. Wagner, Twain was fascinated by the noise, movement and apparent confusion at the sale (MTP:NB34). His public comment was that "wool brokers are just like stockbrokers; they all bounce from their seats and put up their hands and yell in unison—no stranger can tell what ..." (*More Tramps*, p. 106).

The Clemenses sailed for New Zealand via Hobart on the last day of October 1895. Twain returned to speak in Sydney, and Scone, N. S. W., and in Melbourne in late December, again to packed houses. While he could address 8,000 spectators in just four performances in Sydney, it is doubtful that ever was there a more appreciative audience than that at Horsham where only about 300 people could crowd into the hall. Nor was there another offended audience like the group of German gentlemen who attended at Geelong. As the Stawell editor so rightly stated, Twain's "dry mellow fun suits the Australian temperament and environment." The Clemenses had found the Australians "good and kind to us everywhere, and we get a most lively interest in them, and dread leaving them." Of Melbourne, where they had spent about seventeen days altogether, Olivia wrote that they "disliked extremely" having to leave, for they had met several people "that we had come to be really fond of."[10]

"I Myself Am the Latest Marsupial"

When Mark Twain and his wife and daughter Olivia and Clara Clemens sailed on the *Mararoa* from Melbourne on 31 October 1895, for New Zealand, the colony of Tasmania—like Victoria, New South Wales, and the others—thought of itself as belonging to itself, not really to "Australia." Federation was five years away, and the public was far more interested in labor conflict and protectionism than in discussing such a league among the Australasian colonies. Smythe had intended that Twain would be "lecturing in Launceston and Hobart early in November" (*Mercury* [Hobart], 28 Sept., p. 3), but Twain's illness and the resultant rescheduling had reduced those plans to a morning's shore leave. The *Mararoa*, a 2,598-ton cargo ship arrived in Hobart at 5:30 (Olivia said it was four o'clock) on Saturday morning, 2 November, after a day and a half at sea. The weather had been pleasant and the seas smooth, although Olivia wrote her sister that "our food and beds are poor." A little after seven o'clock Mr. Dobson, who

---

10. Potts and Potts, p. 48.

had written to them in Melbourne, came to the ship to invite them to breakfast at his parents' home. This young Dobson was "a great friend of the Days" who were renting the Clemenses' Hartford house.

After breakfast Clara and Olivia went for a ride "to see the country" with young Dobson and neighbors Mr. and Mrs. Walker, while Twain rode around Hobart with Mr. and Mrs. Henry Dobson, hoping "to get a glimpse of any convicts that might still remain on the island."[11] He went to the Refuge for the Indigent which housed 223 convicts, "a crowd, there, of the oldest people I have ever seen," Twain wrote in *More Tramps Abroad* (p. 196). After Mrs. Dobson gave him a "leg-iron (broken) found in the bush—ages of rust on it," the horrors of the convict system seemed to come alive for Twain and, for the remainder of his voyage to New Zealand, he made notes about convicts and the evils of transportation (MTP:NB34).

He also visited with Alexander Morton, a gentleman from New Orleans who was the curator of Hobart's museum (*Tasmanian News*, 2 Nov., p. 2; MTP:NB34). Morton showed him samples of birds, fish, various aboriginal artifacts, and—perhaps most curious of all—the marsupials including the Tasmanian devil. In *More Tramps Abroad*, Twain claimed the distinguishing characteristic of the marsupial "is its pocket."

> In some countries it is extinct, in the others it is rare. The first American marsupials were Stephen Girard, Mr. Astor, and the opossum; the principal marsupials of the southern hemisphere are Mr. Rhodes and the kangaroo. I myself am the latest marsupial. Also I might boast that I have the largest pocket of them all. But there is nothing in that. [*More Tramps*, pp. 195–196.][12]

Of course, his "pocket" and the pun "nothing in that" referred to the much-publicized necessity for the trip: to earn a great deal of money to repay his bankrupt company's debts.

It was in Hobart that Twain "struck the head of the procession of Junior Englands" (*More Tramps*, p. 194) which he would remark throughout his trip to New Zealand. If the Australian people were more American than English, it appears that the towns became more English

---

11. Potts and Potts, p. 47.

12. Cecil Rhodes, English financier and businessman in Africa, was the subject of Twain's shark-fishing story in *More Tramps Abroad*, pp. 84–89. In commenting on writing the South African portion of his book, Twain claimed, "Part of it has been most enjoyable work to me—chaffing Rhodes and making fun of his Jameson Raid" (*Correspondence with Rogers*, ed. Leary, p. 276.)

as the party went farther south. After driving around the city, Twain called Hobart

> the neatest town that the sun shines on; and I incline to believe that it is also the cleanest .... There cannot be another town in the world that has no shabby exteriors, no rickety gates and fences, no neglected houses crumbling to ruin, no crazy and unsightly sheds, no weed-grown front-yards of the poor, no back-yards littered with tin cans and old boots and empty bottles, no rubbish in the gutters, no clutter on the side-walks, no outer borders fraying out into dirty lanes and tin-patched huts. No, in Hobart all the aspects are tidy, and all a comfort to the eye; the modestest cottage looks combed and brushed, and has its vines, its flowers, its neat fence, its neat gate, its comely cat asleep on the window-ledge.[13]

Meanwhile, the ladies "had a most delightful drive into the bush. Up the mountain side to a little chalet where the Dobsons go for about three months during the hot weather. There is a most superb view from this of woods and sea," Olivia wrote to her sister.

> As we drove down we went into Mrs. Walker's for a glass of wine & a piece of cake (or kike as the Australians say).[14] Her house was a bower, it seems to me that I never saw anything more exquisite. A low one-storey house— which very many of the houses are here—with charming drawing-room & dining-room, both leading onto a porch covered with roses, yellow and white, and looking off to the sea and mountains. The porch was very large, being wide and the full length of those two long rooms. Then it was such a perfect mass of roses. [15]

On shipdeck, "apart from the crowd ... with the strong, invigorating breeze," Twain, "with his pilot-cap, his bushy white hair, his cigar," talked to reporters for the *Mercury* and the *Tasmanian News*. He was, he said, "downright sorry" to be leaving Australia, for "all my impres-

---

13. *More Tramps Abroad*, p. 195. Notes from which this passage is taken appear in Twain's notebook (MTP:NB34).

14. Livy noted that in both Melbourne and Hobart people said, "The Lidy will be down in a minute. Would you like to read the piper till she comes? It is on the tible with the kike" (Potts and Potts, p. 47). Twain noted this pronunciation in his Hobart entries, and he used them in *More Tramps Abroad*, writing that the Sydney chambermaid said, "'The tyble is set and here is the piper and if the lydy is ready I'll tell the wyter to bring up the breakfast'" (p. 77). He also recorded that in the smoking room of the *Mararoa* there was a *"good deal of nasal from young English-descended 'natives.' Kaow for cow, naow, for now; &c."* [MTP:NB34.]

15. Potts and Potts, pp. 47–48. Of course, Olivia was describing springtime in the Southern Hemisphere.

sions of this country and of the people are of a pleasant sort, for the reason that it is the human element that makes a country beautiful or otherwise" (*Mercury*, 4 Nov., p. 4). Indicating Mount Wellington and the harbor, Twain told the reporter, "all this is very beautiful, but it seems to me that this could not be beautiful of itself .... You must have the pleasant human element to counteract the effects of climate and circumstances" (*Mercury*, 4 Nov., p. 4). Perhaps this distinction in Twain's mind between the people and the land clarifies the puzzling judgment he would make in his diary after leaving Australia for the last time two months later:

> the truth is that the native Australian is as vain of his unpretty country as if it were the final masterpiece of God, achieved by Him from designs by that Australian. He is as sensitive about her as men are of sacred things—can't bear to have critical things said about her.[16]

Yet the comment about the "unpretty country" was not an opinion of the entire country; especially not of Sydney Harbour which he had likened to Marcus Clarke's description of Hobart's harbor. In the context of his later, convincingly genuine compliments—both public and in his journal—about the New Zealand landscape, one must believe that Twain was here complimenting the "many influential gentlemen" which he had met in Hobart, not trying to be tactful about an "unpretty" landscape. There is no doubt that he appreciated both the "pleasant human element" in Hobart and its beautiful natural aspect.

In response to a query, Twain reiterated his assessment, stated in Melbourne, Ballarat, and elsewhere, that Australians "differ ... from the English people in England; and, just in proportion, they develop a certain similarity to the people of the United States." Twain made explicit a statement first in Hobart which he would reiterate numerous times: " 'No man can understand the life of a community unless he has lived in it' says Mr Clemens, 'and as I cannot do that I intend to confine myself to outside impressions only'" (*Tasmanian News*, 2 Nov., p. 2). Again he would not comment on Australian periodicals except to say that "it's an offence to people or things to criticise them without due reflection." Finally he told the prototype of the tale appearing in *More Tramps Abroad* about how misleading maps can be, particularly when a person doesn't know anything about a place: "Glancing at the maps I had an idea that there was probably a small ferry boat running

---

16. *Notebook*, ed. Paine, p. 265.

eighteen or twenty times a day between Melbourne and New Zealand ...." (*Mercury*, 4 Nov., p. 4).[17] The interview concluded when a man came around trying to show Twain some fossils.[18]

The *Mararoa* departed Hobart at 1:20 P.M., putting in at Bluff, New Zealand's southernmost port, three days later. While on that trip, Twain was called on nightly to entertain the passengers, including Michael Davitt, who was lecturing on home rule for Ireland, and Malcolm Ross, who made a valuable record of Twain's working habits that was widely reprinted in New Zealand newspapers. He complained in his notebook of the poorly tuned piano, on which he himself apparently entertained the smokers in the lounge.

---

17. He jotted this down in his notebook on 2 Nov.: "Supposed they ran a ferry-boat 15 times a day from Australia to New Zealand. The distance is practically the same that it is from St. Louis to N. O.!" (MTP:NB34).

18. Although the *Mercury* printed *"fessils"* (a small bean), this must surely be an error.

CHAPTER SEVEN

New Zealand South

"Most Pleasant and Treasured Memories"

Mr. and Mrs. Clemens, Clara, and Carlyle G. Smythe arrived at Bluff, New Zealand's southernmost port, early on 5 November 1895, aboard the Union Company's *Mararoa*. From there they rode the train to the larger town of Invercargill, with a population of 10,000, where Twain would make his "first appearance in New Zealand" for those who could afford four shillings, two shillings sixpence, or a shilling for the pit. A special train to Bluff after the lecture was advertised for those who wished to travel to Invercargill to hear him.

On the ship from Hobart, he evidently had been reading up on New Zealand, possibly from some of the books given him by Malcolm Ross, the Dunedin journalist. While on the train from Bluff to Invercargill he made notes on the rabbit plague, which he would expand in *More Tramps Abroad*, humorously observing the foolishness of a British law fining a poacher up to £20 for killing a rabbit without a permit. Instead "he ought to be banished to New Zealand. New Zealand would pay his way and give him wages" (*More Tramps*, p. 198). His first impression, recorded in his notebook, was that "New Z consists simply of scenery & civilization" (MTP:NB34). Except for a few unfortunate experiences concerning "civilization," Twain stuck to that opinion throughout his visit.

Advertisements appeared beginning on 31 October, but until 4 November they listed no date or place for the performances, as if those details were not completed until the last minute. It has been suggested that this first performance was in response to local pressure.[1] Of course, Twain had made such appearances in Horsham, Prahran, and perhaps other towns, and receptions in those places had been among the most successful he had experienced. Smythe's promotion piece about his coup in getting Twain to the Antipodes had appeared in the Invercargill paper even before Twain landed at Bluff. The article had appeared in virtually every city Twain visited; not only did it advertise Twain, but it also reminded readers of Smythe's resourcefulness as one of the best-known tour managers in Australasia.

On the fifth, a Tuesday, the Theatre Royal "was crowded in every part, and many turned away from the doors disappointed when they found that ingress would be difficult and comfort a sheer impossibility" (*Southland Times*, 6 Nov., p. 3). The reviewer reported that, because it was "so utterly out of the ordinary track, so unique in material and so delightfully rambling and inconsequential in the method," neither the lecture nor the delivery was susceptible to description. "The audience, after giving him a hearty reception, began to laugh when he started, and so they continued from then till the finish, with a few intervals of rest and relief, mercifully introduced" (*Southland Times*, 6 Nov., p. 3). Rumor had it that a speculator bought out the house for £40 and resold it for £120 at one to four shillings per seat.[2]

In his notebook Twain listed the stories he used for this single performance; many were from the collection he called "For One-night Stands," but he apparently substituted the poem about the weird Australasian animals—both live and extinct—and the one about his Nevada duel for the story of Huck Finn on the raft claiming that his pap had smallpox. His notes included his assessment that he told the continental courier story "too fast," for it lasted only twenty minutes. Intermission was twelve minutes halfway through the performance, and he finished at 9:55, about ten minutes later than he liked to.

A gossipy paragraph in the weekly *Otago Witness* said he

has two or three characteristic poses when on the platform, but the most peculiar one is his habit of nursing his elbow and anxiously pressing his cheek with his hand as if suffering the agonies of an 80-horse power, stump

---

1. R. D. J. Collins, "Sketch Recalls Mark Twain's Visit to Dunedin In 1895," *Otago Daily Times*, 4 Nov. 1977, p. [4].

2. Parsons, "Mark Twain in New Zealand," p. 55.

jumping toothache when on the point of slipping out some particularly ex-
cruciating absurdity. From the time of his stepping out before the footlights
to his leaving, says a contemporary, the lecturer is never guilty of even the
ghost of a smile—he is as solemn all the time as a wart on an undertaker's
horse. [*Otago Witness*, 7 Nov., p. 37.]

Possibly this paragraph was meant to refer to the Invercargill performance, although it was reprinted from *Melbourne Punch* (3 Oct., p. 214).
The *Witness* also reported that Twain had "one of the largest audiences
that ever paid for admission to any entertainment in Invercargill" (7
Nov., p. 28). The daily paper said the "visit of Mark Twain to Invercargill will live long in the recollection of the town, and his lecture
will be among our most pleasant and treasured memories" (*Southland
Times*, 6 Nov., p. 3).

The next day on the train trip out of Invercargill someone gave him
the news of the Melbourne Cup which was that "everybody bet on the
wrong horse—a new horse [Auraria] won." He had earlier lamented in
his notebook that they would miss the Melbourne Cup (MTP:NB34),
but that fact did not keep him from writing about the event as "the
Australasian National Day." The people "swarm in by ships and rail a
fortnight before the day . . . . a hundred thousand strong . . . . Day after
day the races go on . . . . And at the end of the great week the swarms
secure lodgings and transportation for next year, then flock away to . . .
count their gains and losses, and order next year's Cup clothes" (*More
Tramps*, pp. 103-105). Americans, the British, and the Irish had no such
annual "supreme" day as Melbourne Cup Day—neither the Fourth of
July nor the Queen's Birthday nor Christmas. He had already noted
that "everybody that can afford it comes from New Zealand—2,600
miles of rough sea, (going & and coming)" to see the Melbourne Cup
(MTP:NB34). And when the *Cuzco*, the ship which his manager had
taken from Adelaide to make arrangements at Melbourne, was found to
be infected with smallpox and quarantined, Twain had written, "people
on board who came to see the Caulfield Cup (run a couple of days ago)
& the great Melbourne Cup (Nov. 5) & the arrival of the Governor
(next Friday)" would miss all of these (MTP:NB34).

Aboard the train to Dunedin he remarked the "lovely summer morning; brilliant blue sky. A few miles out from Invercargill passed through
vast level green expanses snowed over with sheep" (*More Tramps*, p. 198;
nearly verbatim from MTP:NB34). "A passenger reminds me that I am
in 'the England of the Far South.' "

"Welcome as the Flowers in May"

Dunedin, the second largest city in New Zealand at 48,000 people including its suburbs, was the second stop for the Clemenses. It had been the port city for a former gold-mining area and was in 1895 a thriving commercial center with a museum, two art galleries, and a university. On the day of Twain's arrival, both newspapers carried articles that must have stimulated interest in the distinguished visitor. The morning paper, the *Otago Daily Times*, printed an article by Malcolm Ross, based on various conversations he had held with Twain aboard the *Mararoa* from Hobart. At least some of the conversations took place in the ship's smoking room, and Ross had given him a book he had edited called *New Zealand Alpine Journal* as well as some other "very valuable books" (MTP:NB34). Although not much of Ross's article purports to be direct quotation from the humorist—the reporter eschewed pen and notebook—it is quite valuable as a record of Twain's working habits.

In Sydney, Twain had been asked if it were true that he was the laziest man in the United States. His reply was that "every man has a gift either large or small. It may be to play billiards or to imitate Paderewski." Ignace Paderewski, Polish statesman and concert pianist, had a shock of hair easily comparable to that of Sir Henry Parkes in New South Wales and apparently more unruly than Twain's. Although the New Zealanders were less apt to make specific comparisons between Twain and his maned contemporaries, they were thoroughly aware of the young pianist's skills and appearance. News clips as well as advertisements using his name or face often appeared in the papers, and if the Kiwis had read this interview in Sydney they would immediately have understood the physical similarity between Paderewski and Twain as well as his allusion to the man's "gift." Twain had continued,

> Whatever that gift is man takes a native delight in exploiting it .... In the case of any particular man ninety-nine out of a hundred of these interests may not appeal to him, so that so far as they are concerned he is the laziest of beings .... So I frankly admit that in regard to many human things, I am, if you like to use the term, phenomenally lazy, lazy in every way that you can possibly imagine, until it comes to writing a book. Then there is no more industrious man in the world than myself. [*Argus* (Melbourne), 17 Sept., p. 5.]

Ross's observations on the trip across the Tasman Sea certainly bear out Twain's assessment of his own preoccupation with writing—at least when the "spirit moved him." Ross recorded:

> In his spare time he is engaged in writing a book on his present travels and this will be looked forward to with interest by most colonists. Every day and every night he is hard at work in his cabin, but he is in no danger of becoming "played out," as his method of working is such that there is always a freshness about what he does. As soon as he feels that he has been writing long enough on one subject he leaves it and goes on to another. In the same way with regard to books—when he gets to a point at which writing becomes a labour he immediately throws that book over-board and takes up something more congenial to the inspiration of the moment. He has now two or three unfinished books pigeon-holed in this way . . . . whenever he feels a labour of love becoming a task he puts it aside till he is able to do it more justice, and it once more becomes a labour of love. [*Otago Daily Times*, 6 Nov., p. 4; this article was widely reprinted.]

Twain often wrote "for long hours at a stretch without feeling tired beyond the mere physical exertion entailed" because he did not have "to be particular about facts and statistics, or to get up a very difficult subject." He claimed it was easier to write a work of fiction than a book that required research.

Ross told about Twain's contract with *Century Magazine* to write a dozen articles about the world tour, but "he cannot, or will not, write to order . . . . they wanted them done in a certain way, and Mark Twain got them to let him off the engagement" (*Otago Daily Times*, 6 Nov., p. 4). Clemens had written to his business manager H. H. Rogers (11 June) that he could easily write a subscription book of his round-the-world adventures, "but those 12 articles for the Century at $12,000 would be *horribly* difficult."[3] On 15 June, he said he was "not committed to any magazine yet—and I believe it will be wisest to remain unfettered" for two reasons: first, "to write travels for *serial* publication is hideous hard work," and second, "the Century people actually proposed that I *sign a contract to be funny* in those 12 articles. That was pure insanity. Why, it makes me shudder every time I think of those articles. I don't think I could ever write one of them without being under the solemnising blight of that disgusting recollection."[4] However, Mrs. Clemens had insisted that he was committed for the articles, to

---

3. *Correspondence with Rogers*, ed. Leary, p. 151.
4. Ibid., p. 152.

which he had agreed: "upon examining the documents, she seems to be right. Dam—nation!"

Magazine serialization was not a moot issue, for *Argus* editor Fred W. Haddon had asked him as late as 30 October to write something for publication in Australia. Twain would respond from Christchurch with the outline of his agreement and release from *Century Magazine*. That letter explained that if he did decide to write an article it would be for *Century*, but he "could send a timely Duplicate" to Haddon. He also made clear that his publisher would "pay more to keep all such matter for the book."[5]

Twain told Ross generally the same things about literature that he had told Sydney and Melbourne reporters: he did not read much modern fiction, although he liked Kipling and the Australian Marcus Clarke; he thought Melbourne's *Argus* was a good paper; he was collecting material for his work on New Zealand; and he did not know which of his own books he liked best. Then he spoke on a subject he seemed to have put out of his mind permanently—the loss of thousands of dollars in the Paige typesetting device. Ever since Twain's bankruptcy had been formally announced in close juxtaposition with the failure of Webster & Company, Twain seemed to have blamed everything on Webster—even to the end of his life when he made autobiographical dictations. But when Malcolm Ross mentioned seeing "those wonderful machines the linotypes in Melbourne"—and he could have seen them in Sydney—Twain described his own machine, their competitor. He was interested in a type-setting machine in America,

> a wonderful machine, which, however, could only be produced at a cost of £3000. Ten of those at a cost of £30,000 would be sufficient for a good-sized newspaper, and the Americans would pay the price, but the machine was so wonderfully intricate and so liable to get out of order that it was not a success. Mark Twain lost £40,000 over it. [*Otago Daily Times*, 6 Nov., p. 4.]

When Twain arrived in Dunedin on 6 November, the *Evening Star* greeted the "Silver-haired 'Pilgrim' . . . lynx-eyed traveller" with a poem by Charles Umbers, completed that very day. Umbers saluted many of Twain's most famous creations—innocents, frogs, Mississippians, fighters, and tramps—as well as the star-spangled banner and said that their author was "welcome as the flowers in May" (6 Nov., p. 3). Umbers

---

5. Samuel L. Clemens to Fred. W. Haddon, 14 November 1895, Victoria State Library, Melbourne.

may have been even a newer arrival from the Northern Hemisphere to the Antipodes than Twain was, for Twain had at least gotten the seasons straight when he exclaimed to a Melbourne reporter about having "two crops of spring poets in one year."

Twain arrived in Dunedin only shortly before the curtain went up "punctually" at eight o'clock. A few impatient persons set up "some rapping of sticks at the back of the hall," and when the humorist appeared, it was "the signal for an exceedingly hearty and long-sustained salvo of applause—the most cordial welcome, in short, which has ever been extended to a lecturer in Dunedin" (*Otago Daily Times*, 7 Nov., p. 3). City Hall was full, and, as in Melbourne,

> the members of the Presbyterian Synod, having in the afternoon concluded the business of their annual session, appeared to be present en masse. Whether this was a case of cause and effect can of course be only a matter of conjecture. There was a sprinkling also of members of the Anglican Synod, though that ecclesiastical body was still sitting, and clerical representatives of other religious denominations found themselves on common ground. [*Otago Daily Times*, 7 Nov., p. 3.]

Also present were "professors, bankers, doctors, lawyers, the commercial classes, and the civil service . . . , the youth . . . , [and] ever so many people whom one seldom sees at any entertainment, and only at lectures."

"Merciless Exposer of Humbug"

The Dunedin paper said that "Mark Twain is not, however, a lecturer so much as a *raconteur*," remarking on his "loosely strung together collection of his own written stories," spoken "with just enough of the American twang to give piquancy . . . and with that lazy drawl . . . of which we had learnt from those who had heard him in Australia" (*Otago Daily Times*, 7 Nov., p. 3). The tales were those usually called the "First 'At Home,' " beginning with the truant fishing excursion and concluding with the German language lesson. The *Otago Daily Times* commented that "certainly there could not have been a more merry audience," for "there was apparently only one serious person in the building, and that was the entertainer himself, who told his stories in a matter-of-fact way as if utterly unconscious of their drollery" (7 Nov., p. 3). It appeared that some New Zealanders, like some people who attended in Adelaide, must not have exhaustively studied the works of our illustrious visitor .... Such persons were to be seen amongst last night's audience. They could be detected sniggering prematurely and listening for what was coming. Happy and blest ... to be enjoying for the first time whimsicalities and satires and subtle humor that have set the world a-laughing. With jokes, as with quarrels, the first blow generally leaves its mark. [*Evening Star* (Dunedin), 7 Nov., p. 2.]

The reviewer urged those who "are undecided on the point to go and hear this merciless exposer of humbug, this bright and wholesome humorist, whose special attribute it is to bring to our everyday humdrum lives the joyous relief of a tonic which leaves no distressing after-effects" (*Evening Star* [Dunedin], 7 Nov., p. 2).

On Thursday the seventh, the family went with Dr. Thomas M. Hocken to see his collection of books on New Zealand (which now make up the core of the Hocken Library at the University of Otago) and his antiquities and Maori artifacts, including pictures of their chiefs (MTP:NB34). Twain was greatly impressed with the tattooing, whose "designs are so flowing and graceful and beautiful that they are a most satisfactory decoration .... After that, the undecorated European face is unpleasant and ignoble" (*More Tramps*, p. 198). Hocken gave Twain a copy of "his translation of Tasman's diary," which had just been published in late September (MTP:NB34).

That evening, Twain appeared on the stage "a good deal out of breath, and he explained that his condition was due to the fact that he had lost himself, and had been wandering about for three-quarters of an hour looking for the hall" (*Otago Daily Times*, 8 Nov., p. 3). Whether this was true or whether it was just another of his clever introductions is not certain, but he began his scheme for the moral regeneration of the universe with his watermelon story, which he had been using throughout the tour. The favorite of the evening must have been the Australian poem, which he had promised at the close of the previous performance, for it again "caused roars of laughter" (*Evening Star* [Dunedin], 8 Nov., p. 2).

He introduced a new story "relating how Mrs. M'Williams, in a state of terror, shut herself up in her wardrobe one night during a supposed thunderstorm, and led her husband a merry dance by her frantic appeals to him to resort to all sorts of outrageous experiments to avoid being stricken down by the lightning" (*Otago Daily Times*, 8 Nov., p. 3). This is the first time he had told this story, though after this he used it often, both in New Zealand and in Australia. In two letters written from Timaru on the tenth, Twain explained that he got his "third lecture ready only three days ago."[6] He "had prepared but two lectures, & was 'pat' in only one of them." Although he "badly needed 3," the carbuncle he suffered in Australia kept him from the task and he "lost a valuable part of my best market .... I never got the third lecture in a usable shape till at sea; & I used it first in Dunedin."[7] His journal indicates that he seems also to have considered using either a tale or a short poem about the laughing jackass or kookaburra (MTP:NB35), which may have been the "new Australian poem" advertised in Auckland. He concluded with Uncle Dan'l's tale of the golden arm, which never failed to frighten the ladies in the audience.

Twain may not yet have met William Matthew Hodgkins, president of the Otago Art Society, who on Saturday would take him through the city's art gallery. Hodgkins, a lawyer and the father of New Zealand's premier artist, Frances Hodgkins, was a prolific sketcher. He was sitting in a stall on Twain's right side during the second performance when he sketched two of only very few known illustrations of the humorist *during* a performance. In a rather realistic face, the artist pictured the deadpan expression so often remarked in print by reviewers. He labeled the sketch "the Watermelon Story" and captioned it: "The front seats occupied by members of the Presbyterian and Anglican Synods then sitting in the Town." Evidently the Presbyterian clergymen had liked the first show so much that they came back and brought their Anglican friends the second night. Another sketch by Hodgkins, also labeled "the Watermelon Story" (which Twain told on the seventh), is clearly dated 8 November. Evidently, Hodgkins had sketched it the next day, perhaps after completing the very realistic head on the undated sketch.[8]

Friday the eighth was, Twain recorded, a "rainy day; watched the people .... This is the beginning of N Z summer, I was told" (MTP:NB34). Probably on that day, Livy and Clara "went to a tea at a charming place with fine view & 15 acres in the grounds" (MTP:NB34). This may have been the luncheon party given by Mrs. Royse at Leith House, although the Clemens ladies were not listed among the guests (*New Zealand*

---

6. Samuel L. Clemens to Sam Moffett, 10 November 1895, Mark Twain Papers.

7. Samuel L. Clemens to Henry Huttleston Rogers, unpublished postscript, 10 November 1895, Timaru. Mark Twain Papers.

8. The undated sketch was first published by Sarah Searight, "Mark Twain in New Zealand," *New Zealand Heritage* 13 (1972), 1704.

Graphic, 16 Nov., p. 616). Twain's last performance was that night; the sketchy reports in the *Evening Star* (9 Nov., p. 2) and the *Otago Witness* (14 Nov., p. 37) indicate that he gave the readings usually called the "Third 'At Home,'" consisting of the decadence of picturesque lying, the adventures of the continental courier, the female slave (Aunty Cord), and "'disseminating' the knowledge acquired by him with regard to a cure for stammering." Twain's notes also include the incorporation of mean men, the punch brothers jingle, and the blue-jay story (MTP:NB35).

According to the newspapers, "a very small number of visitors" attended as William M. Hodgkins opened the annual exhibition of the Society of Artists on the evening of Friday the eighth (*New Zealand Graphic*, 16 Nov., p. 616). Twain was shown the museum and public gallery by the lawyer on Saturday, his last morning in Dunedin. Of the annual exhibition he declared:

> Fine. Think of a town like this having two such collections as this, and a Society of Artists. It is so all over Australasia. If it were a monarchy one might understand it .... But these colonies are republics—republics with a wide suffrage; voters of both sexes, this one of New Zealand .... All over Australasia pictures ... are bought for the public galleries, by the State, and by societies of citizens. Living citizens—not dead ones. They rob themselves to give, not their heirs. [*More Tramps*, pp. 200–201.]

Twain had not often remarked on works of art—though he often commented on public buildings. Clearly he was impressed with the Australasians' respect for the fine arts, which in his experience was not always appreciated by democratic peoples. In complimenting Ballarat statuary he had remarked that certain statues in New York City were "disgraceful ... nothing suggestive of art about them" (*Courier* [Ballarat], 21 Oct., p. 4). In the American edition of his travel book he used a picture of a Ballarat statue.

On the morning before Twain's departure, the newspaper editorial expressed complete contentment with the visit: Twain "neither surprised nor disappointed his audiences: he has simply satisfied them. What higher tribute need be paid? The lectures have shown us the Mark Twain that we expected .... and we asked for nothing more." But the paper did point out that "he came for his own profit as well as for ours; but ... we may at least express hearty satisfaction that his face has been seen and his voice heard" (*Otago Daily Times*, 9 Nov., p. 4).

Twain left for Timaru on the morning train, seeing at the station two new young acquaintances (MTP:NB34).

"Humour ... Floating upon ... Liquid Wisdom"

The train brought Twain to Timaru, halfway between Dunedin and Christchurch, on the Prince of Wales's birthday, Saturday 9 November; on Monday, he backtracked to Oamaru. His wife and daughter continued on to Christchurch for the weekend, missing his talk in Timaru that night and the one in Oamaru on Monday night (MTP:NB34). On Monday he claimed they were still celebrating because Australasians loved holidays so much. Back in Adelaide for the South Australian Commemoration day, he elaborated this observation in a luncheon address, and he included it in *More Tramps Abroad*. And in Oamaru on Monday, his manager used the holiday as an excuse for reducing prices in order to fill the unsold seats for the evening performance.

In Timaru, which had nearly 11,000 people living in the town and county, "seats were taken days ago" (MTP:NB34). Apparently, the lecture consisted of the first group of stories, for the *Triad* recorded the truant fisherman and the Mexican plug. But there were somewhat conflicting reports on how the local auditors received his performance. The newspaper reviewer seemed quite happy with the show, "for compared with the recital, the printed story is almost a dead language" (*Timaru Herald*, 11 Nov., p. 3). Country residents had come "from Temuka, Geraldine, and other distant places" and before Twain had talked very long, "what was nominally a monologue became a dialogue, in which the audience took quite a considerable part by contributing repetitions of interjections." Yet, as in occasional audiences in Australia, there were "some present ... who did not get enough in their share of the dialogue. Mark Twain was not 'funny' all the time. Such people must have been misinformed as to the character of the man. Mark Twain is not a mere 'funny' man. His humour is but the foam floating upon a deep stream of serious thought and of liquid wisdom" (*Timaru Herald*, 11 Nov., p. 3).

The monthly literary magazine the *Triad*, published in Dunedin by C. N. Baeyertz, sheds light on this complaint. The editor said he happened to be in Timaru on Saturday night, and Twain "seems to have conquered about ten per cent of his hearers. It says very little for our appreciation of good humour, subtle satire, and wonderful descriptive power, that nine out of every ten who heard Mark Twain were hugely disappointed with him" (*Triad* [Dunedin], 25 Nov., p. 4). Baeyertz seems to have been rather dyspeptic in other criticisms of his neighbors, and his estimate of ninety percent is no doubt exaggerated. But his analysis of the "problem" is illuminating.

> I heard him in Timaru, and when I think of the kind of humour(?) which one hears constantly, and which provokes the loud laugh (I say nothing about the vacant mind) on the streets, in the hotels, and in club-land throughout New Zealand, I am simply amazed .... [Mark Twain] could certainly supply any one of his detractors with sufficient brains to double his intellect, and not be greatly inconvenienced by the loss. [*Triad* (Dunedin), 25 Nov., p. 4.]

Using Timaru "as a type of other places," Baeyertz exclaimed:

> How is it that young men who have never been further than Waimate on the one side, and Temuka on the other, will persist in dogmatically opposing a crude opinion evolved from the "idiotic area" of their puny little "squinting brains," to the judgment of the cultivated world? It is not only Mark Twain whom they have belittled, but all the other great artistes who have visited us. The intelligent few thoroughly appreciated Santley, Toole, Foli, and Wilhemj; but the great majority was disappointed.

Waxing prophetic, he asked, "What went they out for to hear? If they expected vulgarity, the *double entente*, and the *olla podrida* of the nigger minstrel show, then I can understand their disappointment; but if they looked forward to pure original humour and masterly satire from the master-mind that created it, then their want of appreciation is a mystery" (*Triad* [Dunedin], 25 Nov., p. 4).

Baeyertz cited a few specific complaints, the kind young ruffians are likely to make: "One gentleman remarked that Mark Twain would make a good second cook on a [sheep] station." Another "told me he thought Mark Twain was obtaining money under false pretences. Another man told me that the excruciatingly funny story of the 'ten-cent piece' wasn't original, because he had heard it before. One objected to his English, and another to his German" (*Triad* [Dunedin], 25 Nov., pp. 4–5).

> The usual criticism reduced to its elements ran:—I don't see anything in it, therefore there is nothing in it. This criticism is on a par with that of the third standard school boy who, because he cannot get his working of a division sum to tally with the answer given in the book, immediately arrives at the only possible conclusion under the circumstances, that his working is

incorrect? Oh dear, no; that the book is wrong. [*Triad* (Dunedin), 25 Nov., p. 4.]

But Baeyertz's diatribe against his countrymen must be balanced with a look at the only other written review besides his own. It also defends Twain against hasty judgments. Apparently, a significant portion of the audience expected energetic side-splitting one-line jokes, not the "unconscious ... quieter, more modified, and more subtle" expression Twain used to characterize American humor (*New Zealand Herald*, 21 Nov., p. 5). But "he would have quite misrepresented himself," said the *Timaru Herald*, "if he had given his audience absolutely nothing but laughter-moving humour. There was a very liberal share of this, however." Certainly they must not have expected the pathos and seriousness that Twain said were "just trembling on the verge of every [true] jest." In his Timaru performance, this quality was exemplified by Huck Finn's struggle with his conscience, which, Baeyertz reported, someone called "all tommy-rot!"

Twain may have been unaware of these reports, certainly of Baeyertz's which did not appear until he was far away across Cook Strait in Auckland. If he did see the *Timaru Herald* on Monday before he left for Oamaru, he took no notice of it. He had spent Sunday in Timaru (there are no Sunday trains on the South Island), reading in bed, catching up on his journal, which had been somewhat neglected since Thursday, and in general regaining his health, which, after travelling by train and lecturing for five consecutive evenings, was reported to be "not . . . robust." He drove through the "lovely region (farming) around Timaru; *folds* of land with gullies between; green & trim & clean great fields (grain—wheat & oats)—big pastures full of sheep," as his journal recorded (MTP:NB34). He noted "big flouring mills," the snowy mountain peaks, and "wonderful opaline clouds," and he described the varicolored shore and reefs of the sea. He liked Timaru's appearance, a "pretty town & cosy pretty homes all around it. Plenty of greenery & flowers ... broom and gorse." Echoing his question from Adelaide about the botanical gardens, he asked, "Why haven't *we* these?" (MTP:NB34).

He visited a "beautiful bathing beach close to town" (MTP:NB34) and went down to the wharf where he first saw the steamer *Flora*, in which he would sail from Christchurch to Wellington a week later—probably the most memorable voyage of the old pilot's life. He also viewed the wreck of a steamer, grounded in a morning fog on her maiden voyage

(MTP:NB34). This was the *Elginshire*, headed from Oamaru to London with a cargo of 11,000 frozen lamb carcasses and wool. She was reefed just south of Timaru on 9 March 1892. Twain recorded his Australasian acquaintance with the Salvation Army and its "brass music & singing"; but he was "deprived" of the concert because "the ungodly on the outskirts hail me friendly & my stay would not do, unless I were willing to interrupt the Army's work."[9] He ran into the Salvation Army later in Napier and in Hawera on the North Island, and as he left Sydney for the last time he encountered another group, the "rivals of the Salvationists," who "sang the doxology."[10]

On Monday, he backtracked to Oamaru on a train, "express—[which] goes twenty and a half miles an hour, schedule time; but it is fast enough, the outlook upon sea and land is so interesting" (*More Tramps*, p. 201). He confided in his notebook: "charges nearly 10 cents a mile, first class" (MTP:NB34). Generally he was favorably impressed with New Zealand railroads, especially in comparison with western Victorian ones.

"The Trouble Will Begin at Eight"

Backtracking about fifty miles on the train, Twain noted the "exquisite lightgreen brilliant sea, & the beautiful green grain = land, & the snow-mountain views" (MTP:NB34). He arrived in Oamaru early in the afternoon of Monday 11 November, where he found people "still holidaying for the Prince's birthday" (MTP:NB34). When he returned to Adelaide on New Year's Eve, he would make jokes about the extended Australasian holidays, and in *More Tramps Abroad* he claimed it just gave the colonists an excuse for more horse racing. The week before, while Twain was still in Dunedin, Smythe had advertised tickets for Twain's "only appearance in Oamaru" at four shillings for the dress circle. A letter to the *Oamaru Mail*, reminiscent of the one at Bendigo where prices had to be reduced, had complained that "for 4s one could buy one of Twain's books and take him in that form, while if it is a question of seeing him" there was a "counterfeit presentment of the humourist" in a local resident, "Father" Crouch (*Oamaru Mail*, 7 Nov.).[11] When Hugo Fischer, the New Zealand agent, checked in on the eighth,

---

9. *Notebook*, ed. Paine, p. 257; punctuation restored from MTP:NB34.
10. Ibid., p. 263, restored from MTP:NB36.
11. "Father" Crouch was probably Robert Pitt Crouch, Oamaru harbor master.

he was told he would "be frozen out of those prices." The *Oamaru Mail* reported that he was not "running any artic expeditions" and that he would "get a house full if he had to chase all the polar bears and walruses in the district." With Twain's lecture scheduled for the evening before Michael Davitt was to speak on Irish nationalism, and competing with several other shows and concerts on Monday whose prices for admission were as low as sixpence and never higher than three shillings, sales were slow even with a combined population in the county and town of 14,000. So Monday morning's paper advertised "on account of To-day being a holiday, and that all may have the opportunity of hearing the Greatest Humorist of the Age," prices were reduced to the "popular" three-shilling level for dress circle.

With the reduced prices, the "people of Oamaru were not slow to appreciate the opportunity of seeing and hearing the author whose books have been a potent restorative to many a drooping and despondent mind. The theatre was well filled," reported the *North Otago Times* (12 Nov., p. 3). Even so, the *Oamaru Mail* said, the Theatre Royal was "the most sparsely-peopled" so far in New Zealand. But the small audience evidently did not dampen Twain's performance. One reviewer wrote, "To say that Mark Twain is a great man and a brilliant wit is to give him faint praise" although there were some who "affect not to laugh at American wit .... and Mark Twain has no charms for them" (*North Otago Times*, 12 Nov., p. 3). The procedure for the evening could be summarized: "The audience laugh; the lecturer pauses; he proceeds; they laugh; he pauses, and the lecture is at an end. He received an unbounded reception in point of heartiness" (*North Otago Times*, 12 Nov., p. 3). Evidently dogs often went to the theatres in New Zealand, but they "had a fight only once—at Oamaru," Twain wrote in his notebook.[12] And for some reason he noted during the day before the performance that the "trouble will begin at eight"—the advertising slogan for his first lecture series back in 1867. He also confided that the "best thing in the world is the intermission. A trifle of restraint before it—got to be careful or the house may cool—no possibility of cooling *after* it. Try no new thing before it—try *any* new thing *after* it" (MTP:NB34). Perhaps he was giving special thought to his audiences since at least some people were obviously disgruntled in Timaru and Smythe did have difficulty selling all the seats in

---

12. *Notebook* ed. Paine, p. 261; punctuation restored from MTP:NB34.

Oamaru. In response to an interviewer in Christchurch the next day, Twain commented extensively on audiences.

The humorist spent some time with townsmen. On his arrival he was driven "round Claremont way by Mr. W. Evans" (*Oamaru Mail*, 12 Nov.) and the next day before leaving he rode out from town four miles and lunched with Mr. Miles. Years ago, Miles and an American friend Mr. Mear had written Twain "when the M. P. was fooled into reading about the Chamois ... in the N. Z. Parliament" (MTP:NB34).

"Deficiencies of the English Language"

Twain's arrival in Christchurch on Tuesday 12 November 1895, marked the beginning of one of his most pleasant stays in Australasia. In Australia, he had thoroughly enjoyed his visit when he was in good health. The family was especially happy in Melbourne, visiting with squatters in elaborate homes on large properties and going to concerts. Twain seems particularly to have liked the places where he was guest at a "stag" function, like the Yorick Club or the Institute of Journalists in Melbourne, or the visit with members of the Pioneers societies in Ballarat. Being the guests of a particular family, preferably well to do with children of Clara's generation like the Wagners in Melbourne, enhanced the family's enjoyment.

The visit in Christchurch, was, in some measure, similar to that in Melbourne, though much shorter. On Saturday, Livy and Clara had traveled with Twain from Dunedin halfway to Christchurch, leaving him off at Timaru to lecture while they continued to the "City of the Plains" (MTP:NB34). Twain had then gone back south to Oamaru for a lecture Monday night, and on Tuesday he went by train about 150 miles north to Christchurch. Possibly he was in better health and spirits than he had been in some places and than he would be in Auckland. Upon his arrival with Carlyle Smythe, Twain was met at the train by the president and members of the Savage Club and then taken to Coker's Hotel where he talked to interviewers (*Lyttelton Times*, 13 Nov., p. 5). The family spent a considerable amount of time with Mr. and Mrs. Kinsey (later Sir Joseph) and their daughter May, who was near Clara's age. They were shown the town and gardens, and the museum with its skeleton of the extinct giant moa; when they left "after four pleasant days" (*More Tramps*, p. 209), they took with them gifts and treasured souvenirs. Twain was entertained on his last evening at a banquet by the Savage Club, a fraternal organization begun in New Zealand in Christchurch. Like the clubs in Melbourne, the Savages encouraged him to keep on speaking, perhaps longer than he had meant to. On Saturday, the Canterbury Club entertained the humorist.

Twain was impressed with the City of the Plains:

It was Junior England all the way to Christchurch—in fact, just a garden. And Christchurch is an English town, with an English park annex, and a winding English brook just like Avon—and named the Avon .... It is a settled old community, with all the serenities, the graces, the conveniences, and the comforts of the ideal home-life. If it had an Established Church and social inequality it would be England over again with hardly a lack. [*More Tramps*, p. 206.]

If Twain was suitably impressed with Christchurch, so was it with him. Of course, the city had been primed for his visit by reprintings from Sydney and Melbourne papers as well as five days of advertisements and posters provided by his "more-travelled" agent. After three dozen Australasian performances and twice as many reviews, it might almost seem that people would have lost interest, or that reviewers would not be able to think of anything new to say, or that interviewers could not dream up anything else interesting to talk about. But not yet at least.

On Wednesday morning, 13 November, two important interviews appeared in the rival Christchurch papers. Both were reprinted in the area weeklies and excerpted in other cities in which Twain later arrived. It is possible that they were written by the same interviewer; one is almost entirely direct quotation of Twain's words; the other, mostly generalization about the conversation. Both are "by our special reporter," possibly a free-lance journalist.

The interview in the *Press* gives particular insight into Twain's preconceptions and actual impressions about Australasia. He cautioned against making statements without proper reflection, saying tactfully, "I am too close now to give any opinion. By and bye, when I get further off—when I get a perspective so to speak of the colonies,—then I can form some idea of the country" (*Press* [Christchurch], 13 Nov., p. 5). He was still piqued at the treatment some casual "globe-trotters," as he called them, had given to the Americans, and he did not intend to make the same mistake about Australasia. He praised the New Zealand scenery as being "a combination of the fiords of Norway and the scenery of Alaska. There are the same deep crevasses in the mountains, with sea between, that are the charm of the Norwegian scenery, whilst your glaciers and snowclad mountains remind one of Alaska. The only regret is that there is nothing known of your lovely scenery in America" (*Press* [Christchurch], 13 Nov., p. 5). The fiords that had so impressed him must have been those he saw from the sea on the trip into Bluff, and he could have seen mountains in the distance along the rail line from Bluff to Christchurch.

He answered questions on Australasian journalism and literature rather more freely than he had in Australia. He said the character of a paper "is reflected in the editorials," the only part he read. As for Australasian papers, he was "most favourably impressed with the vigour of their style, their scholarly language, and logical conclusions" (*Press* [Christchurch], 13 Nov., p. 5). He was also quite impressed with the sheer number of them, noting privately that Christchurch, "with 40,000 people, has papers enough for a N. England town of—well, I don't know" (MTP:NB34). Most of his public comments on Australian literature were polite and very general; this has led some American scholars to treat them as if he were being more diplomatic than honest. But in Christchurch he did say that an important characteristic of Australian novels, distinct from American and English, was that "the aim of the writer seems to be to give a picture of the place and times; the hero, and still more the heroine, are subordinate" (*Lyttelton Times*, 13 Nov., p. 5).

One of the most interesting points in the interviews—both of them covered this point, but in different contexts—was Twain's distinction between American audiences and "colonial" and British ones. In general, American audiences were "very good," but "they come prepared to demand that you give them the best you have got, and they will therefore feel to you somewhat critical .... They have made a contract with you to give them something and they hold you strictly to your part of the bargain, and all the time they are watching to see that you don't go back on it" (*Press* [Christchurch], 13 Nov., p. 5).

On the other hand, colonial and British audiences are more likely to be "fairly carried ... off with a whoop." He illustrated this point with a story about his trip across the Atlantic when he gave exactly the same anecdotes to Americans in the "first" cabin and the next evening to Britons in the "second" cabin (*Lyttelton Times*, 13 Nov., p. 5). "The colonial audiences at once are friendly with you. They encourage you to give your best. You feel as soon as you step on the platform that they are your friends, that they wish you to succeed, and that puts fire and mettle into you" (*Press* [Christchurch], 13 Nov., p. 5).

His observation here implies an important difference in attitude. The Australasians, who were still colonists, seemed to partake of the generosity and magnanimity afforded by the country of long standing, secure in its worldwide empire. The Americans, on the other hand, with only a century's nationhood behind them, were competitive and perhaps even ungenerous, still having to "prove" themselves, and making everybody else do the same. Although Twain said the Australians at least were more like Americans than like the British, some of his compliments reveal shrewd observation of his countrymen.

The appearance of these two new interviews, covering subjects close to the New Zealanders, probably helped fill the Theatre Royal that evening, when Twain gave the "First 'At Home.'" "It is one of the deficiencies of the English language," lamented the *Lyttelton Times*, "that it has no word for an entertainment like that which Mark Twain gave to his audience" (14 Nov., p. 5). The reception was "hearty, enthusiastic, and friendly in the extreme." Before his appearance on stage, "the chorus of 'For he's a jolly good fellow' punctuated the cheers" of greeting (*Press* [Christchurch], 14 Nov., p. 5). When he did appear, "the people began to stamp and cheer ... for several minutes— more minutes than Christchurch audiences usually devote to that sort of thing" (*Lyttelton Times*, 14 Nov., p. 5). As had been noted in Adelaide, ladies "fully equal in number to the men—laughed as heartily as anybody, proving that Mark Twain is not a 'man's humourist' merely" (*Lyttelton Times*, 14 Nov., p. 5).

Twain spoke "with the accessories appropriate to such distinctively American humour—with a nasal twang, slow deliberation and a kind of absent-mindedness which rendered some of the quaint sayings of the speaker irresistibly mirth-provoking. The odd terms of expression, the humorous contrasts, the whimsical absurdities" all seemed "even better when spoken by their author" (*Lyttelton Times*, 14 Nov., p. 5). He varied from "the dry humour which is so essentially American to the pathos which strikes right home," and all the time "he is the most unconscious man in the whole assemblage" (*Press* [Christchurch], 14 Nov., p. 5). The stories he told were the ones called the "First 'At

Home' "—the truant fishing excursion, Adam with the forbidden fruit, and the Mexican plug, concluding with the German language lesson.

On the first night, Twain "did not profess to teach moral lessons, though he gravely announced that he was building a formidable lay sermon on morals, high living, the conduct of life, and many other great and noble things. He has not finished it yet, and does not seem to have a very clear idea as to when it will be finished" (*Lyttelton Times*, 14 Nov., p. 5). This teaser, which he had used in Australia, prepared for the "Morals Sermon" the second evening. It was well received; and it included as moral illustrations the watermelon story, the "ineffectual efforts of the shot laden [jumping frog] Dan'l Webster to rise to the occasion," the Nevada duel, and Huck Finn, Tom Sawyer, and Jim discussing the Crusades. After the ten-minute intermission, he began with a story, which he had introduced in Dunedin and Timaru, about Mrs. McWilliams and the lightning, telling it "with a good deal of graphic force" (*Press* [Christchurch], 15 Nov., p. 6). In addition to his stock introduction to the Australian poem, the papers recorded a new twist. Twain had found that he had misdescribed the platypus, for "it was trowel-shaped, not at the one end but the other"; moreover, it had no teeth—even though the poem praised them—"but this he suggested might be remedied by the purchase of a false set." The entertainment concluded with Uncle Dan'l's ghost story, "ending in a manner which made all the ladies in the audience jump" (*Press* [Christchurch], 15 Nov., p. 6).

The last entertainment, at "popular prices," began with the explanation that "truth was so valuable that it should be husbanded" and was "a mock-heroic complaint" on the decay of the fine art of lying. Although he had written the maxim "Truth is the most valuable thing we have. Let us economise it" in his journal before he even left Europe (MTP:NB34), it may not have been used until Christchurch. He gave "a new version of the George Washington cherry tree story which tickled the audience immensely" (*Star* [Christchurch], 16 Nov., p. 7). This was also a new item in his program, recorded for the first time in Christchurch. Other examples of picturesque lying included the punch brothers routine, the continental courier, and the stammering cure. One lady correspondent wrote that the talk was "more efficacious, from a moral point of view, than many a church sermon against the vice" (*Canterbury Times*, 21 Nov., p. 7). In bidding farewell, he "remarked that he had spent a real good time whilst in Christchurch, and he left the crops flourishing and everybody prosperous, which was very satisfactory to him" (*Star* [Christchurch], 16 Nov., p. 7).

"As Large as Your Great Moa"

On Friday night after Twain's last performance, about fifty members and guests of the Christchurch Savage Club, established only two years earlier with the charge to foster "the singer, the story-teller, the scribe and the player on cunning instruments,"[13] entertained the American at supper in the Provincial Council Chamber. After the elaborate meal, toasts were made to the queen, to the United States and the American people, to Twain himself, "who for thirty years had kept the world laughing," and to Mrs. Clemens. Twain was elected the first honorary member of the organization, was presented with its emblem, and was thrice-welcomed with the "triple war cry of the tribe, 'Ake ake kia kaha.'" (*Press* [Christchurch], 16 Nov., p. 8).

In response Twain made a humorous speech incorporating compliments about having "mixed a great deal with the lower order of savages, and ... [having] seen them in all costumes and in no costumes— (Laughter)—in all costumes except this one that you wear this evening" (*Lyttelton Times*, 16 Nov., p. 5). No doubt his local references—such as feeling "as large as your great moa" at becoming the first honorary member—and the allusions to the circus and other entertainments in Christchurch concurrent with his were well appreciated by his hearers. A long joke about a "Prohibition State" was told because Twain "did not see much prohibition about the Savages there that evening" (*Press* [Christchurch], 16 Nov., p. 8).

Justice Denniston, in toasting the absent lecturer Rev. Haskett Smith, explained that he had intended that Smith and Twain would reconcile their varying opinions about the straightness of a certain street both had seen. Since Smith had "produced a photograph," the judge "thought the weight of evidence was with Rev. Haskett Smith, and he now offered to Mark Twain an opportunity of saying that he was mistaken" (*Press* [Christchurch], 16 Nov., p. 8). Although it was reported that Twain's explanation "was generally considered to be satisfactory," the reconciliation itself was not recorded until nearly a month later when a reporter in Wellington picked it out of him.

---

13. Letter from S. Bryant to the author, 17 March 1985. Twain's membership began the Club's history of giving honorary memberships to illustrious visitors.

When Justice Denniston had completed his toast to Twain, the Savages drank to R. S. Smythe, who was still under smallpox quarantine in Sydney, and to Carlyle Smythe, who was also a guest at the supper. The "more-travelled" Smythe "regretted that quarantine prevented [his father] from being present with them that evening. He was not, however, wasting his time, but was studying patience and practising it, and he was also studying the German gardens." Of course, this referred to Twain's usual close to the "Morals Lecture"; however, it had been given in Christchurch on the first evening. Smythe hoped to cheer his father up by sending a menu of the supper to him at the Quarantine Station, "where the table was noted for its frugality" (*Press* [Christchurch], 16 Nov., p. 8).

The menu, prepared by Mr. Freeman, included a choice of "Puree Mark Twain" or "Consomme du Vagabond en suite"; followed by "Grenouille sautante a la Smiley, Tete d'elephant blanc derobe, Pate du Prince et du pauvre," and "Mayonnaise Mons. Thomas Sawyer." After these came "Salade sauce omnipresente a la Smythe" or "De os de moa a la Sauvage," and finally they could choose "Gelee au vin Finn Huckleberry, Meringues a la creme de la cour d'Arthur" or "Poudin a la tete de Wilson" (*Press* [Christchurch], 16 Nov., p. 8).

Twain's proposed toast to " 'Journalism,' coupled with the names of two excellent and worthy journalists, Messrs Hart and Exall," again brought the Savages to their feet with raised glasses. Musical accompaniments were given by members Woodhouse, Newman, Willis, and pianist Merton. W. P. Williams gave a recitation.

On Saturday 16 November, Twain was entertained by the Canterbury Club at lunch, but no record of the proceedings has survived (MTP:NB34). However, a local poet hailed him "King of Smiles" on the day of his departure.

> With you we've laughed this many a year,
> We've met your jokes in black and white,
> We knew you not, we held you dear,
> We're pleased that you're "At Home" to-night.
> [*Press* (Christchurch), 16 Nov., p. 8.]

That night was dark and rainy, but Joseph Kinsey and his daughter May accompanied the Clemenses and Smythe on the train to Lyttelton, about twelve miles away, to board their ship to Auckland via Wellington and New Plymouth. With them they carried thirty-five gifts, including bonbons, flowers, books, and Maori artifacts. He also received a stuffed ornithorhyncus (or platypus) that he later claimed to be training for he liked it even better than his "wife beater." While they were in Wellington Kinsey sent them photographs he had made when they were in Christchurch and more books[14]

They boarded the Union Company's overcrowded *Flora* at midnight. In *More Tramps Abroad* Twain described that boat as "the foulest I was ever in" and he claimed to have been put in "a cattle-stall in the main stable" (pp. 210, 209). In his notebook he called it "dangerously overpacked with passengers" (MTP:NB34). He believed that if it had sunk, half the people could not possibly have escaped. In a very heavy sea passengers became seasick and hardly anyone was able to sleep. Twain predicted that no one on that voyage would ever forget it; thirty-five years later, his daughter Clara, though confusing it with the same company's *Mararoa* on which they traveled from Hobart to Bluff, wrote a convincing account of the journey. She said, "Fat people were selected to sleep on the tables, in the belief that they would be less likely to roll off. Curtains were strung from wall to wall, separating the men and women, who had mattresses on the floor."[15] Conveniences like towels, pillows, or sheets were unavailable.

Anniversary Day in Canterbury is celebrated on 16 November, and people returning to the North Island from horse races and shows account in part for the dreadful overcrowding.[16] In addition, a scheduled second ship "had been taken off and ... the passengers intended for two vessels had to be crowded into one," Olivia Clemens wrote to Mr. Kinsey.[17] After describing the conditions, she claimed that the party "comfort ourselves now that if we should at any time be compelled to go steerage it could bring us little of experience that would be new."

"The Most 'Tarnashun' Place"

In Wellington on the North Island at five o'clock on Sunday, they changed to a smaller ship, the 226-ton *Mahinapua*, which

---

14. Olivia L. Clemens to Sue Crane, 24 November (Potts and Potts, p. 48); Olivia L. Clemens to Kinsey, 21 November, Alexander Turnbull Library, Wellington; *More Tramps*, p. 209; Olivia L. Clemens to Kinsey, 13 December, Turnbull Library.

15. *My Father, Mark Twain*, p. 150.

16. Kirk, *Star* (Auckland), 5 July, 1967.

17. 21 November, Turnbull Library.

Twain described as "perfect ... clean and comfortable" (MTP:NB34).[18] About dawn on Monday, the ship, under command of Captain W. J. Newton, passed through French Pass in "half a minute," but then the eddies "picked her up and flung her around like nothing and landed her gently on the solid smooth bottom of sand—so gently, indeed, that we barely felt ... when she came to a stand-still. The water was as clear as glass, the sand on the bottom was vividly distinct, and the fishes seemed to be swimming about in nothing" (*More Tramps*, p. 210). But before they could bait their hooks, Twain wrote later, the ship was off again. The newspapers described the sandbanking as having lasted half an hour around four in the morning.

The Clemenses spent the day in Nelson, back on the South Island, headquartering at the Masonic Hotel. Twain was not "in his best form, being somewhat wearied with travelling, without sleep on the steamer Flora .... Mr. Clemens did not relish the trip on the Flora owing to the large number of passengers 'nineteen deep' he says they were" (*Nelson Evening Mail*, 18 Nov.). He told the reporter that he had enjoyed the South Island cities he had lectured in; as for his opinion of the colonies, he said that "he was too close now to give any opinion—by and bye when he got further off, when he got a perspective so to speak .... then he could form some idea of the country" (*Nelson Evening Mail*, 18 Nov.). He did call the French Pass the "most 'tarnashun' place" he had ever been.

Twain acquired a copy of David M. Luckie's *Maungatapu Mountain Murders*, the story of the brutal slaying of five men near Nelson. He was "mentally absorbed" in this great New Zealand crime and the confession and trial of the desperadoes who perpetrated it. A. A. Grace has written that Twain thought "the trial of the Maungatapu murderers was the most remarkable which had been held in the Southern Hemisphere. He said it presented points of interest which were new, and shed much light on the workings of the criminal mind."[19]

In the afternoon, he enjoyed riding out into the country with Mr. Edward Brown, a cab driver—"the whole region is a garden," Twain wrote (*More Tramps*, p. 210). A crowd went out to the Port hoping to catch a

---

18. "Shipping Intelligence," *Taranaki Herald*, 19 Nov.; MTP:NB34 says the *Mahinapua* was 438 tons; *More Tramps* gives 205; Parsons reports 458.

19. A. A. Grace, "Preface," in D. M. Luckie, *The Maungatapu Mountain Murders* (Nelson: R. W. Stiles, 1924), p. 3. Twain quoted extensively from this book in *More Tramps Abroad*, pp. 210–214. He was probably using the H. D. Jackson publication of 1890.

glimpse of the humorist before he left, but he had slipped aboard and into his cabin, disappointing the well-wishers. The *Mahinapua* sailed overnight from Nelson to New Plymouth.

CHAPTER EIGHT

New Zealand North

"Divine Afflatus Creeping"

Days before Twain's arrival in Auckland, Smythe had seen to the press releases about the successes and honors both in Australia and in New Zealand (*New Zealand Herald*, 16 Nov., p. 5; 19 Nov., p. 5). Especially in Christchurch, the "greatest success on the lecture platform yet introduced by Mr. Smythe, Mark Twain [was] an unprecedented social success in the fullest sense of the word" (*Star* [Auckland]), 19 Nov., p. 2). No doubt—the papers predicted—"our celebrated visitor will be welcomed by an overflowing and enthusiastic audience" (*Star* [Auckland], 20 Nov., p. 5). Reciting the troubles he had already encountered, the papers assured readers that "all these annoyances and disappointments, which would have thoroughly upset many a man, however, had naturally no detrimental effects on the man who wrote 'The Jumping Frog'" (*New Zealand Herald*, 16 Nov., p. 5). As in previous cities, the "town was plentifully decorated with portraits" so that the 60,000 residents might be teased by his doleful demeanor.

The Clemenses approached Auckland from New Plymouth after sailing all day on Wednesday 20 November, on the *Mahinapua*, "a wee little bridal-parlour of a boat—only 205 tons" (*More Tramps*, p. 201). One of the first people Twain met was a "fine large Briton a little frosted with age" who had fought in the West during the American Civil War (MTP:NB34), as Twain himself claimed to have done. He was the hall porter in "the leading hotel in Auckland," the Star Hotel on Albert Street, where the Clemens party stayed. Twain was impressed that Auckland's "situation is commanding, and the sea-view is superb. There are charming drives all about, and by courtesy of friends we had opportunity to enjoy them" (*More Tramps*, p. 214).

The night of their arrival, a representative from the *New Zealand Herald* called along with some others, possibly reporters. Taking "walking exercise while conversing," Twain declined to talk about "how he liked the people of New Zealand, because he said he had been asked that question before" (*New Zealand Herald*, 21 Nov., p. 5). At least thrice before (at Dunedin, Christchurch, and Nelson) he had told reporters that "the man who attempts to describe a country which he sees for the first time after a brief visit to it, and before he has time to digest, as I may put it, what he has gleaned regarding it, is wrong" (*Press* [Christchurch], 13 Nov., p. 5). This sentiment is akin to the major theme of an essay published shortly before he came to Australasia. In reviewing a recent book on America by French "observer" Paul Bourget, Twain had written, "A foreigner can photograph the exteriors of a nation .... no foreigner can report its interior—its life, its speech, its thought .... a knowledge of these things is acquirable in only one way .... years and years of unconscious absorption .... One learns peoples through the heart, not the eyes or the intellect."[1] He would stick with this opinion after he had returned to Sydney when reporters asked him how he thought New Zealanders compared with Australians.

The conversation turned to "Americanisms" in language, a subject that occasionally found space in the colonial newspapers. Twain explained, "there are many expressions said to be American and slang." But they are not necessarily American for "many so-called Americanisms come from the English .... most people suppose that everyone who 'guesses' is a Yankee; the people who guess, do so because their ancestors guessed in Yorkshire" (*New Zealand Herald*, 21 Nov., p. 5). He also commented on his own lack of respect for mere convention. An editor once asked him to change an article he had written for a magazine that had many youthful subscribers. The editor "said I had put a clergyman in a ridiculous position. My reply was he had put himself there. If [the editor] liked to strike the clergyman out he could. But I could put no one in his place" (*New Zealand Herald*, 21 Nov., p. 5).

---

1. "What Paul Bourget Thinks of Us," *Tom Sawyer Detective* (London: Chatto and Windus, 1909), pp. 196–197.

Twain was first "At Home" in Auckland on Thursday evening, 21 November, at the old City Hall, whose "downstairs portion ... was packed, and there were few seats, worth having, to spare in the dress circle" (*New Zealand Herald*, 22 Nov., p. 5). The crowd had begun to gather as early as six o'clock, and the "debtors of Mark Twain for the many pleasant hours and the many hearty laughs his books have afforded them ..., [had] an opportunity of meeting their humorous creditor" (*New Zealand Graphic*, 23 Nov., p. 646). As he came onto the platform,

> it was some minutes before Mr. Clemens could proceed owing to the warmth of the welcome .... He had not spoken four sentences before laughter commenced .... The 'knob' of the tale was never missed, though it came oftentimes in the form of a phrase of two or three words, brought in parenthetically, but with rare effect. [*Auckland Weekly News*, 30 Nov., p. 14; reprinted from *New Zealand Herald*, 22 Nov., p. 5.]

The daily papers acknowledged the long-time acquaintance of the auditors with Twain's writings. But their main theme was that "one must see the man and hear him to enjoy him to the full." "Stenography could easily have enabled one to retain the subject matter of Mark Twain's remarks ..., but to hear them as they fall from his lips is quite another thing .... The grave face, with not a catspaw of a smile on it ..., a mass of grey hair, the clear eyes ... beneath bushy eyebrow ... one cannot describe these things" (*Star* [Auckland], 22 Nov., p. 3).

Only two hints were left in the daily newspapers about which lecture he used: first, the jumping frog, which "although read a score of times, and enjoyed, was never what it was as told by Mark Twain himself," and second, the idle question "Who heard of the forbidden fruit last night will forget the telling of it?" (*New Zealand Herald*, 22 Nov., p. 5). "Prompter," the theatre columnist for the weekly *Observer*, called this story his "best point." Twain was "dwelling on the proneness of human flesh to do whatever was forbidden us. Indeed, he said if the serpent in the Garden of Eden had been forbidden, Adam would have eaten that. And, in his opinion, it would have been a good thing for humanity if he had" (*N. Z. Observer and Free Lance*, 30 Nov., p. 10). These stories usually were in two different routines during the tour; evidently, by this late time, Twain was rather thoroughly scrambling them to suit himself, picking and choosing the crowd-pleasers.

The papers deliberately omitted the "matter" of the stories, instead emphasizing the "manner," for his is "a style of humorous delivery to which Aucklanders are not accustomed, and it was a little time before some of those present 'dropped to it,' or shall we rather say, rose to it" (*Star* [Auckland], 22 Nov., p. 3). Probably taking a cue from the interview printed in the *New Zealand Herald* the morning before, the *Star*, more than most papers, stressed

> the particuliarly effective manner in which the humorist leads his audience quietly up to the point of the joke and leaves them .... His pauses are almost as provocative of mirth as his spoken words. He ... can be silently humorous, and last night the laughter was almost as hearty when he stood saying nothing as when he spoke. [22 Nov., p. 3.]

Twain concluded the first show by promising the "Australian poem up-to-date" for the second night.

"Another vast audience" greeted him on Friday night when he gave his morals sermon. "His annexation of a water melon and the pangs of remorse felt for his act upon discovering it was a green one" and his Nevada duel were "excellently delivered" (*Star* [Auckland], 23 Nov., p. 2). Though some feared that people who were familiar with his works would expect too much, the two evenings showed "conclusively that, however high the expectations of his audiences ... this prince of American humourists is quite able to satisfy them." In fact, it seemed that this very familiarity enhanced the enjoyment, for "every now and then would be heard a sudden solitary laugh—now here, now there,—which could not be restrained .... These people knew the joke before it came, and laughed in anticipation" (*New Zealand Herald*, 23 Nov., p. 5). He gave " 'Artemus Ward and the power of imagination,' ... 'the naming of the baby,' ... 'the thunderstorm,' [and] his own truly wonderful attempt at poetry." The stories were mostly familiar, but "at one time a look, or at another a change in the tone of his voice, or again a gesture, was quite enough to evoke roars of laughter" (*New Zealand Herald*, 23 Nov., p. 5).

That Twain was meticulous in his pauses has been noted before,[2] but it should be stressed that his notebooks are thoroughly sprinkled with entries like the one for the second Auckland performance: "Watermelon, Duel, Crusade, Artemus (too short—only 5 min)—Xning.—8.05

---

2. Parsons, "Mark Twain in Australia," pp. 460–462; Lorch, *The Trouble Begins at Eight*, pp. 218–223, for example.

to 8.57. Then McWilliams & Poem—9.10 to 9.45. Had to leave out Golden Arm" (MTP:NB34).

However, "it was as a poet that Mark Twain most pleased the audience." Having "felt the divine afflatus creeping up his spine" (*Star* [Auckland], 23 Nov., p. 2), he read his "ode upon the peculiar flora and fauna of Australia," evoking "uproarious amusement."

"Travelling and Lecturing ... Don't Mix"

On Friday morning, the family was shown the Public Library by the librarian and the town clerk. In the afternoon Mr. W. Douglas, local President of the Journalists' Institute, took them for a drive to "the grassy crater-summit of Mount Eden" (*New Zealand Herald*, 23 Nov., p. 5). There they viewed "a grand sweep and variety of scenery—forests clothed in luxuriant foliage, rolling green fields, conflagrations of flowers, receding and dimming stretches of green plain, broken by lofty and symmetrical old craters—then the blue bays twinkling and sparkling away into the dreamy distances where the mountains loom spiritual in their veils of haze" (*More Tramps* p. 214; adapted closely from MTP:NB34).

The visit at Auckland turned out to be more leisurely than many of his stops, and the family had ample opportunity to enjoy several drives into the hills surrounding the city. There was no Saturday performance scheduled, for they had planned "visiting the Hot Lakes and spending a day or two thereabouts before returning to Wellington" (*Star* [Auckland], 21 Nov., p. 5), but instead they spent an unexpected weekend in Auckland when they discovered it would be impossible to journey to Rotorua "because [the] train takes 10 1/2 hours to go about 200 & odd miles ... returning, leave at 4 a.m., arrive here at 2.30 p.m.—would be too tired to lecture that night with effect" (MTP:NB34). It seems clear that Twain and Smythe had already booked the third "At Home" before they made the final decision not to go to the hot lakes region, already an important resort. The paper was at least partially correct when it reported that "owing to the thronged houses that have attended," Twain "has abandoned his projected trip to Rotorua" because he had decided to "give a third and new entertainment next Monday evening" (*New Zealand Herald*, 23 Nov., p. 5).

Twain had told the first interviewer in Auckland that "Travelling and lecturing are like oil and water; they don't mix. There are many fine sights in New Zealand that I haven't seen" (*New Zealand Herald*, 21 Nov., p. 5). Saturday's gossip columnist explained that Twain found it "is a difficult matter to travel and to lecture. He must not knock himself up in sight-seeing because then he could not do justice to his audiences." Moreover, "he has passed some of our finest scenery at night, and when he came to Taranaki [near New Plymouth,] he found Mount Egmont shrouded in mist." But, the columnist continued, "I believe he is firmly convinced that the portions of his book which will be the most admired will be those in which he describes the scenery which he had not seen" (*New Zealand Herald*, Supplement, 23 Nov., p. 1; *Auckland Weekly News*, 30 Nov., p. 7). This conversation was possibly a fabrication, but it did echo the same notions attributed to Twain in Sydney Harbour: "I'm going to write a book on Australia .... You know so much more of a country when you haven't seen it than when you have" (*Sydney Morning Herald*, 16 Sept., p. 4), and again in Adelaide: "he wanted ... information about that country, and he did not care whether it was correct or not .... All he wanted was information" (*Advertiser*, 15 Oct., p. 5).

It was probably on Saturday 23 November, that Twain went "to Kauri Gum establishment of Ameri[can] firm of Arnold, Cheney & Co—large exporters to Amer[ica]" (MTP:NB34). In *More Tramps Abroad* he told about the retrieval of the petrified gum from the earth and its manufacture into varnish, based closely on the account recorded in his notebook as having been told to him by Dr. J. L. Campbell (MTP:NB34). Olivia Clemens wrote to her adopted sister Sue Crane on 24 November that they had lunched at an estate called Bishopcourt and then gone to an extensive garden between a lake and the harbor in the afternoon. Afterward Colonel Burton had entertained them for tea on his porch overlooking the harbor.[3]

She also said that "Mr. Clemens does not seem to have as much strength as I could wish to see him have. Yesterday he seemed to feel better, to have more spring, but today he is threatened with another carbuncle. Naturally that makes him feel very much discouraged. However, I still have faith to believe that with Dr Fitzgerald's remedies I shall be able to get it checked. Dr Fitzgerald did do wonders for

---

3. Olivia L. Clemens to Sue Crane, 24 November, Alderman Library, University of Virginia; copy in Mark Twain Papers.

the other one," which he had suffered in Melbourne.[4] Livy had been dressing these eruptions at least once a day since mid-May.[5]

Auckland was one of the few places on the entire world trip where it is known how many people paid to hear Twain. In the same letter to her sister Olivia wrote, "Mr. Clemens continues to have large and very enthusiastic houses. Here he has a large hall, and he has had a thousand people to hear him each night—in fact the two nights counted up to 2172 people who paid for their seats. That did not count the newspaper people nor me." At two to four shillings per seat, Twain probably grossed something over $1500 for the two evenings. Clearly Olivia was pleased with the Australasian audiences, for she wrote, "If Australia and New Zealand had as many big cities as America has he could make his fortune; but the trouble is that there are so few cities, just a *very few* along the coast. I think there are only seven or eight in New Zealand large enough for it to make it worth his while to lecture in them."[6]

The third lecture in Auckland was at the Opera House, apparently somewhat larger, or at least more suitable, than City Hall, for the newspaper advertisements had apologized that it was already engaged for the first two nights. Twain told, "by desire, the marvellous adventures of an amateur courier, which in the Southern towns of the colony was ranked among the ... most successful" (*New Zealand Herald*, 25 Nov., p. 4). The reduced prices assured a large audience and "the enjoyment afforded was as keen as ever, and in almost every sentence his quiet humour told" (*Auckland Weekly News*, 30 Nov., p. 4).

Again the local humorists found Twain a subject for their columns. One said his friend was contemplating a career as a lecturer, but had not yet decided what role he should take.

> To work the religious idea is the easiest, and then there is the historical, the scientific, and various other spheres .... But I am quite sure I would never dream of assuming the character of a humourist, even if I had written as good a book as 'The Innocents Abroad,' or all the other funny works of Mark Twain. [*New Zealand Herald*, Supplement, 23 Nov., p. 1; *Auckland Weekly News*, 30 Nov., p. 7.]

---

4. Potts and Potts, p. 48.

5. Samuel L. Clemens to Joseph Twichell, 29 November, Beinecke Library, Yale University; copy in Mark Twain Papers.

6. Potts and Potts, p. 49.

The reason for such an opinion was that "the character of humourist is so difficult to maintain. You are expected to live up to it, and unless you are always saying good things you are voted flat and a failure." Still, Twain "has come well through the ordeal of the most difficult of all characters. I don't know any man who can claim to have been the author of so much innocent mirth .... [T]here are few writers whose books are so well worth thinking over, few who so consistently communicate impulses to noble, unselfish action" (*New Zealand Herald*, Supplement, 23 Nov., p. 1; *Auckland Weekly News*, 30 Nov., p. 7).

Twain and his family sailed from Auckland on the Union Company's *Rotomahana* at three o'clock on Tuesday. They had arrived at Auckland's western port near Onehunga, crossed through the city and departed from the northeastern shore on their way to Gisborne and Napier on the east coast. In his notebook he commented on the "vast and beautiful harbour," the "perfect summer weather," a "large school of whales," and the "deep blue ... storm-cloud," all described in *More Tramps Abroad* (p. 215). He was fascinated by the story of a notorious shipwreck that had occurred in a fog at the Great Barrier Island a year before, recording some apparently erroneous information about the number of casualties (MTP:NB34n).

"The Profits of ... Gisborne ... Vanish"

Smythe's cooperating New Zealand agent, Hugo Fischer, had passed through Gisborne on 23 November to complete arrangements for Twain's lecture (*Poverty Bay Herald*, 23 Nov., p. 3). All was set; advertisements and promotional articles, including the one that was used in nearly all the papers describing Smythe's twelve-year campaign to get Twain to the Antipodes, began to appear in the local papers. Gisborne also reprinted excerpts from reviews in Auckland. On Wednesday 27 November, the Union Company's *Rotomahana*, which Twain described as "a nice ship, roomy, comfortable, well ordered, and satisfactory" (*More Tramps*, p. 216), was supposed to arrive in Gisborne on the east coast of New Zealand's North Island. After a trip of twenty-three hours in fine weather from Auckland, the ship arrived three hours earlier than scheduled.

However, a heavy sea prevented landing, and the *Rotomahana* anchored about a mile from shore. A crowd gathered to watch the small steam launch, the *Snark*, come out to take about twenty-five passengers ashore, including four prisoners who were to begin jail sentences. It also delivered about twenty-five outgoing passengers, many from the Greenwood traveling dramatic group, while "heavy seas continually broke over the little vessel .... [and] the big steamer was tossing about considerably" (*Poverty Bay Herald*, 27 Nov., p. 2). The passengers changed boats "in a most primitive basket," which seemed very dangerous to Twain.[7]

Twain's lecture was canceled, because, as he told W. Good on the *Rotomahana*, it was "impossible for him to come ashore as the steamer would not wait. Moreover, he did not fancy coming ashore in the Snark" (*Poverty Bay Herald*, 27 Nov., p. 2). The next day he was reported to have said that "he had had many rough experiences in his time, but he had seen nothing to equal the bobbing about of the Snark alongside." When discovering the sentence of one of the prisoners was a year, he was supposed to have said, "Waal, I guess it ought to be shortened to six months after that trip in the tender" (*Poverty Bay Herald*, 27 Nov., p. 2). Later, after Twain had returned to Sydney, the *Bulletin* reported that "it was too rough to land in that unreliable roadstead, so the agonized Smythe saw the profits of the Gisborne visit vanish over the horizon" (21 Dec., p. 8).

No doubt the Gisborne residents, who believed "his brief visit to this port will find a place in the book which the humorist is now writing," would have enjoyed the illustration included in the American edition and later as the frontispiece of the "authorized" edition of *More Tramps Abroad*, depicting the transfer of passengers in the basket. But they were to see only a page, a rather poetic and highly complimentary one nevertheless, in the English edition.

Livy Clemens celebrated her fiftieth birthday aboard the *Rotomahana*, unable to land because of the heavy seas. However, Twain, with characteristic foolishness, "claimed that her birthday has either passed or is to come; that it is the 27th as the 27th exists in America, not here where we have flung out a day & closed up the vacancy."[8] Although this joke about time differences from North America was restricted to his notebook and the family, the humorist did make jokes about the "upside-down" seasons in the Antipodes. To a Melbourne reporter he had expressed dismay at the prospect of "two crops of spring poets" in

---

7. *Notebook*, ed. Paine, p. 257.

8. *Notebook*, ed. Paine, p. 257; punctuation restored from MTP:NB34.

a single year; and as the southern summer wore on, he found his Sydney audiences especially receptive to jokes about the "December heat." Of course, many—perhaps even most—of his Australasian auditors would actually have come from England themselves; having mastered their own early confusion at such time changes made them superior to Twain's apparent befuddlement.

"What a Calamitous Thing ...
to Be a Professional Humorist"

Early the next day, they reached Napier where Twain was scheduled to lecture twice. He noted the new pier and "beautiful green bluffs" with the town on top. Although he liked Frank Moeller's Masonic Hotel, which looked over the sea with its "solemn deep" breakers and "luxurious lullaby" (MTP:NB34), he had no use for the three cages of canaries decorating the long porch. As far as he was concerned, "A cary's [sic] 'music' is but the equivalent of scratching a nail on a window-pane. I wonder what sort of disease it is that enables a person to enjoy the canary" (MTP:NB34).

That evening, 28 November, he spoke at the Theatre Royal. Two surgeons, Drs. de Lisle and Bernau, had looked in on him before his show and "advised Mr. Clemens to spare his audience—by sparing himself"; but because it was really too late to cancel, Twain went on anyway. There was a sign on the theatre in Napier informing literate canines that " 'Dogs [were] positively forbidden in the Dress Circle.' " This implied, Twain reasoned, "tacit permission to fill up the rest of the house."[9] Apparently in several places "Plenty dogs attend my lectures," but only in Oamaru did they get into a fight. He seemed a bit "long-winded and prosy" at the beginning as he told his story of the truant fishing excursion.[10] But the Mexican plug was "a horsey item which seemed especially to tickle the ears of the local groundlings"; Huck Finn's conscience and the lost dime followed. Newspapers reported a very short joke about some missionaries. Their "heathen congregation ...ate 'Him ..., her too,' and promised the friends who went to 'Fetch away the thing' not to do it again" (Hawke's Bay Herald, 29 Nov., p. 3). Although this probably had been used before, since it was recorded

---

9. Notebook, ed. Paine, p. 261.
10. Parsons, "Mark Twain in New Zealand," p. 71.

in the American portion of the tour as part of the lost dime story,[11] Napier's is the first Australasian recording of the joke.

Twain said he had a "Lovely time with the audience" (MTP:NB34). The reviewer said his style was

> unique, and so characteristic as to be quite familiar to those who delight in his writings, for the diction seems to be inseparably wedded to the matter .... 'What a calamitous thing it must be to be a professional humorist!' Last night we witnessed the facility with which a heaven-born genius of that ilk could so twist words and contort phrases as to keep an audience in an agony of amusement. [*Hawke's Bay Herald*, 29 Nov., p. 3.]

Though he canceled his second performance, Twain and at least some of Napier's 9,000 residents hoped for a matinee on the afternoon of the thirtieth, but that was not to be. Twain's fourth carbuncle, no doubt aggravated by the hot weather, forced him to lie around for a while.[12] He took the opportunity to describe the "smooth and placidly-complaining sea at our door, with nothing between us and it but twenty yards of shingle—and hardly a suggestion of life in that space to mar it or make a noise." He commented on the "unfamiliar ... foreign ... melancholy ... unvisited solitudes" of the Antarctic seas.[13] All things considered, Twain thought it "a good stroke of luck that knocked me on my back here at Napier, instead of some hotel in the centre of a noisy city." Besides dealing with some correspondence, he spent the days examining the local newspapers, reading Indian history in preparation for his visit to that country, and studying and remarking on rail timetables.

It was evidently in this last activity that he discovered that "the New Zealand express train is called the Ballarat Fly" (*More Tramps*, p. 217), although there is no information to that effect in his notebook. Rather, he recorded there only that "this morning we had one of those whizzing green Ballarat flies in the room" (MTP:NB34). He

---

11. See Fatout, *Mark Twain Speaking* (, p. 12.

12. In a letter to Twichell, Twain calls this his third carbuncle. The second, he says, was at Melbourne; at Adelaide he still had the remnants of the Melbourne eruption. But at Horsham he was "in perfect health," he said, and apparently so in Stawell. Then in Ballarat (20 October) he was "down on the blankets" for the third time, recovering while on board ship to New Zealand. The Napier ailment had begun in Auckland around 20 November, making it the fourth boil. His first one had been in Sydney in mid-September.

13. Samuel L. Clemens to Joseph Twichell, 29 Nov., *Mark Twain's Letters*, ed. Paine, (New York: Harper and Brothers, 1917), p. 630.

did elaborate on the annoying pest, and in his book he described more fully "his stunning buzz-saw noise—the swiftest creature in the world except the lightning flash. It is a stupendous force that is stored up in that little body. If we had it in a ship in the same proportion, we could spin from Liverpool to New York in the space of an hour" (*More Tramps*, p. 217). In claiming that he travelled from Napier to Wanganui on the "Ballarat Fly," he took the opportunity to praise the railroads: "nothing that goes on wheels can be more comfortable, more satisfactory, than the New Zealand trains. Outside of America there are no cars that are so rationally devised. When you add the constant presence of charming scenery and the nearly constant absence of dust—well, if one is not content then, he ought to get out and walk" (*More Tramps*, pp. 218–219). Partially inspired by acquaintances he had met in Victoria, he had not had such kind words for the Australian rails, whether occasioned by change of gauge, rough spurs in rural Victoria, or that state's refusal to accept his return ticket on the leg between Castlemaine and Maryborough.

Apparently his doctor called again and told him about some drunkards reclaimed by the Salvation Army, and a "citizen" told him that the colonists, rather than having their teeth filled, merely pulled them out and substituted false ones. Even young ladies sometimes had a full set (*More Tramps*, pp. 216–217; MTP:NB34). If "colonists" also included Australians, it is no wonder that the audience howled when he read his poem about the duckbill platypus who "has got to have teeth, if it is only a false set" (*Age* [Melbourne], 28 Dec., p. 7). Twain passesd his birthday "under world time" in Napier, where he turned "60—no thanks for it."[14]

"A Clear Case of Mental Telegraphy"

Twain, his family, and Carlyle Smythe left Napier for Palmerston North on Monday 2 December, "a perfect summer day [with] cool breeze, brilliant sky" (*More Tramps*, p. 217). From Napier he had written that Clara and Livy tolerated "this nomadic life pretty well; certainly better than one could have expected . . . . [showing] heroic endurance that resembles contentment."[15] Twain remembered this train

14. Ibid.
15. Ibid.

trip as having taken about five or six hours; it took one hour to go the twelve miles from Napier to Hastings.

They stopped about twenty minutes for lunch at Waipukurau, where Twain was reminded of his faith in mental telegraphy. Since its appearance in *Harper's Magazine* in September, Twain's article "Mental Telegraphy Again" had been excerpted by Australasian newspapers as part of their editorializing prior to his various arrivals. Twain illustrated the phenomenon with examples from his personal life; one of these was the account of his contracting with R. S. Smythe for his tour around the world. New Zealanders had probably already read Twain's story of having mailed a letter to Smythe on 6 February; "three days later I got a letter from the self-same Smythe, dated Melbourne, December 17. I would as soon have expected to get a letter from the late George Washington" (*Australasian* [Melbourne], 5 Oct., p. 650). This was a clear impossibility unless Smythe knew by thought transference what Twain was asking—namely, to give him the same terms as he had given their mutual friend, explorer H. M. Stanley, who had recommended Smythe's management. There is little doubt that Twain believed in at least some occurrences of thought transfer, for he had told this story to his New York business manager before he wrote the article he sold to *Harper's* for a much-needed $200.

At Waipukurau, Twain could see a picture that he mistook for the death of Napoleon III's son. Prompting his wife Livy about "when the news came to Paris," she thought of the death of Napoleon's son "Lulu." She could not see the picture, and, instead of thinking of news that had occurred while they recently lived in Paris, she had thought of the event sixteen years earlier. Twain was convinced this "was a clear case of mental telegraphy ... of my mind telegraphing a thought into hers. How do I know? Because I telegraphed an *error* .... She had to get the error from my head—it existed nowhere else" (*More Tramps*, p. 218; adapted closely from MTP:NB34). He included this episode in his travel book, further to illustrate his belief.

After lunch the journey continued through "rich vegetation" under the "brilliant sky." He noted again forests, vines, and ferns as he had remarked them near Auckland. They entered a "romantic gorge, with a brook flowing in its bottom, approaching Palmerston North," probably the Manawatu River (*More Tramps*, p. 217; adapted closely from MTP:NB34). Twain lectured in Palmerston North on 2 December, but the newspapers of this period have been destroyed by fire; therefore, it now seems impossible to discover what stories he told or how his audience reacted to them. The only surviving record of his visit to the city was discreetly omitted from *More Tramps Abroad*. But in his notebook he had written, with some obvious literary revision and exaggeration:

Club Hotel. Memorable hotel. Stunning Queen-of-Sheba style of barmaid always answered the bell & then got up on her dignity & said lighting fires, brushing clothes, boots, &c., was the chambermaid's business. Would she please tell the chambermaid? (No answer. Exit.) "Why do you *answer* the bell?" Sign up, saying landlord not hold himself responsible for baggage. No keys to the doors. Drunken loafers making noise down stairs. Said he *had* keys but didn't know they was going to be wanted, & it would take a long time to sort them out; hadn't any labels or numbers on them. Elderly & not very handsome woman said she'd a given up *her* room if she'd know people was so particular—*She* wasn't afraid to sleep without a key. Got a key at last—midnight.

Early in the morning baby began—pleasantly—didn't mind baby—then the piano tin kettle, played by either the cat or a partially untrained artist— certainly the most extraordinary music—straight average of 3 right notes to 4 wrong ones, but played with eager zeal & gladness—old, old tunes of 40 ys ago, such as I heard at Timaru—& considering it was the cat—for it *must* have been the cat—it was really [a] marvelous performance. It convinces me that a cat is more intelligent than people believe, & can be taught any crime.

Rooms astonishingly small—partitions astonishingly thin—parlor the size & shape of a grand piano. Very funny hotel. Landlord shows ladies through with his hat on. Fat, red, ignorant, made of pretty coarse clay, possibly mud.

"Anything the matter with your head—or is it custom to keep it covered?"[16]

Perhaps the most disappointing thing about this hotel was that "Smoking [was] not allowed in the rooms." Unfortunately, no other record exists from which to determine how other of the 12,000 residents of Palmerston North responded to Twain or to his stories.

"Not Usual to Laugh at Sermons"

The four-hour trip from Palmerston North to Wanganui on 3 December was again remarkable for the most comfortable, satisfactory, and rationally devised train cars outside of America (*More Tramps*,

---

16. *Notebook*, ed. Paine, pp. 259–260; punctuation restored from MTP:NB34.

pp. 218–219; MTP:NB34). However, Twain thought it a bit awkward to arrive within six minutes of Wanganui and then spend twenty mintues changing cars (MTP:NB34). Around the town he noted the horseback riding, the "comely girls in cool and pretty summer gowns," and the Maoris, whose older members were "very tastefully frescoed" (*More Tramps*, p. 219; MTP:NB34). He was greatly impressed that women and Maoris were able to vote and that the latter had seats in the government. In a letter dated 5 December Livy described a drive she and Clara took "along the Wanganui River to a Maori settlement." They met several older Maoris including a "woman with her lips all tattooed," and they were shown the council house.[17]

The weekly newspaper promised that Twain "will speak for himself this evening to a packed audience in the Oddfellows' Hall; he himself being the oddest fellow in it, or we are very much mistaken" (*Yeoman*, 7 Dec., p. 12). Even at four shillings for a stall, and two shillings sixpence for the dress circle, the hall "was packed, many having to stand" that same night when a "hearty welcome [was] extended to [Twain] by a large and appreciative audience" (*Wanganui Herald*, 4 Dec., p. 2). His preface indicated that he was

> hunting up facts for a grand sermon on morals. At least he said so .... He hadn't tried his hand at sermonising before, and he was just going round picking up the necessary facts. There was no hurry. If he hadn't got enough by the time he had been round the world—well, he could go round again, and then if he was still short of facts he could invent a few to fill up.

From then on the audience was "convulsed ... with laughter for nearly two hours" (*Wanganui Chronicle*, 4 Dec.).

This lecture was not the "morals sermon," which had a different introduction and usually began with the stolen watermelon story. He claimed in Wanganui that the facts he was collecting were determined by the impression made on him at age thirteen. He went fishing instead of going to school; when he returned, he found a dead man in his father's office. Missing school "was wrong; very wrong. If it hadn't been wrong he would not have done it." He discoursed for a while on "his native village, where half the people were dead and the other half asleep, and where it was impossible to distinguish one half from the other" (*Wanganui Chronicle*, 4 Dec.). Next he told

---

17. Harnsberger, p. 157; Harnsberger's book misdates this letter 2 December; her transcription in the Mark Twain Papers, Bancroft Library, is dated 5 December.

about the Nevada silver mines where he nearly got into a duel, and, warning his hearers about trusting strangers, he told about the Mexican plug horse and the man with the wandering mind. Huck Finn and the runaway slave Jim demonstrated that "a sound heart is better than a half-educated conscience." After the intermission, Twain extolled the value of studying the German language as a means of cultivating patience. He himself had been at it for twenty-eight years and expected not to learn it in this life. The moral gleaned from the story of the serpent and the missionary, told during the first performance, " 'fetched' them all" (*Wanganui Herald*, 4 Dec., p. 2; *Yeoman*, 7 Dec., p. 9).

That afternoon, Wednesday 4 December,

> a lunatic burst into my quarters and warned me that the Jesuits were going to 'cook' (poison) me in my food or kill me on the stage at night. He said a mysterious sign [illustration] was visible upon my posters and meant my death. He said he saved the Rev. Mr. Haweis's life by warning him that there were three men on his platform who would kill him if he took his eyes off them for a moment during his lecture. [*More Tramps*, p. 220.][18]

When queried about whether the assassins would be present that evening, the lunatic hesitated, but finally said they would not; instead they would trust to the poison. Twain's opinion was that "this lunatic has no delicacy. But he was not uninteresting. He told me a lot of things. He said he had 'saved so many *lecturers* in twenty years that *they put him in the asylum.*' I think he has less refinement than any lunatic I have met" (*More Tramps*, p. 220).[19]

The *Wanganui Chronicle* did not offer much criticism of the lecture, but it did give detailed and valuable accounts of the contents of the performances, which were not recorded elsewhere. It pointed out that "it is not usual to laugh at sermons, or the matter upon which they are to be formed. Mark Twain, however, did not ask anyone to laugh. He talked seriously, deliberately, and without a smile." Especially useful is the record of the introduction about "hunting up" facts for a sermon (cited above) and of Uncle Dan'l's ghost story, which

---

18. This is taken nearly verbatim from MTP:NB34; see *Notebook*, ed. Paine, p. 260.

19. Only the words quoted from the lunatic are taken verbatim from the notebook. His daughter Clara misplaces this episode in Melbourne. She tells of reading a book in the hotel's reception room when a "maniac .... with blood-shot eyes" hissed at her. He offered to save her father's life with "a little bottle ... Mark Twain must drink" (*My Father, Mark Twain*, pp. 145–146).

gave every man, woman and child a "Yankee start." He was finishing off with a ghost story—the story of the golden arm—and as it progressed he gradually worked up the feelings of his hearers to such a pitch that one and all appeared to be breathlessly awaiting the terrible conclusion. It came, and in a manner that was totally unexpected, for with a sharp, sudden and loud exclamation he broke abruptly off, the ladies especially nearly jumping out of their seats at the resultant shock. [*Wanganui Chronicle*, 5 Dec.]

Twain and Smythe left at eight o'clock on 5 December for speaking engagements in Hawera and New Plymouth. However, on Sunday they were back in Wanganui, a rather large population center of nearly 14,000 people, taking a riverboat ride. Twain was disgusted with another passenger, a "filthy old maid with two fat horrible .... slimy muddy half-caste pugs in her lap" (MTP:NB34)—an episode he suppressed from *More Tramps Abroad*.

Twain often lashed out against injustice in its various forms. In Ballarat, for example, he praised the revolt at Eureka Stockade as a "victory won by a lost battle." After studying Australasian history back in London, in *More Tramps Abroad* he would condemn transportation and the convict system and the genocide practiced in some places against the Aborigines, as well as aboriginal atrocities against white settlers. Although in general he thought the Maoris and the treatment of them by the English superior to parallel situations in Australia, in Wanganui he found one violation of this principle.

The monument to the Maori wars seemed to Twain "the most comical monument in the whole earth" because it praised the whites who died for "law & order against fanaticism & barbarism,"[20] implying that the Maoris who died defending their homeland were ignoble and unworthy. The other monument, the one to the Maoris who died on the side of the English, was a "disgrace to both parties—the traitors & those who praise them" (MTP:NB34). It could be "rectified" only "with dynamite," he wrote, because it invited "treachery, disloyalty, unpatriotism" (*More Tramps*, p. 221). That the British had merely subdued, not exterminated the Maoris; that they had not taken all the best land; and that they allowed the natives to vote showed the enlightenment of both races. But the inadvertent satire in the monument clearly disturbed him.

---

20. *Notebook*, ed. Paine, p. 261.

New Zealand North   171

"Government Lands ...Open for Occupation"

At Hawera, where Twain lectured on 5 November, the newspaper carried advance publicity from Wanganui. The Drill Hall held "such an audience as ... is seldom seen in Hawera," a town of only 2,200 residents, including its environs. The "whole country around from Stratford to Opunake and to Patea was ... strongly represented." Reserved seats, which cost four shillings, "were promptly filled, [and] soon no more three shilling seats were available." Back seats, at two shillings, overflowed into standing room only, and the crowd "welcomed him in the flesh because in spirit it had long appreciated the man." The paper commented that there was "a good deal that was new and there was some that was familiar" including Huck's struggle between an " 'educated' conscience and a heart unfettered by the teachings of civilisation" (*Star* [Hawera], 5, 6 Dec.). Twain wanted "to put in the 'heavenly sand-pile' but dasn't" because he thought the Southern Hemisphere audience "wouldn't have understood; they have never seen the Milky Way" (MTP:NB34).

The next day he traveled about fifty miles at an average—he said— of twelve miles per hour. The Taranaki peninsula was known as the "garden region," Twain noted in his journal; "they never had a drouth; the grass is green & fat the year round" (MTP:NB34). He thought it "looks like one vast 'clearing'—[it was] covered, stretch after stretch, with prone & charred great trees & vast roots." The reason for all this new clearing of land was that "the government lands have been thrown open for occupation" and "little frame cottages, old & paintless" were now interspersed with "neat new painted ones." He was told that white settlement "was retarded by Maori hostilities, but peace has reigned for years, now."[21] Reporters in Auckland claimed he had missed seeing Mount Egmont because it was shrouded in fog when he had sailed through the Taranaki Bights, landing at New Plymouth on his trip northward from Nelson. This time it was capped by a cloud.

It was on 6 December, the day he traveled from Hawera and lectured in New Plymouth, that he wrote the somewhat ambiguous entry "Plenty dogs attend my lectures."[22] In Oamaru and Napier (he wrote in Hawera), dogs had attended his performances, and it may have been that they stayed away from his lectures on the west coast. But probably

---

21. *Notebook*, ed. Paine, p. 261; punctuation and spelling restored from MTP:NB34.
22. *Notebook*, ed. Paine, p. 261.

he meant that they did come in New Plymouth, for the next journal entry also linked Napier and New Plymouth whose public parks and promenades were "ahead of time" in both towns. "Where else in the world," Twain asked himself, "do villages & towns take so much interest in noble botanical gardens, pleasure grounds, art galleries, museums, libraries & race-tracks as in Australasia? It is wonderful & creditable" (MTP:NB34).

Besides the parks and gardens, New Plymouth's 3,800 citizens (and another 10,000 in the surrounding county) also had "a large, lofty building" in Alexandra Hall, which would hold a thousand people. Twain was "advertised for a fortnight in *The Budget*" to lecture there on 6 December.[23] "Seldom has the Alexandra Hall been so packed," and seldom "perhaps has the audience so thoroughly enjoyed the entertainment." He met "such a welcome as is usually accorded only to old favorites . . . . Monologue entertainments, as a rule, do not offer very great attractions to the general public . . . , but there was a strong admixture of curiosity" to see Twain. He used the excerpts which were so welcomed in the Victorian country towns—his Mississippi River childhood, Huck and Jim, and the German language lesson. These stories and his "droll witticisms kept the audience in a perpetual state of half-subdued laughter, disturbed now and then by a spontaneous and uncontrollable outburst, as a particularly fetching point found its way home" (*Taranaki Herald*, 7 Dec.).

After the evening's program, New Plymouth joined the large Australian capitals as well as Christchurch, Auckland, and other places, in providing Twain with entertainment at the local men's social club, the Taranaki Club.

"A Certain Class of Goods"

The shortness of his stay in Wellington, already a city of 37,000 plus about 4,300 in the suburbs, must have been one of the disappointments of Twain's trip to New Zealand. Passing through the harbor on Sunday, 17 November, the family and Carlyle Smythe docked just long enough to exchange their places on the overcrowded and foul *Flora* for berths on the "darling little" Mahinapua, a "perfect little bijou," which was "clean & comfortable" with "good service, good beds"

---

23. Parsons, "Mark Twain in New Zealand," p. 73. No copies of the *Budget* are now extant in New Zealand.

(MTP:NB34). After "doing" the North Island, including Napier on the east coast, the family returned on the train by way of Wanganui; then Twain went north to Hawera and New Plymouth. The trip back south from Wanganui to Wellington took nine hours, but Twain expected it to be "pleasant & unfatiguing" (MTP:NB34). The reason a trip of only a hundred miles took such a long time was that there were only "two express trains *a week*; that is what fooled us; there was a line in very fine type in the midst of the public time-table, stating that this train[']s on Tuesdays & Fridays *only*" (MTP:NB34).

One result of this confusion was that Twain's talk in Wellington scheduled for Monday night, 9 December, was canceled, and seats already sold were transferred to the next night. Similarly, Tuesday's tickets were moved to Wednesday, but—unlike the other major cities where he had spoken—there was no time left to book an "extra" performance, for the family had to board the *Mararoa* for Sydney on the thirteenth. No doubt Twain and his manager were disappointed to lose the income from another performance, but their sight-seeing and socializing were also curtailed.

Twain received excellent press coverage in the Wellington papers throughout his visit. A month before his arrival there, the weekly columnist "Scrutator," in commenting on Twain's Australian poem, had quoted Bret Harte's poem on the emu (to prove that a poem on the Australian animals was possible) and suggested:

> When Mark gets up to the North Island he ought to try his hand at some Maori rhymes. For instance, can he find a rhyme to Paikakariki, a word whose quaintness of sound so tickled the fancy of Rudyard Kipling that he had told a friend of "Scrutator's" he had jotted it down for "use somehow, somewhere, someday." I read my Kipling pretty diligently but I haven't come across Paikakariki yet in any of his new work. [*New Zealand Mail*, 14 Nov., p. 23.]

Both the *New Zealand Times* and the weekly *New Zealand Mail* reprinted an interview from Christchurch, and the *Mail* said of that city's coverage of Twain's visit, "We have not ... read anything better in their way than these articles in the *Lyttelton Times* and *Press* for some time" (21 Nov., p. 2).

Most Wellington papers devoted portions of gossipy columns and several "leaders" to biographical anecdotes about Twain. It was reported in Wellington that at the Savage Club supper in Christchurch

Twain had explained how his description of a certain street as being "like a corkscrew" could be reconciled with another description that it was a street "called straight." "But we have not been able to find out quite how. One report," the paper teased its readers, "says that the explanation was given by the American humorist and was found quite satisfactory by the company. Unfortunately it seems to have been too satisfactory for the reporter to deal with .... We want this discrepancy reconciled" (*New Zealand Times*, 21 Nov., p. 2).

In some ways Wellington's interest in Twain was reminiscent of the country towns of Victoria, for despite its position as the capital of the colony, it treated the pilgrimage as a noteworthy event. The fact that Wellington was the last stop in New Zealand was conducive to such coverage; and, of course, the Victorian country tour occurred at the end of the Australian itinerary. The papers, as in Victoria, noted the visit of the New Zealand agent Hugo Fischer who had come to town to make arrangements the week before Twain and Smythe's arrival. And the intention of the governor and his wife to be present at the first "At Home" was deemed newsworthy. Such publicity in addition to the paid advertisements and the delay of the first show filled the Opera House on 10 and 11 December.

The Manawatu train arrived at ten, and after having supper, Twain received "with the urbanity of a journalist and the courtesy of a man of the world," one "R. A. L." whose interview appeared in the weekly *New Zealand Mail* after Twain's last performance. Much of the conversation was about Twain's own books, and many of the topics had already been discussed with other reporters. To the criticism that *Innocents Abroad* had been "just vamped out of books of travel and encyclopedias," Twain answered:

> There's a Freemasonry about dealing with things you see yourself which can't be counterfeited. There is an ease and certainty of touch in describing what you see which you can't get artificially .... Only in that way could you get the firmness of touch ..., the thing depends on your personal observation. How could a man describe that battered and faded last supper of Leonardo da Vinci's who had not seen it? His touch would be uncertain, his grasp weak, his description faulty. [*New Zealand Mail*, 12 Dec., p. 51.]

He also explained that he had "tried to put down that rebellion" in the southern states. He thought he could "do it in two weeks by taking service in the Confederate Army as second lieutenant." His strategy when getting near General Grant's United States Army was to retreat "to another point in view—somewhere out of danger .... I was very fond of exercise in those days .... But fourteen retreats in two weeks ...was too much exercise."

The interviewer did, however, uncover the great mystery of the Christchurch Savage Club supper on 15 November. Another of the "much-travelled" Smythe's clients, the Reverend Haskett Smith from England, toured throughout Australasia almost simultaneously with Twain. He had magic lantern pictures (similar to slide transparencies) to accompany his lectures on the Holy Land, and he was fond of showing pictures of a certain "street called Straight" in Damascus. As Twain clarified it in Wellington:

> "It was at supper," says he, "in Christchurch. We must settle this matter, says I, Mr. Smith. You have kind of reduced my reputation for veracity. Let's settle at once.—With all my heart, says he.—Now what did you have to drink, says I, when you went on that street?—Nothing, says he.—I had something different, says I, and that settles it." [*New Zealand Mail*, 12 Dec., p. 51.]

Although it makes a good yarn, the story is still not quite right. If it does refer to the supper given by the Savage Club, Twain was challenged by Justice Denniston "to 'put himself straight' as to his difference with Mr. Haskett Smith over 'the street called Straight' " (*Star* [Christchurch], 16 Nov., p. 8). Denniston

> had hoped to hear Rev. Mr. Haskett Smith and their distinguished guest fight out the question .... they saw this street differently. Mark Twain said it was like a corkscrew, whilst Rev. Haskett Smith produced a photograph which showed it was straight. Speaking judicially, he thought the weight of evidence was with Rev. Haskett Smith, and [Denniston] now offered to Mark Twain an opportunity of saying that he was mistaken as to the street. [*Press* (Christchurch), 16 Nov., p. 8.]

Neither Christchurch paper reported Twain's remarks, but the *Press* said he had given "an explanation of the reason why he stated that the street in Damascus was not straight, which was generally considered to be satisfactory." The supposed conversation between Twain and Smith, while it may have taken place somewhere at supper, probably did not occur at the Savage Club supper because "apologies were ... received from the Rev. Haskett Smith, who had been obliged by business engagements to leave Christchurch" (*Star*, 16 Nov., p. 8).[24] Even though the yarn as reported to R. A. L. is one version of the truth, at least the mystery, which had been reported as far away as Auckland, was cleared up.

Twain also clarified his own experience as the writer of the "leading" article, or the editorial. When his editor left town suddenly, "the pressure of my first leading article weighed with more and more solidity, until I remembered that it was the 22 April, 1864. Tomorrow would be the 23rd, the third centenary of Shakespeare's birthday. There was my subject," he told R. A. L. "But as every day was not the third centenary of the birth of the immortal bard, the practice of the daily article proved sufficient after a week" (*New Zealand Mail* [Wellington], 12 Dec., p. 51).

Speculation about the authorship of *The Personal Recollections of Joan of Arc*, which was being serialized in *Harper's Magazine*, had been rife when Twain left North America. Its authorship would not be announced for another year when it appeared in book form. When asked if it were his, Twain had told reporters, "That question has already been asked me several times, and I have always said that I considered it wise to leave an unclaimed piece of literary property alone until time has shown that nobody is going to claim it. Then it's safe to acknowledge that you wrote that thing whether you did or not" (quoted in *Australian Star* [Sydney], 14 Sept., p. 7). R. A. L. was able to get Twain to shed some light on why he would publish a book anonymously when just his name on the cover would ensure a huge sale. Of *The Prince and the Pauper* Twain said he had intended it to be anonymous "to test the value of the book on its own merits." But more importantly, Twain said,

> the distinctive badge "Mark Twain" was a trade mark which advertised a certain class of goods—low comedy goods all of them. I had no right to introduce tragedy under that mark and swindle people .... Some here and there in America said they had paid their three dollars under false pretences, and made a fuss. But the thing went all right after all. [*New Zealand Mail*, 12 Dec., p. 51.]

"A Terrible Sameness"

The next day a representative from the *Evening Post* called on Twain at the Occidental Hotel. The conversation, though not reported verbatim, mostly concerned the tour itself. The nine-hour train

---

24. However, the *New Zealand Times* [Wellington] (21 Nov., p. 2) says, "Smith (who was present, by the way) .... "

trip from Wanganui, Twain told the reporter, was made up of "continual stoppages at little stations, where apparently nothing was done, and which appeared to him to be simply arranged to fill in time, and the gentle, albeit sometimes jolty, ride from station to station, as though the train were out for an easy constitutional" (*Evening Post*, 10 Dec., p. 3). In his diary he had claimed that between Stratford and New Plymouth. "it was difficult to stay in your seat, so tremendously rough was the road." That country, which had many butter and creamery factories, was called New Zealand's "garden." Twain concluded that "they ought to put the milk in the train—that would churn it. This was my only unpleasant experience" of a New Zealand train (MTP:NB34).

Apparently, Twain was thinking about the book he planned to write when he got home, which would go a long way toward the discharge of his debts. The reporter wrote that he was interested in "colonial character, with a view to the inevitable book, but finds the urban population much like the urban population elsewhere, for travel is reducing the world to a terrible sameness." Toward the end of the conversation, Olivia Clemens was supposed to have interjected the hope that they might "find some nice quiet spot in Africa where crocodiles and irritating insects of the genus homo would not be too numerous, and where the customs of the country would allow interviewers and autograph hunters to be shot on sight, and there, under the gentle protection of the family Maxim gun, composition might go on undisturbed" (*Evening Post* [Wellington], 10 Dec., p. 3).[25]

Outlining the remainder of his tour, which now had a rather specific itinerary with no more "Queensland" appearances promised, Twain said the main anxiety was his "own health. It is anything but robust. Twice he has been ill since coming to Australia, but to-day he says he is feeling better." The carbuncle had erupted yet again in Auckland, and Mrs. Clemens had begun applying "Dr. Fitzgerald's remedies .... to get it checked. Dr. Fitzgerald did do wonders for the other one."[26] Although Twain had kept up a busy touring and lecturing schedule, he had been able to rest somewhat in the last three days, riding the train ten hours on Saturday from New Plymouth to Wanganui, where he took

---

25. Although the reporter attributed this to Olivia Clemens, it surely sounds more like one of Twain's hyperboles.

26. Potts and Potts, p. 48.

a riverboat excursion on Sunday, and riding the train to Wellington all day Monday.

Twain spent "three days partly in walking about [Wellington], partly in enjoying social privileges, and largely in idling around the magnificent garden at Hutt .... I suppose we shall not see such another one soon." He called Wellington "a fine city, and nobly situated. A busy place, and full of life and movement" (*More Tramps*, p. 222). After his interview with the *Evening Post*, Twain called on Lord David Glasgow, governor general of the colony, who attended the "At Home" that night. Lord Glasgow must have been the only governor he saw; as he explained in *More Tramps Abroad*, Australia "has four or five governors, and I do not know how many it takes to govern the outlying archipelagos; but anyway you will not see them .... I was in Australasia three months and a half, and saw only one governor, the others were at home"—which, he explained, meant "England" (*More Tramps*, p. 83).

After the lecture Twain was entertained by the Wellington Club (MTP:NB34), and the evening of the eleventh he was out until 1:30 a.m. at a supper at the Club Hotel with only eight other people, mostly prominent Maoris. He called this the "Modesty Club," though this may have been only a Twain invention. There he learned some Maori words and discovered that he should have addressed both the governor and the audience of which he wrote, he "didn't know it was custom" (MTP:NB34). On his last full day in Wellington, he and Smythe went to Hutt to enjoy Mrs. Ross's gardens; he played billiards, a favorite pastime of his; and in the evening he went to a concert (MTP:NB34).

His own "concerts," as reviewers occasionally called them, were fully as successful as any he had given in New Zealand. The Opera House was "filled in every part." Twain's opening remarks—when he should have been saluting the Governor's party—assured his audience "that he proposed to give them various moral lessons," which consisted of stories like Jim and Huck on the raft. The reviewer praised his "quiet power of description, and facility for putting in local colour, local character, and local scenery in a few graphic touches" (*Evening Post* [Wellington], 11 Dec., p. 2).

Twain told "that inimitable horse yarn relating to [his] purchase of a Mexican plug, and when he, with infinite feeling, arrived at the point in the narrative where, having ascended for the last time to mid-air, from the back of the bucking 'plug,' he descended to earth only to find that someone had struck his purchase with a strap and the horse 'wasn't there,' the ripple of laugh that was rolling round the Opera House became a roar." Of the German language, Twain claimed he "never hoped to 'learn' it; he had tried for 20 years, and got no further than those terrible genders and dreadful separated verbs, but he had gone too far now to lay it down, and perhaps in another life—if there was time enough—he would advance another stage" (*Evening Post* [Wellington], 11 Dec., p. 2).

All who saw Twain, one reviewer promised, would remember the "bright and genial, shrewd, philosophical, and deliciously fresh and humorous personality of the author," and when they read his books would remember "they heard it in the hesitating, deliberate, quiet voice which, while not appearing to accentuate one thing more than another, brings out new points in every phrase" (*Evening Post* [Wellington], 11 Dec., p. 2).

Twain's personal appearance was integral with his performance: "When the man himself walked on to the stage, we accepted him at once. We all marked that strong face, the powerful head with its masses of tumbled hair, that seemed to be still tossing in sympathy with the seething brain, the keen eyes, the determined countenance" (*New Zealand Mail*, 19 Dec., p. 32). While some found the leonine head, as it was sometimes called, a part of his humorous costume, others felt it connoted wisdom and demanded respect:

> What a grand head the man has .... It is fashionable with a certain class of the genus idiot to sneer at a man who wears his hair long ... and maintain that long locks signify conceit .... but that fine grey head of hair of Mark's seems peculiarly fitting in his case. It is the head of a shrewd, clear-brained social philosopher, whose mordant wit flashes out and wraps itself round the frauds and shams of life, enveloping them in a garment labelled "Humbug," so that they may be known of all men for what they really are. And there is no conceit about Mr. Clemens. [*New Zealand Mail*, 12 Nov., p. 43.]

The Clemenses left New Zealand on the Union Company's *Mararoa* at 3:15 p.m. on Friday 13 December, bound for Ceylon, India, and Africa. Aboard was a "menagerie of mannerless children," which greatly annoyed Twain. Apparently in retaliation, he confided in his diary, he hoped for a heavy storm. On the ship was the manager of the Greenwood Acting Company which had disembarked in a basket with tons of scenery and costumes in a severe storm at Gisborne. He told Twain that the population was so sparse that it was hardly worthwhile financially for such a company to tour New Zealand. Still they did it, no doubt because—like Twain—they found appreciative audiences. In *More Tramps Abroad* Twain elaborated his notebook entries about the tranquil summer weather, calling it "three days of paradise. Warm and sunny and smooth; the sea a luminous Mediterranean blue" (p. 223).

CHAPTER NINE

Farewell to Australasia

"Highly Respected by All Classes"

The trip across the Tasman Sea from Wellington to Sydney was so pleasant that Twain said only poetry was appropriate. He read Mrs. Julia A. Moore's *The Sentimental Song Book*, which, along with Goldsmith's "deathless story" *The Vicar of Wakefield*, he always carried with him (*More Tramps*, p. 223). In fact he read both of these and a work by Jane Austen, which he called "thoroughly artificial" (MTP, pp. 2-3). While the Clemenses were still at sea, the Sydney newspapers again began heralding his arrival. The *Australian Star* published an article about events that evidently had taken place in the smoking lounge of the Australia Hotel during Twain's September sojourn there. It was written most likely by young Herbert Low, who claimed to have been in Twain's company nearly every day he was "here"—either in Sydney or in both Sydney and Melbourne (*Worker* [Sydney], 2 Apr., 1909). Twain had spent an evening "with a few attentive listeners," telling an anecdote printed for the first time on 16 December, the day before Twain was scheduled to return from New Zealand.

According to the report, toward the close of the seventies, when the Clemenses were living in Connecticut, Mrs. Clemens used to do Twain's correspondence. One day she found "a letter with a mourning border from an English gentleman, a great friend of her husband .... This gentleman, who was a younger son, had developed an adventurous turn of mind, and had gone out to Melbourne a few years before."

When Olivia read the letter she was astonished to find sympathy for "her bereavement at the death of her husband, which, the writer [of the letter] went on to say, took place in Melbourne." A "large and representative gathering" attended the funeral, and the widow would be consoled

> to know that the deceased was highly respected by all classes of the community. In fact the corpse had one of the most touching and demonstrative valedictories ever accorded a rising literary man who had strayed so far from home and died a stranger in a strange land. The writer himself did not appear to have met Mr. Clemens, who, he explained, was on a lecturing tour, but he vouched for the high-toned character of the funeral, and the esteem in which the late lamented was held by all who pretended to have known him. Whose the fraudulent corpse was or what the explanation of the affair was never revealed, for the writer of the letter soon afterwards died of fever or perished prematurely in some other way. [*Australian Star*, 16 Dec., p. 20.]

The mystery, so far as Twain knew in September when he told it, was never unraveled.

This might have been a Twain yarn, but if it was, the *Australian Star* reporter certainly seemed to believe it. And Twain claimed in *More Tramps Abroad* to have discovered the solution during his visit to Bendigo in western Victoria. Although the first published record of this story is the 16 December article in Sydney, just before Twain sailed from England on his way to Australia, he had already told the story to his friend and publisher Henry Harper in May 1895.[1] Still, it was an Australian story and it served to pique interest for Twain's farewell to Sydney.[2]

Smythe began advertising Twain's performances for 20 and 21 December as soon as it was certain he would arrive in time, even though "the Hall has not yet been decided on" (*Australian Star*, 16 Dec., p. 3). By the day of Twain's arrival, R. S. Smythe had hired the School of Arts in Pitt Street, "no other hall being available" (*Sydney Morning Herald*, 17 Dec., p. 2), and was advertising "an entirely new entertainment" at "holiday prices" of one, two, and three shillings because it would be "the country visitors' only chance" to see the great man (*Australian Star*, 18 Dec., p. 3). The Schools of Arts or Mechanics' Institutes through-

---

1. Paul A. Doyle, "Henry Harper's Telling of a Mark Twain Anecdote," *Mark Twain Journal* 15 (1970), p. 13.

2. See chapter 3; chapter 5.

out Australia were a phenomenon largely of the eighties and nineties and the product of the labor movement. They provided a subscription library for working class people as well as a meeting hall for members and the public. All the towns in Australia Twain visited had Mechanics' Institutes, and he spoke in these buildings in Horsham and Ballarat.

In late 1895, the School of Arts on Pitt Street in Sydney was in deep financial trouble. It had a membership of 1308 men, 688 women, and 257 life members and had recently abandoned the practice of allowing 1400 women at a half-rate subscription because "the wear and tear of the books was so great that the cost of re-binding was too large an item." The library, which was augmented monthly, contained 55,000 volumes, "not only the latest works of fiction, but all the up-to-date standard works on science, travel &c." Louis Becke's *By Reef and Palm*, which Twain claimed to have read three times and praised in several interviews, was among the most popular borrowings. The library had thirty copies of Du Maurier's *Trilby*, the year's best seller, which Twain said he had not yet read (*Sunday Times* [Sydney], 15 Sept., p. 5).

Members of Sydney's School of Arts were in the process of deciding what to do about its decrepit building. The School of Arts had been deficient in revenues for the last three years, and members were discussing renovation, "so that most of the frontage to Pitt-street might be let or leased to advantage." They voted to convert the library into shops and the large hall into an enlarged library; profits from the commercial space were intended to pay for such changes. The hall was already being let out to raise funds, and Twain's manager was able to get it for his second Sydney season. But members also had considered selling the building and site, moving only the library and reading room off the prime commercial location to a building in less need of repair (*Sydney Morning Herald*, 19 Dec., p. 6; see also *Australian Star*, 19 Dec., p. 6). It is no wonder, then, that the *Bulletin* called it "musty as well as shabby" and suggested that it "badly wants to be burnt down by some judicious incendiary, and a new one built out of the insurance money" (21 Dec., p. 8).[3]

Arriving in Sydney at nine on the morning of 17 December, Twain recorded that the weather had turned cool after a "burster" (*More Tramps*, p.   ; MTP, pp. 3–4). Evidently he was met practically instantly by reporters looking for a story. In his notebook he expressed

---

3. This building is still standing, now housing several businesses.

contempt for their questions and what he now saw as petty colonial jealousies:

> The interviewer is pathetically persistent in trying to worm out of you your "impressions" of N. Z. & her people & audiences, & "which city did I like best, there; & which audience; & are the audiences there as quick & bright as in Austral; & which do I think the most remarkable city, Syd or Melb; & which newspapers do I consider the best; but don't I think them *all* remarkable["]—& a dozen other questions of the same guilelessly idiotic sort, which only another idiot would answer. [MTP, p. 4.]

The interview that appeared in the *Daily Telegraph* (20 December 1895) clearly fits the description that Twain—disgusted—left in his journal. Twain said he had "not formed an opinion at all: 'I just went through the country at a fast rate, and had no time to form an opinion. I thought the people were particularly fortunate in living in a country with such a grand climate.'" He used the example of Timaru, which he claimed had a wind storm while he was there: "I guess if I had left Timaru before the gale abated my opinion would have been that that was a windy place" (*Sydney Daily Telegraph*, 20 Dec., p. 6).[4] Giving his impression of the "verdant appearance of the different places," he said he noticed no particular difference between the audiences in New Zealand and those in Australia.

Twain had learned his lesson in Sydney about discussing politics; but he also had become tired of casual visitors passing on their hurried impressions of places, including the United States, as if such opinions were to be relied on as facts. When the reporter asked about New Zealand politics, Twain responded, "I have no impressions ... if I had, they would just likely be erroneous ones. I don't think it is right to hurry through a place and form impressions. I have none—no publishable ones, anyway" (*Sydney Daily Telegraph*, 20 Dec., p. 6). Twain was disappointed even with his friend Herbert Low, who seems to have been back in Sydney from Melbourne; it is probable that he had written the article in the *Daily Telegraph*, for no other interview appeared in the papers: "Low is immensely capable fellow with his pen, yet *he* asked me questions wh it would have been brutal in me .... to answer to a newspaper. These towns & people are full of jealousies of each

---

4. In fact, there is no evidence in his journal or in *More Tramps Abroad* that Timaru experienced a gale while he was there. He must have confused it with Dunedin the day before, where there was a rain and wind storm that Twain noted in his journal.

other, & perfectly ready to out with them in print or anywhere" (MTP, p. 4). Perhaps the *Bulletin* had sent its own reporter to see Twain, but the only report it carried was a gossipy one that could have originated almost anywhere: in Maoriland, "he did well nearly everywhere save at Gisborne," where it "was too rough to land .... Twain will lecture in Sydney School of Arts .... It is to be a new lecture, and will embody the Australian poem which was unfinished on his previous visit, and which has since been completed with much greater difficulty than the results seem to be worth" (21 Dec., p. 8).

Probably on Tuesday evening, the family attended a melodrama based on Marcus Clarke's *For the Term of His Natural Life*, which was playing at Her Majesty's Theatre in Sydney. Twain's reaction to the dramatization implied that a play could not examine the convict system with the depth that Clarke's novel had done. In his notebook he wrote, "Even when the chain-gang were humurous they were still a most pathetic sight .... that old convict life .... [was] invented in hell & carried out by Xian devils."[5] Clara called the play "gruesome."[6] Apparently on Tuesday or Wednesday, Twain went to the botanical gardens, which he thought as fine as the other gardens he had seen throughout Australasia. He also noted the cricket ovals and other grassy spaces in the Domain (MTP, pp. 5–7).

Sharks were a problem in Sydney that season, and the newspapers advertised rewards for their capture. For example, the Reliance Oil Company offered five guineas for the largest one caught between Christmas and Easter, and "as an incentive to the destruction of these monsters," it would give one pound for all sharks over twelve feet long (*Australian Star*, 28 Dec., p. 1). In *More Tramps Abroad* Twain wrote a wonderful shark story that explained how Cecil Rhodes got his start as a businessman. The notebook entry gives several abbreviated anecdotes about the watches, money, and even Prayer Books that people found in sharks after they had been killed, but Twain considered these stories "doubtful." Although there is no hint of it in *More Tramps Abroad*, Twain's journal records a shark-fishing excursion to Bondi (he thought) in Sydney Harbour where "I ... caught one myself, but he thought he caught me—& as he was doing most of the pulling I conceded the argument & let go" (MTP, pp. 5–6). J. F. Archibald, then editor of the

---

5. Gribben, *Mark Twain's Library*, I, 145; *Notebook*, ed. Paine, pp. 262–263.

6. Clara misplaces this in Melbourne. See *My Father, Mark Twain*, p. 145.

Bulletin, is supposed to have enjoyed regaling people with the "story of his fishing expedition to Manly with Mark Twain, when an accomplice, planted among the rocks below, continually saw to it that the visiting American had a weighty schnapper on his hook."[7] Another account records that Twain made rather extended visits to Archibald's house in Cronulla district, where the editor was famous for schnapper fishing. Although this account does not make clear whether Twain joined him in the hobby, the context implies that he did.[8]

"The 'Little War Cloud' ... the Fruitful Peace"

On Thursday, 19 December, a "blazing hot afternoon" (*More Tramps*, p. 226), Twain and Carlyle Smythe rode in a first-class car to Scone, a country town some 125 miles north and west of Sydney, coming back the next day. On the trip, he evidently read in the papers about the threat of war between England and the United States because of a border dispute over British Guiana. President Cleveland invoked the Monroe Doctrine, which declared that the United States would not tolerate meddling in the Western Hemisphere by European powers. For several days it looked as if the two countries were close to blows, which would have probably involved Australians against the Americans.

On the train, he met a slovenly young man who "was living in a dude dreamland where all his squalid shams were genuine, and himself a sincerity. It disarmed criticism, it mollified spite, to see him so enjoy his imitation languors, and arts, and airs, and his studied daintinesses of gesture and misbegotten refinements" (*More Tramps*, p. 225; adapted closely from MTP, pp. 7–6). Eventually the "imitation dude" left at a small town and was replaced by a bishop and two clergymen.

They traveled through various scenery—the nearby Hawksbury River in the National Park with its woods, stream, and lake; then the "green flats thinly covered with gum forests"; past "huts and cabins of small farmers"; dry, lifeless grasslands; and then Newcastle a bustling coal-mining center where Twain had to change trains for Scone (*More Tramps*, pp. 225–226; adapted closely from MTP, p. 7). Along the way Twain noted "pretty frequent glimpses of a troublesome plant,"

---

7. Vance Palmer, p. 94.

8. W. E. FitzHenry, unpublished history of the *Bulletin*, Australian National Library, p. 195.

the prickly pear, and he began collecting unusual Australian names for the theme of an Australian poem, "A Sweltering Day in Australia," to be included in *More Tramps Abroad* (pp. 226–227; from MTP, p. 7). Of all he collected he said, "the best word ... the most musical and gurgly, is Woolloomoolloo."

On Friday, Twain, having ridden the train down from Scone, arrived late for his performance in Pitt Street. He apologized, explaining "that he had just arrived in Sydney after an eight-hours railway journey, and the train was 'only half an hour late.' Perhaps on the whole, he said, it was fortunate that he had arrived at night, since he had been compelled to change his clothes in the cab as it went through the streets" (*Sydney Morning Herald*, 21 Dec., p. 7). He elaborated on this experience as the introduction to his lecture.

> Whew! it was sweltering .... I don't know where the other clothes are. They've gone in the cab. And I don't know where the cab is gone. It's probably melted. The only heat that I've experienced like this was what I once got in the Sandwich Islands. But there they don't trouble themselves much with superfluous clothing. The women wore—well, I don't remember what they wore. There wasn't enough of it. And the men—well, just on ordinary occasions they didn't wear anything. But on State occasions they did. They wore smiles, and they even smiled too much. If you in Australia have this kind of weather in the middle of December, what must you have in July? [*Sydney Daily Telegraph*, 21 Dec., p. 10.]

No doubt this joke, which many of the Australians could easily sympathize with, "warmed" his audience to one of his happiest receptions. He told the story (which he had introduced in Dunedin) of Mortimer McWilliams in his pajamas and military helmet during the lightning storm, and the one about the continental courier; but "owing to the lateness of the hour" he could not give his Australian poem, as had been promised. Instead, he "referred to the strained relations which had recently sprung up between England and America. Advancing to the edge of the platform, and speaking with great earnestness," Twain said that,

> in bidding his audience good night, he wished to express his belief, as well as his earnest hope, that the 'little war cloud' which had been lowering over England and America during the last few days would be quickly blown away under the influence of cooler and calmer counsels (Loud cheers.) He trusted sincerely that the fruitful peace which had reigned between the two nations for 80 years would not be broken—(cheers)—and that the two great peo-

ples would resume their march shoulder to shoulder, as before, in the van of the world's civilisation. (Prolonged cheering.) [*Sydney Morning Herald*, 21 Dec., p. 7.]

On Saturday night, "the hall was packed, and the great humorist met with a splendid reception," and at times "the whole audience was convulsed" (*Sydney Daily Telegraph*, 23 Dec., p. 6). Even though "many grim-looking men, elderly and dignified, held out for a time ..., eventually they had to succumb, and when the fit took them they were worse than their more volatile companions." Ladies were not spared, and as he "gently waved his hand to amplify the points, to the accompaniment of wildly hilarious noises, it seemed as though he were conducting some maniacal orchestra" (*Sydney Daily Telegraph*, 23 Dec., p. 6). This time he did read the Australian poem, but otherwise he gave a repetition of the previous entertainment. Australians again appreciated his remarks about "an early removal of the friction which now prevails between his country and England. 'I hope,' he said, 'that we shall soon cease to be annoyed[9] by all this unpleasant, unprofitable,[10] and unbrotherly war talk'" (*Sydney Morning Herald*, 23 Dec., p. 3).

After Twain was long gone from Sydney, the *Bulletin* could expatiate at leisure,

> Mark Twain returned to Sydney last week for a two-night season, and lifted up his slow, pensive voice in the shabby old hall of the School of Arts .... The humorist on this occasion broke loose from his old groove and gave a rather newer set of reminiscences than before, and he has a sinful "pome" on hand, which is probably the most remarkable thing ever composed concerning this country. The present brief season is announced as Twain's very last Australian appearance, which possibly means that after his book is published it won't be safe for him to come back, and the public will have to vent its fury on Smythe, who is stout and can't run away very fast, as a substitute. [28 Dec., p. 9.]

The next week, when Twain was in the Indian Ocean and Smythe was safely back in Melbourne, the *Bulletin* was still joking about the manager's success in introducing Twain to Australia. "Hop" drew Smythe pasting up billboards advertising lectures by the Duke and Duchess of York. The same issue carried an excellent interview with Twain, quite possibly by A. G. Stephens, then associate editor of the *Bul-*

---

9. *Sydney Daily Telegraph*: plagued.
10. *Sydney Daily Telegraph*: unnecessary.

letin, who would very shortly begin the "Red Page" reviews in that journal. Twain told the interviewer about a ghost he had seen, a humorous dream he had experienced, and his "passion for the theatre." They talked about Twain's own books as well as those of contemporaries. He liked Marcus Clarke's novel because "all the time I felt that I was reading history." He called Gabbett, the cannibal, "as strongly-drawn a character as I ever met." *By Reef and Palm* is good because Becke "seems to be chronicling facts and incidents he's seen—things he's lived amongst and knows all about." But Charles Reade "makes an awful botch" when he uses secondhand material (*Bulletin* [Sydney], 4 Jan. 1896, p. 8.)

"A Great Colonial Epic"

The Clemenses sailed from Sydney for Ceylon aboard the P&O liner *Oceana* on Monday, 23 December at one o'clock. As they were leaving about twenty "male & female cranks—rivals of the Salvationists—in no uniform but waterproofs (it was raining) sang hymns on the dock," begging money.[11]   The ship was manned by Lascars, who had "rich dark brown" complexions, "short straight black hair," and "whiskers fine and silky; lustrous, and intensely black." He found them attractive in their "white cotton petticoat and pants; barefoot; red shawl for belt; straw cap, brimless, on head, with red scarf wound around it." Twain thought the ship with its "spacious promenade decks; large rooms"; "well selected" officers' library; and "sweet bugle call to dinner" to be "surpassingly comfortable" (*More Tramps*, p. 229; closely adapted from MTP, pp. 10–12). They arrived in Melbourne on Christmas morning and were driven to the estate of John Wagner, with whose family they had spent many pleasant hours in October. Christmas dinner was taken at Highgate on the Hill with the R. S. Smythe family.

As early as 19 December, Smythe had begun advertising "Farewell Appearances" for Boxing Night and the next, in the Athenaeum Hall, "no other hall being available" (*Age* [Melbourne], 19 Dec., and 23 Dec., p. 8). He quoted from the Wellington papers and promised that, with the exception of the "Australian poem in its finished form," which was "The Funniest Thing Ever Written of the Colonies," it would be "an entirely NEW MARK TWAIN 'AT HOME'" at holiday prices of one,

---

11. *Notebook, ed. Paine, p. 262.*

two, and three shillings. And although there was no review of the holiday show, Smythe pointed out in his last advertisement that the revised poem was "received last night with shouts of laughter" (*Argus* [Melbourne], 27 Dec., p. 8).

On Thursday and Friday, 26 and 27 December, Twain gave the same lecture—a bit shorter than most of his performances—"without change." It consisted of the punch brothers jingle, the Lucerne girl, the McWilliams story, the sandpile, and the Australian poem (MTP, pp. 13, 48). The poem was "making progress, and might, if the author had only remained here a little longer, [have] developed into a great colonial epic," reported the *Age* (28 Dec., p. 7). The poem appears for the first time in Twain's journal among the entries made on board the RMS *Oceana* between Sydney and Melbourne; according to the review in the *Age*, that is the version he read in Melbourne in December.

The introduction was similar to the versions recorded in other renditions, but his list of animals had grown to include the dugong and the dingo; he was told the lyre "was a bird, but he did not believe it" because he had "met plenty without feathers" (*Age* [Melbourne], 28 Dec., p. 7). The poem now contained verses not previously reported in the newspapers, and, if the reviewer is to be trusted, his interpolated remarks included a quartet not recorded even in his notebook. Perhaps these are reconstructed verses he claimed in September to have given to the beggars he met Sydney while walking around the wharf with Herbert Low. He had found so much trouble, he claimed, trying to rhyme "boomerang with kangaroo that he gave it up in despair."

> At last he consulted a professional poet, who advised him to drop these words of four syllables and try two syllable words. In order to test the capacity of the poet, he gave him two words, "Geelong" and "Prahran" [nearby towns Twain had visited on 28 and 29 October], to put into rhyme, and quick as lightning the poet reeled off the following:—
> Lo! there is Geelong.
> Where the righteous belong;
> And there is Prahran,
> Where they don't give a ——

The reporter quoted the second stanza, and three lines of the third; it was "an ode to 'the kangaroo good and true, foreshortened as to legs and body tapered like a churn,' the physiological absurdity of which threw the audience into roars of laughter" (*Age* [Melbourne], 28 Dec.,

p. 7). A completed version of the poem was attributed in *More Tramps Abroad* to a New Zealand companion aboard the *Warrimoo*.[12]

Twain spent Boxing Day and the next one in Melbourne playing billiards with young Jack Wagner and his sister, Mrs. S. McCulloch. On the day of his departure, the weekly *Australasian* theorized: "If he has been very little lionised it is because the Australian public recognise that lionising is for saunterers and official visitors, not for busy men, whom such attention bores. And a lecturer who puts himself in the hands of Mr. Smythe cannot serve two masters. Mr. Smythe is suave and gentle, with most delicate touch, but inexorable, and the rule is 'business first and pleasure afterwards,' for the reasons given by Mr. Weller," a character in Dickens's *Pickwick Papers* (*Australasian*, 28 Dec., p. 1247).

Boxing Day was so widely celebrated that the newspapers did not even appear, nor did they send reviewers to the show that night. However, Twain seems to have answered a reporter about his views on "the anglo-American situation." He claimed to know little on the subject of politics but he did foreshadow remarks he would make publicly a few days later in Adelaide: "He declares unmistakably that the United States people are anxious to avoid war with any nation but particularly with England; and at the same time he declines to believe that the action of the President was in any way an election move" (*Star* [Ballarat], 27 Dec., p. 3; *Advertiser* [Adelaide], 27 Dec., p. 5). Still, he thought President Cleveland "probably takes a strained view of the Monroe doctrine."

Twain and his party left Melbourne for India on Saturday, traveling in a "very heavy sea all night" (MTP, p. 13). With him he took "the good wishes of thousands of Australian friends, to whom it has been one of the pleasures to make his acquaintance. And they know that if he should hereafter write about this country it will be to say much that is funny and nothing that is otherwise than good natured" (*Australasian*, 28 Dec., p. 1247). He left behind him "many pleasant recollections of that quaint genius which has made [him] known throughout the world" (*Age* [Melbourne], 28 Dec., p. 7).

---

12. A rather complete account of the poem is given by Coleman O. Parsons in "Mark Twain in Melbourne," *Mark Twain Journal* 22 (Spring 1984), 41–42; rather than repeat his account, I have tried to fill in gaps. See also Arthur L. Scott, *On the Poetry of Mark Twain, with Selections from his Verse* (Urbana, Ill., University of Illinois Press, 1966), pp. 29, 111.

"Where It Is Always a Holiday ... or ... a Horserace"

Sailing weather was better on 29 December, and early in the morning of 30 December, the 3175-ton RMS *Oceana*, captained by Commander E. Stewart, anchored in Largs Bay, South Australia. Twain, Carlyle Smythe, Livy, and Clara arrived in Adelaide in time for Commemoration Day, celebrated on Monday the thirtieth rather than on Saturday, the actual anniversary of the proclamation. Fifty-nine years before, on 28 December 1839, the province of South Australia had been proclaimed by Governor Hindmarsh at the Old Gum Tree about seven miles from present-day Adelaide, a few hundred meters from Glenelg. The latter resort, a popular seaside watering place, was the site of the celebration.

All the other major Australian colonies—those that would become known as the state capitals after federation—had simply "grown up" as products of the convict system, the mining boom, or the search for land. But the proclamation of South Australia as a province before settlement began had made it "radically and essentially different" from the other colonies. The discreteness of the various colonies is underlined by the South Australians' celebrating Proclamation Day as their "national birthday." The leader in the Adelaide *Advertiser* pointed out that the early settlers of South Australia

> did not indulge in visionary imaginings of a new Utopia, but came to carve for themselves homes out of the wilderness by diligent and honest toil. Their aspiration was not to make rapid fortunes, but to live a freer and better life. Many of the emigrants in the early days were impelled by motives not dissimilar from those that sent the Pilgrim Fathers across the Atlantic two hundred years before. They sought to escape from the atmosphere of Toryism, from the tyranny of the squirearchy, and the iron-bound conventionalities of the old world. [30 Dec., p. 4.]

The weather was perfect for such a celebration—sunny, but, although midsummer, "never uncomfortably warm." Glenelg was "thronged" with the 50,000 people who rode special trains from Adelaide at fifteen-minute intervals, as well as "several thousands" who drove their own vehicles. Despite its being a Customs holiday as well as a public holiday, the *Oceana* and four other ships were allowed in the harbor, "for holidays are never allowed to interfere with the inward clearing of vessels" (*Advertiser* [Adelaide], 31 Dec., p. 4). Mark Twain showed up at Glenelg just in time for the festivities.

Attractions included "the wonderful and fascinating merry-go-rounds, the gaily-decked steamers, the newly-renovated baths, the strong-lunged showmen, the fair women, the brawny sons of Australia, the swingboats soaring up to giddy heights, the beautiful promenades, and the cool, clean beach" (*Advertiser* [Adelaide], 30 Dec., p. 5). Transport was provided to convey visitors to the historic gum tree, and cheap sea excursions from the jetty were popular enough to keep three launches busy all day. An exhibition of historical relics and an autograph book for the names and dates of arrival of senior members of the colony were on public display. Twain, by special request, signed the book. In the afternoon there were swimming contests for various ages, boat races for all classes of crafts, greased pole climbing, and other mirth-provoking activities (*Advertiser* [Adelaide], 31 Dec., p. 6). After dark "a thousand lights twinkling like stars" along the beach and the "flash [of] the electric searchlight" thrilled the spectators.

An official ceremony was held at Town Hall at one o'clock to welcome the governor of South Australia, Sir Thomas Fowell Buxton, and Lady Victoria Buxton. Afterward, Glenelg's mayor, G. K. Soward, honored him at a luncheon in the Town Hall. It was attended by about 200 guests, including Premier C. C. Kingston, Commissioner of Public Works J. G. Jenkins, Mayor G. Tucker of Adelaide, and others Twain had met when he visited Adelaide in October. As Jenkins had "finished toying with the wing of a chicken," a "spontaneous burst of applause" greeted two late arrivals, the American Consul C. A. Murphy and his friend Mark Twain (*Advertiser* [Adelaide], 31 Dec., p. 4).

About halfway through the proceedings, Premier Kingston proposed a toast to the "Old Colonists," of whom there were six in attendance. The original old settlers, H. T. Morris, W. L. Beare, J. A. Hill, William Hodges, John Thorne, and the president of the Australian Natives' Association, F. P. Auld, each responded briefly. When Twain wrote about them in *More Tramps Abroad* he claimed they were so old they "could remember Cromwell." "They showed signs of the blightings and blastings of time in their outward aspect, but they were young within; young and cheerful, and ready to talk .... They were down for six speeches, and they made forty-two." The reason for such confusion, Twain explained, was that they were deaf;

> when they see the mayor going through motions which they recognise as the introducing of a speaker ..., they all get up together and begin to respond,

in the most animated way; and the more the mayor gesticulates, and shouts "Sit down! sit down!" the more they take it for applause, and the more excited and reminiscent and enthusiastic they get (*More Tramps*, pp. 124–125).

After the Old Colonists, American-born J. G. Jenkins, in toasting the navy, "apologised for the absence of the Minister for War—(laughter)— ... who was at present looking after the oyster-beds." Concerning the threatened war between Britain and America, he said "that as South Australians if we lived in happiness and prosperity until the outbreak really occurs we would live for centuries yet to come. (Cheers.)" However, he had "feared that the war scare had led to the absence of Mr. Murphy, the American Consul, but he was glad to see that gentleman had ventured in under the guardianship of Mark Twain. (Laughter and cheers.)" (*Advertiser* [Adelaide], 31 Dec., p. 6).

Sir Richard Baker, president of the Legislative Council, was asked to toast the visitors including Twain, and in so doing he said he believed there would be no war between Britain and America, and the people could thank the Stock Exchange of London for a telegram sent to New York. Baker was evidently referring to London dispatches of 19 and 20 December about the America's Cup. Twain's notebook records the joke: "A few days ago among the cables was: 'The Board of Trade has cabled the N. Y. Chamber of Commerce: "Pleasure boats will not be allowed to obstruct the movements of the British war-ships." Reply of Chamber of Commerce: "we hope your war-ships will be better than your yachts."'"[13] If Twain would "fill up that frog with the shot of ridicule" when he got back to New York, "there would be no war" (*South Australian Register*, 31 Dec., p. 6).

In responding to Sir Richard's remarks Twain agreed that there would be no war, "for certainly never in the history of mankind would any war or was any war so disastrous as this suggested war would be .... Blood is thicker than water, and there must be no bloodshed between England and America. (Applause)." Twain said he did not realize there was another of his countrymen at the luncheon until he "heard him lift up his voice, and when he lifted it up I knew by certain signs that there was another American here." The signs were his sentiments for peace, the fact that "he made more noise than the other seven speakers," and his "cast-iron veracity" (*South Australian Register*, 31 Dec., p. 6). In

---

13. *Notebook*, ed. Paine, p. 263. These dispatches were reprinted in the *Sydney Morning Herald*, 21, 23 Dec. See also MTP:NB36.

concluding, Twain congratulated the South Australians on their perfect climate, "where you have beautiful spring weather in midwinter
[December], and where snow is unknown .... where it is always holiday ... [and], when you have no holiday, or nothing else to do, it is
always a horserace" (*Advertiser* [Adelaide], 31 Dec., p. 6). He liked the
arrangement Australians had of placing "holidays not only to dates but
to what suits your own comforts." He claimed to have passed through
Australia "when they celebrated the Prince of Wales's Birthday. They
celebrated it on the 8th, the 10th, and the 11th, and skipped the 9th
altogether. (Laughter.) I suppose there was a horserace on the 9th.
(Loud laughter.)" (*Advertiser* [Adelaide], 31 Dec., p. 6).[14]

In his second Adelaide lecture in October, Twain had introduced his
"morals sermon" with the droll observation that "it was a difference
of opinion that led to horseracing" (*South Australian Register*, 15 Oct.,
p. 6). But *Quiz and Lantern* had the last word on this subject: "Mark
Twain made a mistake in saying that when we have no holiday we have
a horse race. If he wants to be absolutely truthful in his book on Australia he will say that when we are not lying and cheating our fellows
we are going to church and putting threepences in the collection-plate"
(9 Jan., 1896, p. 4).

Twain went to the Zoological Gardens on Tuesday, 31 December,
where he saw a dingo and "the jackass (bird) laughed for us";[15] at last
he had seen "the only laughing jackass that ever showed any disposition to be courteous to me. This one opened his head wide and laughed
like a demon, or like a maniac who was consumed with humorous scorn
over a cheap and degraded pun. It was a very human laugh. If he had
been out of sight I could have believed that the laughter came from
a man" (*More Tramps*, p. 122). Try as he might in New South Wales,
he had told a reporter just as he had crossed the border into Victoria,
he could not get the kookaburra to laugh for him. A cartoon in *Melbourne Punch* (3 Oct.) suggested that in Victoria he had found birds
which would laugh, but no known record corroborates that joke, and
the *Bulletin* of the same week, although it had a similar cartoon, has
no reference to subsequent laughing birds. Twain claimed the laughing
jackass was kept around, unlike many native animals, because he was

---

14. In reality he had been in Timaru and Oamaru, New Zealand, on the Prince's
birthday, and had written the same joke in his notebook.

15. *Notebook*, ed. Paine, p. 265.

useful to man: he killed snakes. "If L. J. will take my advice," Twain offered, "he will not kill all of them" (*More Tramps*, p. 122).

Twain also lunched with Dr. Samuel J. Way, the lieutenant governor with whom Clara and Livy had been carriage riding on their previous visit to Adelaide (MTP, p. 14). He called and left his card at Government House, missing the governor who had invited him to spend the night, an invitation Twain had to decline (MTP, p. 14).

Twain, Olivia and Clara Clemens, and Carlyle Smythe sailed for Ceylon from Adelaide at noon on the 1 January 1896, on the P & O liner *Oceana*. For three more days, they traveled westward along the southern Australian coast. On 4 January, Twain recorded in his notebook that they were tied up in the "perfectly landlocked roadstead—the most desolate-looking rocks & scarred hills" at Albany, Western Australia (MTP, p. 14). Ship arrivals were plentiful, "full of people rushing to the mines," many of them intending to return "home" as soon as they had struck it rich. At last in the morning of 5 January, the ship passed Cape Leeuwin, turning from its westward direction to "take a long straight slant nearly N. W. without a break for Ceylon" (MTP, p. 16).

The humorist, taking a final look at a country he had thoroughly enjoyed, wrote almost the only unpleasant thought he seems to have had about it:

> One must say it very softly, but the truth is that the native Australian is as vain of his unpretty country as if it were the final masterpiece of God, achieved by Him from designs by that Australian. He is as sensitive about her as men are of sacred things—can't bear to have critical things said about her.[16]

This passage, known since 1935, should not be taken as a judgment on the continent, or even as the last word. For he continued—and with more astuteness than the Australians displayed with their petty jealousies and the grave problems of resources, social unrest, and fraud: "Thinks he is going to build a mighty nation there, & some day be an independent one—a republic—cut up his 60 & 100,000-acre sheep runs into farms, maybe—irrigate the deserts, &c—Federation is *sound*; but better not hurry to cut loose from England" (MTP, p. 17). Comparing it to India and, no doubt, to problems the Americans had when they broke from England, Twain's final word was that "Australasia is the modern heaven—it is bossed absolutely by the workingman" (MTP, p. 18).

---

16. *Notebook*, ed. Paine, p. 265.

CHAPTER TEN

Mutual Admiration

"Humour ... Distinctively Her Own"

When Mark Twain arrived in Australia he was a thirty-year veteran of humorous writing and lecturing. Australians—native ones as well as transplanted Britons and Americans—had been reading his printed works for nearly as long as he had been writing them. From what they wrote in their newspapers, it seems that one or two editors may even have heard him on stage as far back as the Sandwich Islands lecture of 1866–1867. J. L. Dow in Melbourne, "Tom Touchstone" in Ballarat, "Scrutator" in Wellington, and others testify to acquaintance with his works measured in decades before they became journalists.

Australians and New Zealanders consistently saw Twain as "synonymous with," in the "front position of," or displaying "staying power in" what they called "American" humor. Therefore, their comments may give a reasonably good picture of late nineteenth-century "American humor," at least as exemplified by Mark Twain. Moreover, looking at what Australasians said as well as what Twain said can give some idea of why Twain was so willing in the Antipodes to grant interviews "more steadily than during any other phase of his career," and to "push his thinking at least a little beyond the conventional wisdom" regarding humor.[1]

---

1. Louis Budd, "Mark Twain Talks Mostly about Humor and Humorists," *Studies in American Humor* 1 (April 1974), 4.

In the Antipodes, Twain did use some original material—like the Australian poem, numerous topical one-liners about his carbuncle, the December heat, sheep-farmers-turned-journalists, his manager's quarantine, and so on. But most of his lecture stories had been read for years. In general, the newspaper writers recognized and credited Twain's right, even necessity, to use his old material. In Sydney, a reviewer said the "oldest of the gems .... were amongst the best" (*Sydney Daily Telegraph*, 20 Sept., p. 5). "Menander" in the *Australasian* pointed out that two lectures (and Twain gave three) would amount to "a small volume," which "is not a commodity at sale for a few hundreds." He appropriately illustrated his point by telling about fund-raisers who write to litterateurs and say that they "do not ask for a money contribution from you; but if you will kindly write us an original sketch or essay of three or four columns, which will cost you nothing, our committee will be deeply grateful" (5 Oct., p. 655).

There are, of course, two distinct parts to Twain as humorist in 1895—what Australasians often referred to as "the matter" and "the manner." Reviewers frequently assumed their readers were familiar with the "matter," either from having read Twain's books or from having read other reviews of his performances. And so they tended, particularly as the tour neared its close, to emphasize the "manner" of his presence, stage business, and delivery. The early reviews, along with Twain's notebooks in which he listed a good many of the programs he used, have satisfied American scholars that they know what Twain said and that it was well received. Similarly, the notebook entries in which Twain recorded the length of time it took him to deliver various stories in different performances and the reviewers' insistence on describing his mannerisms have likewise assured scholars that they know how he acted. But the magic between Twain and his audiences that developed to make the Antipodean tour so successful—despite Twain's continued and sometimes extremely painful ill health—has not been properly appreciated.

Scholars have not stressed enough either what the Australasians could tell them about "that humor which is peculiarly American," ignoring or sometimes expressing annoyance with "the many interviewers [who] posed many of the same questions."[2] Louis Budd, in his early examination of Twain's interviews, even suggested that some Australasian

2. Ibid., p. 5.

reporters may have been "mediocre journalists [trying] to compete as humorists with the master . . . . " Budd valued those who "were professional enough to lie low," but he dismissed others because their interviews were "sloppy or even counterfeit." Nor have American scholars examined what it was in the colonial temperament that Twain was responding to when he wrote in his notebook comments like "lovely time with the audience" at Napier or "delightful audience" at Horsham; or when Olivia Clemens wrote their daughter that "Papa never talked to a more enthusiastic audience."

The *Argus* in Melbourne editorialized that "the criticism of humour varies with the time and the country; it varies also with the individual, his age, his culture, and his digestion . . . . attempts at estimating the relative value of different kinds of humour are scarcely worth the paper spoiled in their production" (21 Sept., p. 6). Adelaide's *Quiz and Lantern* wrote, "If Mark as a lecturer is only as funny as he is as a writer, there ought to be no doubt as to his success on Australian soil. Australian humor approximates more closely to the humor of America than that of England" (3 Oct., p. 3). Stawell's *News and Pleasant Creek Chronicle* said, a fortnight prior to his arrival, that his "dry mellow fun suits the Australian temperament and environment especially of those living in the 'bush'" (12 Oct., p. 2). These comments clearly reflect a knowledge of Twain's published works.

"When some complained that they knew most of the stories and jokes as well as Mark Twain does himself they paid him a compliment," opined the *Australasian*, "for they showed that they had read and remembered what he had written, which is more than can be said of many very popular authors" (28 Dec., p. 1247). Not only were the educated familiar with Twain's works; even the unread knew them, as is exemplified by the man in Timaru who complained about grandfather's old ram, so the editor wrote, "that the excruciatingly funny story of the 'ten-cent-piece' wasn't original, because he had heard it before" (*Triad* [Dunedin], 25 Nov., p. 5). And in Adelaide, the reviewer claimed— "wildly improbable as it may sound . . . , rash as it may appear"—there seemed to be "some . . . to whom Mark Twain's stories were actually new," for they indulged in "uncontrollable laughter" (*South Australian Register*, 14 Oct., p. 6).

But perhaps more typical were statements like the ones in Auckland: "they knew him, his thoughts, and his personality. And they knew his

style and stories .... every now and then would be heard a sudden
solitary laugh—now here, now there,—which could not be restrained
.... These people knew the joke before it came, and laughed in anticipation" (*New Zealand Herald* [Auckland], 22 Nov., p. 5; 23 Nov.,
p. 5). As Dunedin journalist Malcolm Ross observed, the occasional
criticism "that he has told [his auditors] nothing new" was "really one
of the highest compliments that could be paid to him, because it shows
how universally his stories have been read" (*Otago Witness*, 14 Nov.,
p. 37). Several papers suggested that "he has given the world more
hearty laughs than possibly any man of his day and generation" (*Argus*
[Melbourne], 1 Oct., p. 6).

Halfway through Twain's Australasian tour, the leader in the Christchurch *Press* began, "In all other departments of art and literature America has so far been content to follow European models; her humour is
distinctively her own. We labour to imitate it in our own 'New Humour'; but between the two there is a great gulf fixed" (16 Nov., p. 2).
The *Press* offered several "reasons for this difference" between American and British humor, arising from "the conditions of their life and
growth." This article was mainly concerned with the content, or what
some papers called the "genial philosophy," of Twain's humor. While
English literature has a "strong Conservative instinct," American literature is—like her cities—"the growth of decades, not of centuries; it
is all brand new." This gave it a rough-and-tumble frontier attribute
with which the Australians, perhaps more than the New Zealanders,
seemed to empathize. It was probably this bumptiousness that made
A Connecticut Yankee in King Arthur's Court one of the Australian favorites and made the uprising at Eureka Stockade one of Twain's favorite
Australian events. Twain himself remarked upon the modernness of
Sydney and Melbourne, for example, in their using hydraulic lifts that
made possible skyscrapers of a dozen stories, as opposed to the English elevators in which "you arrive at old age on your trip to the sixth
floor" (*Age* [Melbourne], 27 Sept., p. 6). It is this same spirit of "raillery
and good-natured ridicule" that would allow Twain in *More Tramps
Abroad* to spoof the six Old Colonists at Adelaide's Commemoration
Day celebration.

Another important factor in defining American humor was that the
"Yankee mind is critical of everything"—"the religious, political and
social traditions of the land they left. And that same critical spirit

... to-day finds expression in an attitude of light raillery and good-natured ridicule towards everything that is sacred only by antiquity or sanctioned by convention" (*Press* [Christchurch], 16 Nov., p. 2). The newspapers often remarked stories in Twain's lectures that demonstrated the "critical spirit" of America, especially Huck Finn's struggle with his conscience and final decision not to return the slave Jim to Miss Watson. Another favorite was Huck, Jim, and Tom Sawyer's contemplated crusade to rescue the Holy Land, a project halted by the discovery that it was a " 'religious' practice to take the land away from the people it belonged to" (*Age* [Melbourne], 1 Oct., p. 6).

Two other themes that the Christchurch editor identified were closely allied: "keen commercial rivalry" and a "passion for bigness." He explained that it was a part of the "national disposition to 'lie over' and 'go one better' " than one's neighbor. This, of course, can account not only for humorous exaggeration in yarns like the one that tells how Cecil Rhodes made his first fortune by shark fishing (*More Tramps*, pp. 84–89). But it also provides the very basis of favorite stories like "The Notorious Jumping Frog of Calaveras County" and Twain's narrowly escaped duel while acting as newspaper editor in Nevada. Twain had the reputation of being "unable to hit a cathedral" with a six-shooter, but the rival editor withdrew when Twain's friends said he could shoot the head off a sparrow "five times out of six." "There you see," Twain concluded, "Fame was forced upon me by them young editors. Fancy my position had it come to that duel! The man wasn't as big as a cathedral ..." (*Evening News* [Melbourne], 1 Oct., p. 1).

The "passion for bigness," the *Press* said, accounts for exaggeration like Twain's description of the Washoe Zephyr in the Nevada territory as "a roaring dust drift, about the size of the United States set up edgewise." Such overstatements were no doubt pleasing to Australians in their big country. In writing his travel book he copied from a well-known Australian history to describe a Dubbo dust storm, which, he wrote, "tallies very well with the alkali dust storms of Nevada" (*More Tramps*, pp. 69–70). In an interview in Auckland, Twain used such an exaggerated metaphor to explain that "simple extravagance" can be saved from being "utterly reprehensible" by being "happily phrased": "For instance ..., the captain of a ship is describing the perils his vessel went through; 'Why,' says a listener, 'You must have shipped a great deal of water'; 'Sir,' says the captain, 'we pumped the Atlantic Ocean through my ship sixteen times'" (*New Zealand Herald* [Auckland], 23 Nov., p. 5). He told Melbournians that in the United States horses were so fast and storms so heavy that he "knew of one being chased by a storm for 18 miles. 'That horse ... never got a drop of rain and yet the dog behind the cart was swimming all the way'" (*Evening News* [Melbourne], 1 Oct., p. 1). Twain claimed that Australians told him that in Queensland it is so hot "the hens lay fried eggs," and in New Zealand he learned that the great moa "was still in existence when the railway was introduced ... and carrying the mails .... The company exterminated the moa to get the mails" (*More Tramps*, pp. 68, 60).

"Picturesque But Unmistakeably Vulgar"

Besides a critical mind and a competitive spirit, a third source for the new American humor arose from what the Christchurch *Press* called "a piebald nation—or, rather, a medley of nations." This is a penetrating comment, not merely in its refusal to generalize about that vast country, but also in seeing that the "incongruity" in the very fabric of the nation gave a would-be humorist a ready-made advantage. Certainly, in the humor that preceded Twain an important element often was the "bumpkin," the "city slicker," or the "dude" who finds himself in the city, in the country, or on the frontier, respectively—in another world whose customs he does not understand. Such incongruity at the heart of humor is, of course, easily demonstrated. The *Press* continued, "In the violent contrast of nationalities and religions, forms of dress and forms of speech, arise those incongruities which are the source of humour. The elements mingle in the irascible and combustion follows—the collision of races kindles the spark of humour." The editor cited the "bespectacled German, with a turn for metaphysics ..., against the background of astute practical Yankeedom," "the negro ... clothed in a suit of Stars and Stripes ..., [with] his quaint dialect ..., aping the manners of the Yankee," and "the Heathen Chinee." He might also have mentioned the Nevada silver miner, the unsuspecting bumpkin who buys an untamable Mexican horse, the would-be poet, and a host of other characters Twain depicted (or even acted) in his lectures.

In fact, each of the three separate lectures used on the world tour employed a wide variety of locales, character types, dialects, and modes. He used at least four stories in black dialect, two different spoofs on the German language, three frontier "tall tales" as well as other frontier adventures told as the truth, and at least four different stories in which cultivated clergymen or journalists get their come-uppance. The heterogeneous mixture in each of the three lectures may have been best described, probably by Herbert Low, in the *Sydney Morning Herald* after Twain's very first performance:

> It is difficult to describe Mark Twain's style, chiefly because he hasn't one. He possesses many. One moment he is ... a burnt-cork combination ..., the next ... peculiarly sly and visionated, [then] .... almost burlesque .... It is necessary [to follow closely] ... for he loves to dart back on himself and surprise you in the midst of a deep-welling laugh with something quite otherwise. [20 Sept., p. 5.]

"This picturesque commingling ... in a heterogeneous mass not merely supplies the humorist with ready-made incongruities of thought," the Christchurch paper pointed out, "but provides him with a language which is comic in itself independently of its meaning. Dialect in America is a never-failing material of humour" (16 Nov., p. 2).

Various examples of the dialects possible in the American language, including "those lumbering polysyllables which Mark Twain called 'alphabetical processions'; ... the quaint dialect of the plantation, the picturesque story of the diggers' camp, richly garnished with vivid metaphor ... help, perhaps, more than anything else, to contribute its peculiar flavour to American humour." Others referred to Twain's "odd and paradoxical style" (*Argus* [Melbourne], 1 Oct., p. 6), "quaint expressions" (*Age* [Melbourne], 28 Sept., p. 7), "some distorted phrase or daring expression of untutored slang" (*Advertiser* [Adelaide], 17 Oct., p. 4), "dryness and pithiness of expression" (*Australasian* [Melbourne], 5 Oct., p. 655), and "quaint drollery" (*Star* [Ballarat], 22 Oct., p. 4). Such comments, while referring in part to Twain's performances, are obviously applicable to his written works, such as *The Adventures of Huckleberry Finn* and "The Jumping Frog."

While reviewers repeatedly remarked on Twain's vocabulary, they did not often record the examples of homely expressions or frontier slang that he used, for example, in "Buck Fanshawe's Funeral." In fact, one reviewer was pleased that "the introduction of gold field 'slang' terms in ... Buck Fanshawe was effected without allowing the 'slang'— so often objectionable— to be anything but very amusing" (*Evening News* [Sydney], 23 Sept., p. 4). The writer for the *Press* preferred

the eastern humorists, such as Washington Irving and Oliver Wendell
Holmes, to some of Twain's closer predecessors because the easterners
"have caught the cosmopolitanism of all literature; culture has modified their peculiar national traits .... And that is a type of American
humour that will outlive the obscure slang of Artemus Ward or the irritating misspellings of Josh Billings. We hope so at least, in the interests
of that 'well of English undefiled' which American humour is rapidly
polluting" (16 Nov., p. 2).

It was feared, mainly in England, that "the English language ... will
lose more in elegance than it gains in vividness when such locutions
as 'biled shirt' and 'cownecked shoes' are stamped with the hall-mark
of literary acceptance," wrote the *Press*. "The corruption that is to be
feared is inelegancy of diction, the substitution of the slipshod jargon—
admittedly picturesque but unmistakeably vulgar—of the camp and
the plantation, the street and the saloon for the authorised language
of the schools" (16 Nov., p. 2). Previous humorists had also relied
on "an unsparing use of the words 'stranger,' and 'guess,' and 'calcu-
late,'" pointed out the *South Australian Register* (14 Oct., p. 6). But
Twain's humor, the consensus indicated, did not depend on such tricks
of "extravagant orthography" (*Advertiser* [Adelaide], 12 Oct., pp. 4–5)
or clumsy vocabulary for its effect. Instead it was his use of dispro-
portionately high-flown language that tickled the Australasians. Three
such "hifalutin" examples reported from his lectures will illustrate.

In his "First 'At Home'" Twain often yammered on with a perfectly
pointless story in which he described Uncle Lem's animal "as not a
'mongrel dog,' but a 'composite' or a 'syndicate' dog" (*Sydney Morning
Herald*, 25 Sept., p. 5). "A composite dog is a dog that's made up of all
the valuable qualities .... kind of a syndicate; and a mongrel is made
up of the riffraff that's left over."[3] In the performance usually called the
"Second 'At Home,'" Twain told a story about the first time he stole
a watermelon. Newspapers all the way from Adelaide to Christchurch
reported his telling about his "annexation of a watermelon" (*Star* [Auck-
land], 23 Nov., p. 2). "Perhaps the word 'stole' was a little harsh; but
at any rate he 'withdrew' it—'retired' it—while the farmer was waiting
upon another customer." Of course they also reported that when he
discovered "it was the greenest melon grown that year," he took it back
and told the farmer "he should be ashamed to work off green melons

---

3. *Mark Twain Speaking*, ed. Fatout, p. 291.

on people who had confidence in him, and also that if he did not reform, his (Mark's) custom would be withdrawn" (*Courier* [Ballarat], 23
Oct., p. 4).

A final example of overstated diction is seen in the offhand remark
about "the maiden lady who lent her No. 6 glass eye to another maiden
lady who was 'excavated' for No. 7" (*Australasian* [Melbourne], 5 Oct.,
p. 655). This grossly exaggerated and slightly askew diction is followed immediately by the anti-climactic erroneous verb form: "and so
that eye wouldn't lay still; every time she winked it would turn over."
Then follows a truncated adverb, absurd appositive, inappropriate person shift, and the redundant, and possibly inelegant, colloquial "back
side": "It was a beautiful eye and set her off admirable, because it was
a lovely pale blue on the front side—the side you look out of—and it
was gilded on the back side."[4] The ultimate compliment about Twain's
language may have been made by the *Advertiser* in Adelaide: "One of
the anecdotes of his opening lecture fell almost flat, simply because a
term in it, quaint enough when first penned, has now found a familiar
place in the spoken language" (17 Oct., p. 4).

Australasians also liked Twain's clean, unsullied fun. They praised
him for making "the world laugh more heartily and more innocently
than any other man—and that is no mean achievement in this age of
sordid and strenuous preoccupation" (*News and . . . Chronicle* [Stawell],
12 Oct., p. 2). Some writers went so far as to say "the most remarkable
feature of American humor is the freedom from sewerage . . . . it is pu-
rity itself" (*Press* [Christchurch], 16 Nov., p. 2). They called Twain the
"originator of a once new, pure, unvulgar fun—a man who could always, and can, make one laugh honestly and without shame . . . , a man
whose mirth has never descended to the low . . . . " (*Melbourne Punch*,
26 Sept., p. 203). No doubt it was this quality that made the women
who attended his performances laugh "as heartily as anybody" (*Lyttelton Times*, 14 Nov., p. 5). His humor was "mentally sanitary," (*Evening
News* [Sydney], 20 Sept., p. 4), and if auditors "expected vulgarity, the
double entente, and the *olla podrida* of the nigger minstrel show," as
seems to have been the case in Timaru, then they would experience
"disappointment" (*Triad* [Dunedin], 25 Nov., pp. 4–5).

Another element of the humor was a successful linking of unexpected
or apparently unlike concepts. The number of times the Australians re-

---

4. Ibid., p. 90.

ported these is testimony to the pleasure they took in them. Of course, "he can be as direct as he pleases, as in his description of graduating in the art of lying: 'I tried it, and became an instantaneous success.'" As early as his second lecture, the *Sydney Morning Herald* identified "the thoroughly typical Twainesque linking together of opposites." He told of his "experiences amongst lawyers and bars, newspaper editors, horse-thieves, and Congressmen" (23 Sept., p. 6). The same opening was reported with variations in Melbourne, Adelaide, Ballarat, Timaru, and Auckland. In Wellington, the paper even noted "two or three 'gentlemen of the long robe' ... who looked very uncomfortable" at being linked with horse thieves and liars (*New Zealand Times*, Supplement, 14 Dec., p. 1). In Melbourne, he told the Yorick Club that "age has its own value, but that is to other people, not to those who have it" (*Australasian* [Melbourne], 5 Oct., p. 615). These jokes depend in part on the linking of opposites, but they also employ multiple meanings, or even punning, as in "lawyers and bars."

Close to such unexpected opposites is Twain's use of an incongruous, often anti-climactic, ending. In Christchurch the *Star* said, "the point of his joke [was] a seeming afterthought, or anti-climax" (15 Nov., p. 5). Adelaide's *Quiz and Lantern* identified a similar element: "Australian humor approximates more closely to the humor of America than that of England. We are fond of anti-climaxes" (3 Oct., p. 3). A Sydney interviewer said that in private conversation Twain

> has plenty to say, but he is not in a hurry to say it, and it takes a little while to find out that when you think he has answered a question he is merely thinking whether he has done so or not, and generally finishes by rounding it off, clinching it, as it were, by some sapient or incongruous addendum, these addenda being like a lady's postscript, often the most important part of the communication. [*Sunday Times*, 22 Oct., p. 4.]

This trait may be most clearly seen in the first story of the first "At Home." When he was thirteen, he claimed, one day it was "too wet for school—*and just wet enough to go fishing.*" He did not go home, but instead went to his father's office, which doubled as the coroner's office, to "*wait until things cooled off at home.*" When he discovered a corpse glistening in the moonlight, Twain said, "*I went away. I don't mean that I went in a hurry. I just went—through the window. I took the sash with me, not that I wanted it, but it was easier to take it than to leave it*" (*Triad* [Dunedin], 25 Nov., pp. 4–5).

If the sources of Twain's humor could be traced to the vast het-erogeneous human and natural landscape of Twain's homeland, and the antiseptic qualities of its style and diction to the rebellious Puri-tan fathers, the Australasians also offered insight into various modes of humor that he used. Christchurch's evening paper had said edito-rially, "That the man was a born humorist, we knew, but we had not realised all the subtlety of the humour" (*Star*, 14 Nov., p. 2). The Ade-laide *Advertiser* said Twain was most successful and most influential in "that vein, half invention, half narration" (12 Oct., p. 4). Welling-ton's editorialist summarized his humorous writing: "Some of his work amuses merely, much suggests, instructs, stimulates, strengthens the best that is in us by presenting wholesome necessary truths in whimsi-cal and striking, original and terse fashion. That is a great side of him" (*New Zealand Mail*, 12 Dec., p. 32). And in Timaru he was "by turns philosophical, descriptive, humorous, and satirical" (*Triad* [Dunedin], 25 Nov., p. 4).

"The Springs of Pathos"

Twain's own comments about comedy, wit, and humor are concentrated in four interviews granted in 1895, two of them in Australia and one in New Zealand, and in his essay of about the same time called "How to Tell a Story." To borrow Louis Budd's words, these "may form the richest body of [Twain's] commentary on humor."[5] A very good question arises: why, after over three decades of writing humor-ous anecdotes, novels, and lectures, did Mark Twain suddenly begin in Australasia to talk about humor itself? A few possible reasons have been offered. As he prepared for his world tour under conditions of bankruptcy, he may have wondered "how he could still manage to make others laugh in his dejected frame of mind and how anybody could laugh in such a treacherous world," and he probably worried whether he still had his "almost infallible sense for the audience."[6] Budd also suggests that the interviewers asked him about humor more often than anyone had before, in part because they wanted to know whether the Australians were becoming more like the Americans and less like the British. However, Budd did not not examine the rapport between Twain

---

5. Budd, "Mark Twain Talks Mostly about Humor and Humorists," p. 4. Budd includes an interview given in Paris, in January 1895.

6. Ibid., p. 5; Budd cites Lorch, pp. 185ff.

and his interviewers; and in another article he dismissed reports whose authors had tried to intrude their own personalities into their conversations with Twain.[7] Whether Twain was merely catering to his public more willingly than he ever had because he needed their good will and their money, or whether he just liked the Australasians better than he liked most newspapermen, the fact remains that he *did* give himself to them more generously than he ever had before.[8] And he did compliment the Australasian publications, both publicly and in his notebook.

In Sydney young Herbert Low asked Twain to distinguish between wit and humor. No doubt, what Twain said in that interview, which was widely reprinted, influenced what some of the reviewers wrote about Twain. That is, when they realized for the first time what he thought humor was, then they were able to see those very things more clearly in his performances. " 'What is humour?' " Twain repeated Low's question. "I suppose no man ever knew why he had humour, and where he got it from, exactly what constituted a humorous idea, or in what way it first appealed to him." But, Twain continued,

> I maintain that a man can never be a humourist, in thought or in deed, until he can feel the springs of pathos. Indeed, there you have a basis of something material to go upon in trying to comprehend what this impalpable thing of true humour is. Trust me, he was never yet properly funny who was not capable, at times of being very serious. And more; the two are as often as not simultaneous .... Look at all the humourists and their creations, their subtle contrasts and their exquisite breaks of laughter—can't you see behind it all the depth and the purpose of it? [*Sydney Morning Herald*, 17 Sept., p. 5.]

Each of his three performances used at least one extended "pathetic" episode: Huck Finn feeling sorry for having tricked Jim in the fog; the slave Aunty Cord searching for her lost son; and Huck struggling with his conscience over returning Jim. He also had other stories he sometimes substituted, but these were the major ones, and his reviewers cited them as "the choky bit," which usually came just before the intermission. Some of his stories were "purely humorous and others pathetically humorous" (*Melbourne Punch*, 3 Oct., p. 218). Twain explained to Low,

---

7. Budd, "A Listing of ... Interviews," *American Literary Realism*, (1977), pp. 1–10.

8. Budd, "Working the Newspapers," in *Our Mark Twain: The Making of His Public Personality* (Philadelphia: Univ. of Pennsylvania Press, 1983), pp. 96–119, somewhat modifies his earlier views.

Probably there is an imperceptible touch of something permanent that one feels instinctively to adhere to true humour, whereas wit may be the mere conversational shooting up of "smartness"—a bright feather, to be blown into space the second after it is launched .... by general, if tacit, consent Wit seems to be counted a very poor relation to Humour. I suppose that Pope was one of the wittiest writers who ever put pen to paper; and yet most of us agree that he was "artificial." Now, humour is never artificial. [*Sydney Morning Herald*, 17 Sept., p. 5.]

Not all readers agreed with Twain that humor was superior to wit, nor that pathos and humor "are as often as not simultaneous." On Saturday 21 September, both the *Argus* in Melbourne and the *Australian Star* in Sydney carried editorials discussing Twain's comments on humor that had appeared in the *Sydney Morning Herald* and in the *Argus*. The *Australian Star*, possibly because it was piqued with a supposed insult to Sir Henry Parkes, was rather severe with Twain:

We have amongst us now, lecturing to us, a very famous author, who describes much of the work by his greatest rival as "shoddy" literature. The adjective is good to dwell on, and good to apply, if necessary, not only to Bret Harte, but to Mark Twain himself, to Max O'Rell, and to all their tribe; for no profession is so likely to make even a genius forget himself and lose his balance as the profession of a humourist. [21 Sept., p. 4.]

"A wit, on the other hand," the *Australian Star* concluded, "may often be guilty of ill-humour, but seldom of bad taste .... How fortunate are those whose reputation exceeds their performance, whose jokes are applauded before they speak, whose audiences ever laugh at as well as with them." However, once the *Australian Star* had seen Twain in operation, it was gracious in its treatment of him.

His remarks on wit and humor may have shaped the way editors expressed their own ideas. For example, "it is impossible to say where humor ends and wit begins, or which is in the greatest abundance. All that one can be sure of, though the wit and humor cannot always be differentiated, is that both are there" (*Independent* [Bendigo], 23 Oct., p. 3). This is not to imply that these small-town editors and reviewers would have been incapable of making such judgments about Twain's writings without the interview in Sydney, or that their appreciation is less than genuine. But it does seem reasonable that they would have taken into account the man's own remarks, especially when they had been reprinted in their hometown papers.

At least twice in Sydney, Twain said "without hesitation that he did not think [his own works] witty, but that he did think they were humorous. Wit, he thinks, is something that flashes itself upon the hearer; humor something that scintillates and meanders. Wit need not be funny; humor must be funny" (*Sydney Daily Telegraph*, 17 Sept., p. 5). Those who apparently did not agree that humor was superior to wit would often write that Twain "is something more than a humorist" (*Independent* [Bendigo], 23 Oct., p. 3). Or they would explain; "Wit has been likened to a flash, and humour to an abiding light. In [Twain's] compositions there is both wit and humour; the light of humour shines steadily throughout, and the wit is constantly flashing. That explains the perpetual accompaniment of laughter and interest" (*New Zealand Mail* [Wellington], 12 Dec., p. 32).

The underlying theme in Twain's humor—in addition to some purely whimsical stories like Adam's diary or the Australian poem—was, as his "Morals Sermon" pointed out, "reformation" of the human race. But the reform hoped for was not the traditional "moral" or even "social" one. It was more a reform of sham, cant, pomposity, foolishness, inequity—in short, what a Wellington paper called "Humbug." As the *Age* [Melbourne] pointed out, his audience came to hear "something which was not altogether what the author himself has described in the forcible language of Master H. Finn as 'rot and slush and hogwash'" (28 Sept., p. 7). A few examples will demonstrate. A favorite story used in his "one-night stands"—in the country towns—warned against "the disposition to jump at conclusions on circumstantial or insufficient evidence," telling about "the clergyman who made a great oration when christening a child, but forgot to start by finding out whether it was a boy or a girl" (*Maryborough and Dunolly Advertiser*, 28 Oct., p. 5).

Several more yarns can be easily seen as attempts to point out a fundamental wrong, or at least a nonsense, in the world. The favorite in that category was not satiric, for nothing could be done to "correct" the problem. So Twain's treatment was entirely humorous and good-natured, and it had been familiar to his readers since *Innocents Abroad*. It is the story of the difficulties in learning the German language. Usually included in the "Morals Sermon," the "moral" it taught was "patience is such a virtue." Twain himself had been studying the language twenty-eight years but no longer had any hope of learning it unless in the afterlife if there is time. He called attention to the " 'split' verbs, the extraordinary terminations, and the mixing up of the genders .... an unmarried lady was of the neuter gender—no sex at all; while a turnip was feminine. That was showing idolatrous worship of the turnip, and very little respect for the lady. It was also observed that the neck, bosom, elbows and body were of the masculine gender, and the head neuter" (*Courier* [Ballarat], 22 Oct., p. 4). "It does seem to me," Twain opined,"that the languages on the continent are harder on the cat than on the girl. In France a cat is a male; in Germany a cat is a female. [In all other countries it is neuter.] Why, if I were a cat I would sooner die than live in such a condition of uncertainty" (*Maryborough and Dunolly Advertiser*, 28 Oct., p. 5). He observed that "a fish was 'he,' and 'his' scales 'she,' but a fishwife was neither" (*Courier* [Ballarat]). Sometimes he concluded with the language lesson, but sometimes he read the tale of the German fishwife, which ends with the "hope that a deceased fishwife would be rewarded for the uncertainty of gender during her life in Germany by having in her eternal home 'only one good square sex and have it all to herself'" (*Evening News* [Geelong], 30 Oct., p. 1). Sometimes he used the fishwife's tale to illustrate the language lesson.

"Depends ... upon the Manner"

Twain agreed with an Auckland interviewer that American humor "is different entirely to French, German, Scotch, or English humour."

> And the difference lies in the mode of expression .... As a rule when an Englishman writes or tells a story, the "knob" of it, as we would call it, has to be emphasised or italicised, and exclamation points put in. Now, an American story teller does not do that. He is apparently unconscious of the effect of the joke .... In any other country but America the part at which you should laugh would be put in italics and with exclamation marks. [*New Zealand Herald*, 21 Nov., p. 5.]

An illustration of Twain's point has already been seen: C. N. Baeyertz in Dunedin followed the European convention when he "put in italics" at the laugh lines in his printing of the truant fishing story.

The "manner," then, is the second part of Twain's humor that was so successful in Australasia, the part that so "took" his auditors. It is obvious from the reviews that Twain had, in addition to the amusing words themselves, several well-rehearsed techniques to make his audience laugh. In the conversation with the Auckland journalists he said that "the similes used in America may be a little more extravagant than in England, but the method of treatment is modified. The method is quieter, more modified, and more subtle" (*New Zealand Herald*, 21 Nov., p. 5). Some of these words are the same ones his reviewers had already been using for nine weeks to describe his acting. Twain's clearest statement about performing seems to have been in the essay published in October 1895, while Twain was in Australia, but apparently unseen in that country while he was there. Although it begins with a disclaimer about his own ability to tell a story, it is rather clear that what he describes is very nearly what he did, at least in Australasia.

Twain supplied, apparently at the editor's suggestion, the essay "How to Tell a Story" to *Youth's Companion*.[9] "I do not claim," he begins, "that I can tell a story as it ought to be told. I only claim to know how a story ought to be told."[10] Only the humorous story is difficult to tell, because it "depends for its effect upon the *manner* of the telling; the comic story [which is English] and the witty story [which is French] upon the *matter*" (p. 161). Twain does not really develop definitions of or distinctions among "humor," "wit," and "comedy," although he does, by illustration, contrast them. He insists, though, that the humorous tale "was created in America."

Instead, he describes the way to tell the three kinds of amusing stories: "The humorous story may be spun out to great length, and may wander around as much as it pleases, and arrive nowhere in particular; but the comic and witty stories must be brief and end with a point. The humorous story bubbles gently along, the others burst." This description employs the same language Twain used with Herbert Low in Sydney and again with journalists in Auckland. Probably taking a cue from the *New Zealand Herald* interview, the Auckland *Star*— more than most papers—stressed "the particuliarly effective manner in which the humorist leads his audience quietly up to the point of the joke and leaves them" (22 Nov., p. 3). And in Wellington, the familiarity of his works did not diminish their effect, for his "stories, anecdotes, sketches—call them what you please—are not like riddles, which de-

---

9. Budd, "Mark Twain Talks Mostly about Humor and Humorists," p. 20.

10. "How to Tell a Story," in *Tom Sawyer Detective*, (London: Chatto and Windus, 1909), pp. 161–171.

pend for their success upon one point (the answer) kept carefully in reserve till the end" (*New Zealand Mail*, 19 Dec., p. 32).

One of the characteristics of humorous story-telling is that it is "told gravely ... [unsuspicious] that there is anything funny about it."[11] The Wanganui paper pointed out that Twain "did not ask anyone to laugh. He talked seriously, deliberately, and without a smile"; he "himself resembles a graven image. He never laughs; he never even smiles—at any rate, not visibly" (*Wanganui Chronicle*, 5 Dec.). Of the Irishman Twain visited in Bendigo he said, "he had a deep fondness for humour, yet he never laughed; he never even chuckled; in fact, humour could not win to outward expression on his face at all. No, he was always grave—tenderly, pensively grave; but he made me laugh all along" (*More Tramps*, p. 160). In Christchurch, the audience did not laugh "*with* him, for the humourist comported himself with as much gravity of demeanour as the gravest judge that ever presided over dry-as-dust procedure. And if any one of the audience were to be asked what the lecture was about, ... no definite answer would be obtained" (*Star*, 14 Nov., p. 2). This exactly fits Twain's description of the humorous story as "rambling and disjointed," though it often "finishes with a nub ... [dropped] in a carefully casual and indifferent way." A comic story, he said, will take ninety seconds, while the same story told in the humorous mode "takes ten minutes, and is about the funniest thing I have ever listened to." Some of its other attributes include an "innocent and happy" teller filled with "sincerity and unconsciousness."[12] Christchurch reported that "he is the most unconscious man in the whole assemblage" (*Press*, 14 Nov., p. 5). About half of the material Twain used in Australia employed a narrator other than himself—Huck Finn, Jim or another black, or a silver miner, for example. These were usually told in heavily illiterate dialect—a characteristic apparently so prevalent that more than one interviewer remarked on Samuel Clemens's good English.

"Wrong by the Five-Millionth of an Inch"

Twain said there are four parts to successful yarning: "To string incongruities and absurdities together in a wandering and sometimes purposeless way, and seem innocently unaware

---

11. Ibid., p. 161.
12. Ibid., pp. 161–163

that they are absurdities, is the basis of the American art."[13] That Twain was a master of this quality surely has been amply demonstrated already, but to the examples might be added the *Sydney Morning Herald*'s report that "he rambles on with the set purpose of rambling .... he starts out ... stops halfway through ... digresses a little more, and at the widest circle of this boomerang recital drops back of a sudden on the tag, or the moral, or the lost point of his anecdote" (23 Sept., p. 6). *Melbourne Punch* described the story about an old man who lost his dime "and wanders off to the relations of an eye-witness, describing with a particular minuteness their relations, &c., etc., and never, never, never, coming back to his original yarn. We wait in vain for the conclusion—it doesn't come, and finally the story-teller goes to sleep ..." (26 Oct., p. 203). These papers were referring to something like the following tale:

> Next morning he went down to have a look at [his ram], and accident'ly dropped a ten-cent piece in the grass and stooped down—so—and was a-fumblin' around in the grass to git it, and the ram he was a-standin' up the slope taking notice; but my grandfather wasn't taking notice, because he had his back to the ram and was int'rested about the dime. Well, there he was, as I was a-sayin', ... and Smith—Smith was a-standin' there—no, not jest there, a little further away—fifteen foot perhaps— ... the ram he bent his head down, so ... Smith of Calaveras ... no, no it couldn't ben Smith of Calaveras—I remember now that he—b'George it was Smith of Tulare County—course it was, I remember it now perfectly plain .... Well, Smith he just stood there .... why sho! it *warn't* Smith of Tulare at all, it was Smith of Sacramento.

And from there he wanders to the borrowed glass eye, the missionaries and the cannibals, the composite dog, and so on.

The second technique was slurring the point, by which Twain seems to have meant fumbling around for the correct Smith or, later on, trying to describe the mismatched glass eyes, concluding that "that warn't any matter—they worked together all right and plenty picturesque .... as soon as she begun to get excited that handmade eye would give a whirl and then ... a-flashing first blue and then yaller and then blue and then yaller, and ... the oldest man in the world couldn't keep up with the expression on that side of her face."[14]

---

13. Ibid., p. 166.
14. Quoted from *Mark Twain Speaking*, ed. Fatout, pp. 289–292.

The third device, Twain said, was dropping in a "studied remark," act-ing as if one is "thinking aloud." Except for his tour with George Wash-ington Cable, when he read from the then-unpublished *Huck Finn*, Twain always memorized his speeches so that he could use "those stud-ied fictions which seem to be the impulse of the moment ..., fictitious hesitancies for the right word, fictitious unconscious pauses, fictitious unconscious side remarks, fictitious unconscious embarrassments, ficti-tious unconscious emphasis placed upon the wrong word with a deep intention back of it."[15] Although the Sydney reporters did not have ac-cess to Twain's essay, they picked up this trick right away: the *Sydney Morning Herald* had figured out by the second performance that "no doubt all the impromptus are carefully studied[, but] the preparation is not detected behind the final result." In Wellington, he was praised for "the effects, apparently unstudied, most naturally produced" (*New Zealand Times*, 11 Dec., p. 2).

Finally, there was the pause, which Twain called "an exceedingly im-portant feature ..., frequently recurring ..., dainty ..., delicate, and also uncertain and treacherous; for it must be exactly the right length—no more and no less—or it fails of its purpose and makes trouble."[16] Of his techniques for "delivery," his "timing," of which the pause is a part, seems to have been the most striking and precise. His notebooks from the trip are filled with entries giving the precise amount of time used in telling certain stories. He controlled their length at least in part by his "frequently recurring" pauses. Two examples will demonstrate.

In Invercargill, his first New Zealand appearance, he noted in his journal: "Nov. 5. Shortened Dead Man. Old Ram as usual. Read Courier too *fast*. Began it at 8.30; ended it at 8.50; added Xning, & called intermission—8.55. At 9.07 did the Poem; then the Duel; then German (full length); then Whistling, & closed at 9.55."[17] And for his first performance (of five) in Melbourne he made elaborate plans: "I want to end at 9.25. I don't believe Sollermun is necessary if Old Ram will run to *9*. P. S. *Next Day*. Old Ram (?) *did* run to *exactly* 9. Then 7

---

15. *Mark Twain in Eruption*, ed. DeVoto pp. 214, 224, quoted in Edgar M. Branch, " 'The Babes in the Wood': Artemus Ward's 'Double Health' to Mark Twain," *PMLA* 93 (1978), pp. 955-972; see also Lorch, *The Trouble Begins at Eight*, p. 217. It seems that on the world tour the portion of "Adam's Diary" may have been read.

16. "How to Tell a Story," pp. 166–167.

17. Miriam J. Shillingsburg, "American Humour in an Inter-Cultural Context: 'Dis-tinctively Her Own,'" *Australasian Journal of American Studies* 6 (July, 1987), 41.

m. intermission; re-began at 9.07, & *think* Smallpox must have reached past 9.30 (I did not hurry it); I added nothing to the German, (but talked very slowly) & it lasted till 9.48 or 9.50" (MTP:NB35).

If that is what Twain said about the usefulness and practice of the pause, is it possible to tell from written reports how it actually worked? This seems more difficult, but a humorous passage from his speech to Melbourne's Yorick Club may be helpful. Presuming the dashes to be pauses, a reader can get some idea of how the piece would go:

> My friend on the right (Mr. Deakin) and I were talking just now about that very thing [growing old]. I said I thought that if I had created the human race— ... oh! I could have done it. (Laughter.) I was asked nothing about it, and I didn't suggest anything. (Laughter.) But I thought that if I had created the human race, and had discovered that they were a kind of a failure—(laughter)—and had drowned them out—(loud laughter)—well, I would recognise that that was a good thing. And then, fortified by experience, I would start the thing on a different plan. (Laughter.) I would have no more of that 969 years' business. I wouldn't let people grow that old. I would cut them off at 30. [*Australasian* (Melbourne), 5 Oct., p. 615.]

On occasion, too, he used an extremely long pause, just before the "nub" of the story. For example, his daughter Clara, who saw at least two dozen performances in Australasia alone, reports the platform version of the Mexican plug story: "Well, that horse gave such a buck-jump at last that it sent me out of the saddle up and up—up so high I came across birds I never saw before. I kept on going and just missed the top of a steeple. But when I got back, the horse .... was gone."[18]

But the best example of the long pause must be the ghost story about the woman with the golden arm. This is the story that Twain used to illustrate his essay "How to Tell a Story"; as he told it throughout Australasia, it never failed to frighten the ladies. Told in black dialect, it was about the man who robbed his wife's grave of her golden arm. She comes to haunt him night after night, until finally

> de voice say, *right at his year*—"W-h-o—g-o-t—m-y—g-o-l-d-e-n—*arm*?" (You must wail it out very plaintively and accusingly; then you stare steadily and impressively into the face of the farthest-gone auditor—a girl, prefer-ably,—and let that awe-inspiring pause begin to build itself in the deep hush. When it has reached exactly the right length, jump suddenly at the

---

18. Lorch, *The Trouble Begins at Eight*, p. 220, note 35.

girl and yell, "*You've* got it!" If you've got the *pause* right, she'll fetch a dear little yelp and spring right out of her shoes. But you *must* get the pause right.[19]

"If the length of the pause was wrong by the five-millionth of an inch," he said elsewhere, "it fell flat."[20]

What, then, did the reviewers say about his use of the pause? A Wellington paper said his style "depends much on pauses for its effect" (*New Zealand Mail*, 19 Dec., p. 32). Of his first performance, Sydney's *Evening News* said:

> The deliberate dawdling American fashion of allowing points of humor to seem to occur, as it were, has to be indicated in print—the speaker gives the real thing. The drawl and the pauses have the effect of making it seem as though the jokes were being made, or rather were generating themselves, on the spot. "The best part of a doughnut is the hole, and the bigger the hole the better the doughnut." Well, the pauses and hiatuses are not the best part of Mark Twain's "lecture," but they add greatly to its charm. [20 Sept., p. 4.]

In Auckland, Twain was "silently humorous, and ... the laughter was almost as hearty when he stood saying nothing as when he spoke" (*Star*, 22 Nov., p. 3).

"What American Humour Actually Is"

Most of the auditors came prepared for a laugh, although it was reported here and there that some humorless persons attended. They knew what to expect because the publicity posters featured a "truculent-looking fellow scowling ... all round" who looked like "some tragic actor ... taken in the character of King Lear as he was uttering the curse upon his daughters .... it would never do for an American humourist to be drawn with a broad grin on his face. That would be out of character; they are not built that way" (*New Zealand Herald*, Supplement, 23 Nov., p. 1). Even before Twain opened his mouth he had the "guests" at his "At Home" in gales of laughter, for he "slouched" onto the stage from behind the "Stars and Stripes," walking "with a 'toddling motion,' ... like the lines on his face, part and parcel of his drollery" (*Sydney Daily Telegraph*, 20 Sept., p. 5), and bowed to his audience. "With the exception of an occasional curious trot, as when recounting

---

19. "How to Tell a Story," pp. 170–171.
20. Lorch, *The Trouble Begins at Eight*, p. 221, note 37.

his buck-jumping experiences," he "stands perfectly still in one place .... He rarely moves his arms, unless ... to show by action how a certain thing was done" (*Critic* [New York], 25 Apr. 1896, p. 286). He wore the "conventional claw-hammer outfit" (*Australian Star*, 20 Sept., p. 8), the "regulation evening-clothes with the trouser-pockets cut up high, into which he occasionally dives both hands" (*Critic* [New York], 25 Apr., 1896, p. 286). His shock of white hair looked like "an amazed gum-tree," according to the *Bulletin*. He stood with his feet apart, and he placed his glasses, a watch, and in some performances a book and a caraffe on the small table that, along with a chair, was his only stage furniture.[21]

Then, reported *Melbourne Punch*,

> he composes himself to sleep, like a horse standing up. He closes his eyes, rests his head lightly on his right hand, which in its turn is supported by the left arm folded across his chest, and then—commences to talk in his sleep. And what deliciously, pleasantly dreamy talk it is—all flowing forth in an easy conversational way, as if the sleeper fancied himself away in some quiet place with a few friends to whom he was telling a few yarns and experiences .... Every now and again a burst of laughter wakes him from his doze, and makes him blink his eyes and put his hands in his pockets; but he is soon asleep again, and rambling again in his own land of dreams and shadows .... For nearly two hours he keeps in that sleep, from which the audience wish he would not wake before morning, and then he suddenly wakes. [3 Oct., p. 218.]

The main theme of the reviewers was stated best in Auckland: "One must see the man and hear him to enjoy him to the full," and that would require "nothing short of some ingenious combination of photography and the phonograph, similar to that which Mr. Edison has just constructed, [to] furnish even a faint reproduction of his appearance last night, and it would be a very faint reproduction indeed" (*Star*, 22 Nov., p. 3).

Finally, the auditors seem to have been fascinated with his "Murkan" accent, a combination of a "slow, weary ..., calm, languid, slightly monotonous drawl" (*Evening News* [Melbourne], 28 Sept., p. 4) and the flat pronunciation and "country" grammar of the American South. Even in Ballarat, with its large population of Californians, it "took a little while for the audience to understand their man" (*Evening Echo*

---

21. The reference to the chair, the carafe, and a traveling clock appears only in Melbourne's *Evening News*, (28 Sept., p. 1).

[Ballarat], 22 Oct., p. 4). The reviewer for the Auckland *Star* revelled in the "smooth and — except to a fine ear that can catch its modulations — the somewhat monotonous voice with its decided American accent" (22 Nov., p. 8). In Melbourne, Twain talked

> in short sentences, with a peculiar smack of the lips at the end of each. His language ... [shows] an utter disregard for the polished diction of most lecturers. "It was not" is always "twarn't" with Mark Twain, and "mighty fine" and "my kingdom" and "they done it" and "catched," and various other purely trans-atlantic words and phrases, crop up profusely during his talk. He speaks slowly, lazily, and wearily, as a man dropping off to sleep, rarely raising his voice above a conversational tone; but it has that characteristic nasal sound which penetrates to the back of the largest building. [*The Critic* (New York), 25 Apr. 1896, p. 186.]

Other Melbournians reported "an eccentric little jump on the last syllable of a sentence" (*Evening News* [Melbourne], 28 Sept., p. 4).

He spoke "with the accessories appropriate to such distinctively American humour—with a nasal twang, slow deliberation and a kind of absent-mindedness" (*Lyttelton Times*, 14 Nov., p. 5). Melbourne's *Argus* said "that inimitable drawl" gaves his stories, "new or old ..., a strange fascination in 'Mark Twain's' way of telling them—a quaintness that exactly suits the odd and paradoxical style of humour" (1 Oct., p. 6). He spoke in "a hesitating, yet confidential manner ... an ordinary conversational tone, and [he] has a strong nasal twang" (*West Wimmera Mail*, 25 Oct., p. 5). The country towns claimed "his drawl, which all have heard of, was recognised as an old friend .... together with the general quietness of his attitude" (*Advertiser* [Bendigo], 24 Oct., p. 3; reprinted in *Maryborough and Dunolly Advertiser*, 28 Oct., p. 5). And although interviewers were a bit surprised at his correct grammar, they commented on his delivery even in private conversations: "Judging from the manner of speech adopted, one unaccustomed to Americans would conclude that Mr Clemens is a phenomenally lazy man, one word following the other as though each was being mentally turned over, and its full worth in the sentence weighed" (*Courier* [Ballarat], 21 Oct., p. 4).

The *Argus* summed up the wedding of matter and manner by saying that "for the first time one really realised what American humour actually is":

> There was the quiet, lazy drawl, the half-closed eye, the confidential manner, leading one slyly away from the point of the story, so that it might be

thrust in unawares amongst the small ribs by a sort of addendum or afterthought. And then a patient, resigned silence, until the laugh was over, as if it was all an annoying interruption which had to be endured, though why they laughed the lecturer did not know. [28 Sept., p. 7.]

CHAPTER ELEVEN

More Tramps Abroad

"Trying ... to Make a Good Book of It"

Samuel, Olivia, and Clara Clemens continued their triumphant lecturing and sightseeing tour through India, Ceylon, South Africa, and back to Paris. When they arrived in England, no doubt exhausted, the news came that the oldest daughter Olivia Susan Clemens, who had stayed with her sister Jean in Hartford, was seriously ill. Mrs. Clemens and Clara immediately started for America, but before they reached her, Susy had died of meningitis. The story of Twain's grief and bitterness has been told many times over.

It was during the first year after this loss that Twain set himself to writing his last travel book. In a leased house secluded from all but the most intimate friends, Twain was steadily working on the only book he would ever write entirely in England.[1] In his deep grief Twain must have found solace, or at least occupation, in writing the book that would be published simultaneously in America as *Following the Equator* and in England and Germany as *More Tramps Abroad*.

Twain wanted Frank Bliss of the American Publishing Company to publish the American book because his recent publisher, Harper, appealed mainly "to people who are accustomed to read. That class are surfeited with travel-books. But there is a vast class that isn't—the fac-

---

1. Welland, p. 170. Although I have compared the English and American versions, I rely on Welland's fascinating account of their composition and textual relationship.

tory hands and the farmers. They never go to a bookstore; they have to be hunted down by the canvasser. When a subscription book of mine sells 60,000, I always think I know whither 50,000 of them went. They went to people who don't visit bookstores."[2] He believed Bliss best pursued this non-literary audience with his "canvassers," and that he would earn "$30,000 in the first six months." He also had in mind half a dozen or so other schemes, which included lecturing as well as publishing. He was already beginning to sound like the old Twain stung over the failed typesetting machine.

Twain intended the book to be about 180,000 words, and he wrote the first chapter on 24 October 1896.[3] On 18 December, he wrote Rogers that he was keeping "cheerful" because of his work. "I work seven days in every week, and seldom go out of the house .... I got to work on the book at the earliest possible moment ... and I have not missed a day since." He was now considering 250,000 words, of which he had written 65,000; he intended to "turn out 30,000 a month."[4] By 15 January, he had "written 130,000 & could finish by March 1st; but I expect (as usual) to write a good deal more than necessary, so that I can scratch out as much as I want to."[5] Two weeks later he had finished it, "but I have covered only about half of the trip. 180,000 words does not allow me room enough. So I think of going on and making it a 2-volume book of 140,000 words each."[6] But as soon as he "concluded to go on and make 2 volumes of this book [he] broke down." It was now his plan "to write a third more matter for the one volume than necessary, then weed out and leave one compact and satisfactory volume .... I am going to write with all my might on this book."[7]

By 1 March, he had completed a draft, "then spent a week gutting it. I gutted a third of it out, & then began a careful revising & editing of the remaining two-thirds. I shall complete this revision in two or three days."[8] In mid-March he reported of the remaining two thirds that he was "getting them into very satisfactory shape. Am very much pleased. I think I shall be through by June 1. I am trying my very

---

2. *Correspondence with Rogers*, ed. Leary, p. 249.
3. Welland, p. 170.
4. *Correspondence with Rogers*, ed. Leary, p. 255.
5. Welland, p. 171.
6. *Correspondence with Rogers*, ed. Leary, p. 263.
7. Ibid., p. 264.
8. Welland, p. 171.

best to make a good book of it."[9] To his English publisher he wrote, "I wouldn't trade it for any book I have ever written."[10] On 14 April, he wrote Rogers that he had finished "yesterday," but he had excluded the South African material. His major advisors, including Livy, urged him "that South Africa ought to be in,"[11] and finally he began that part. On 18 May he wrote, "I have just this minute finished this book *again*. I have added 30,000 words."[12] He submitted forty chapters in manuscript to Andrew Chatto of Chatto and Windus on 15 June, and Frank Bliss of the American Publishing Company had a typescript of the same portion.[13]

The title remained unsettled until very near the end of composition. At various times, he had referred to the book as *Round the World, Imitating the Equator, Another Innocent Abroad, An Old Innocence Abroad, A Tramp Abroad Again*, and *The Latest Innocent Abroad*;[14] it was actually announced as *The Surviving Innocent Abroad (Triad* [Dunedin], 1 Feb. 1898, p. 8). Two months prior to his deciding on the title of either edition he had written out the dedication to young Harry Rogers: "with recognition of what he is and apprehension of what he may become unless he form himself a little more closely the model of The Author." Rogers was the son of Twain's friend and business manager, who had not only dragged him out of the bankruptcy but, before the year was out, would have Twain well on the way to financial security. Twain claimed he would "know the title to give it" when he had finished the book. Finally, after consultation with friends, he decided by 15 June on *More Tramps Abroad* for the Commonwealth and European editions; on 27 July, he wired to Bliss in America "Following Equator."[15]

Several lengthy passages, usually those reprinted from Australasian histories, appear in *More Tramps Abroad* but not in *Following the Equator*, making the two texts distinctively different, and in some cases rendering critical commentary obscure if a reader is holding the wrong

---

9. *Correspondence with Rogers*, ed. Leary, p. 267.

10. Welland, p. 172.

11. *Correspondence with Rogers*, ed. Leary, p. 275.

12. Ibid., p. 276.

13. For a detailed account of the progressive submission of the two setting copies, see Welland, pp. 173ff.

14. See ibid., pp. 170–173; *Correspondence with Rogers*, ed. Leary, pp. 269, 275.

15. Welland, p. 173.

edition. Virtually all of these American excisions occur in the Australasian part, making the two books even more different if one is reading only the report on the Antipodes.[16] Evidently Bliss thought Americans would not be interested in Australian history, and he excised even more than the "whole raft of reprint matter [which was] ripped out" by Twain and Chatto.[17] Chatto made two long deletions, one explaining the shipboard game of shuffleboard, the second possibly seeking to avoid a libel suit from an Australasian shipping company. This latter change is particularly interesting, because several reviewers and later critics have called attention to the trip from Christchurch to Wellington on the *Flora*. The American edition prints nearly two pages that Chatto excluded from the version which went to Australia and New Zealand.[18] In those missing paragraphs Twain called the ship the "equivalent of a cattle-scow" and charged that the Union Company found it "inconvenient to keep a contract and lucrative to break it" when they crammed 200 people into a vessel licensed to carry 125. He said it was "a powerful company, it has a monopoly, and everybody is afraid of it—including the government's .... conveniently-blind representative .... [who] winked a politic wink and said nothing" at the overload of passengers.[19]

Because the American edition was elaborately illustrated, Twain wanted it circulated around the world. But Chatto and Windus, within its copyright privilege, prevented that. Four days after publication, it was making its second printing in spite of "the lukewarmness or even hostility" of some reviews in England. On both sides of the Atlantic, "thirty thousand copies [were sold] right away; the royalties and the other earnings Rogers had invested for Clemens added up, by the end of that January, to enough to pay off the creditors in full and still leave thirteen thousand to spare."[20] The English book was available in Australia by New Year's Day, and in New Zealand around mid-January.

---

16. Volume I of Harper's authorized edition, from which the Penguin reprint was made.

17. Welland, p. 173.

18. Ibid., pp. 172–182, details the changes between the two books and between the books and their respective copy texts.

19. *Following the Equator* (Hartford: American Publishing Company, 1897), p. 301; (New York: Harper and Brothers, 1899), I, 316–317.

20. Kaplan, p. 350. Other accounts say there was $18,000 to spare.

"Amusing ... Serious and Instructive"

More Tramps Abroad was published on 12 November, but orders could not be filled by Chatto and Windus until a second printing was completed on 25 November 1897.[21] The "long promised history of Mark Twain's lecturing tour" was announced by the London correspondent of the *Sydney Daily Telegraph* on 26 November. About a month later, advance copies began arriving at the newspaper offices in New Zealand and Australia, and editors scurried to scoop their rivals in reviewing the book. Such hurried glances formed the bases for its critical reception in the Antipodes. Critics neither hailed nor damned the book; most, like the *Bulletin*'s Red Page reviewer, A. G. Stephens, were satisfied to use extended quotations with a few bridging comments between them. Some, however, offered intelligent remarks about Twain's observations of the countries and people who lived in them.

In a long review, the *Sydney Morning Herald*, which had given Twain thorough coverage when he was in the city, expressed disappointment in the "attempt of the humorist to draw water from the ancient springs that once welled forth so spontaneously" (1 Jan. 1898, p. 2). In comparison with his earlier travel books, especially *Innocents Abroad*, he seemed "an old man fallen on evil times, trying to joke .... But the public that so often laughed with him has learned the trick of his humour, and has become familiar with the mechanical processes of its production." The reviewer was echoing remarks Twain himself had made when he was in Sydney. He had praised W. S. Gilbert and Lewis Carroll, but of Dickens he said, "with the years I have lost much of my youthful admiration."

> I don't know where it is exactly, but I cannot laugh and cry with him as I was wont. I seem to see all the machinery of the business too clearly .... The true and lasting genius of humour does not drag you thus to boxes labelled "pathos," [and] "humour," and show you all the mechanism .... And time, it seems to me, is the true test of humour. [*Sydney Morning Herald,* 17 Sept. 1895, p. 5.]

Now the paper said that Twain's newest work "reminds us that there is a fashion in humour as well as in clothes, and that the one can become as archaic and old-fashioned as the other. The reception of this book will be dictated rather by a genial recollection of the past than for what the author has to offer in the present."

---

21. Welland, p. 182.

This is a curious beginning, for the "archaic" humor of twenty-five years before (in *Innocents Abroad*) had been extremely funny when Twain had read it to Sydneysiders only two years earlier. Calling the chronological "design of the volume ... pleasant enough," the reviewer did not point out a single instance of the "something pathetic" that he said characterizes *More Tramps Abroad*. The nearest he came to a specific example of Twain's failure occurs when he said, "There is a burst of unconscious humour which the long-suffering pastoralist will best appreciate in the remark that in Australia, when you speak of a squatter, you are always supposed to be speaking of a millionaire" (*Sydney Morning Herald*, 1 Jan. 1898, p. 2).

Instead, the reviewer summarized some of the most clever foolishness in the Australasian portion of the book. He called attention to the New Zealander's explaining that "the only game bird in Australia is the wombat, and the only songbird the larrikin, and that both are protected by Government" (*Sydney Morning Herald*, 1 Jan., p. 2). He noted Twain's interest in Australian pronunciations and his belief that a person who signs the visitors' book at Government House "will receive an invitation to the next ball ... if nothing can be proven against you." For a review that starts off sounding like it will damn the book, several of the phrases do not seem very unfavorable. His "stories about sharks do more than credit to the imagination," and he "scores distinctly" in his economic and political observations about the change of rail gauges at Albury. The reviewer concluded that the humorist's warning about believing local people who give a visitor free information could be applied to Twain himself, as well as more generally to "visitors who have this unfortunate itch to write about us."

On New Year's Day, the *Age* in Melbourne devoted several inches to publicity for the new book. The reviewer there likewise "hurriedly skimmed" the book and decided "whether I am stupid or Mark is dull, I shouldn't like to be certain. I can only say that the book, at a casual glance, seems to me absolutely commonplace and (to Australians) uninteresting" (1 Jan. 1898, p. 2). Although "occasionally the keen observation and racy humor of the 'Innocents Abroad' flares up agreeably," for the most part Twain's reliance on Australian historians annoyed the reviewer. All the rest of the article consisted of direct quotations from some of the most felicitous of Twain's descriptions: Sydney Harbour and his praise of Australian freedom, equality, and the resultant lack of reserve. The reader quoted Twain's remark that Adelaide had an extremely healthy religious atmosphere because "anything can live in it—Agnostics, Atheists, Freethinkers, Infidels, Mormons, Pagans, Indefinites" (*Age* [Melbourne], 1 Jan., 1898, p. 2). Finally, he quoted at length Twain's judgment that the governors of the various colonies, with no war and no veto, were always going "home" to England because they did not have enough to do. Therefore, they became the Australasian heads of "culture, refinement, elevated sentiment, polite life, religion . . . , [and] fashion."

Melbourne's other morning paper, the *Argus*, printed a complimentary review from the *Home News* that said the book "has a great deal to say that is amusing and much that is serious and instructive regarding Australia" (8 Jan. 1898, p. 4). Instead of charging against him his extensive use of Australian histories, this reviewer said these histories had a "strong attraction" for the author. The article cites Twain's disapproval of the exploitation of Kanak labor in Queensland, his comparison of Australians with Americans rather than with the English, his description of the Melbourne Cup (which he did not see), his disappointment with the Southern Cross constellation (which should have been the Southern Kite), and some comments on aboriginal drawings he had seen. Although there is more quotation than review, the tone of the article is entirely pleasant and appreciative. And the *Sydney Daily Telegraph*, having taken time for reflection, remarked that the book "contains one or two inaccuracies, but it is stunning reading all the same" (22 Jan. 1898, p. 8). The writer agrees that the "humorist must not be trammeled by slavish adherence to mere facts." Mainly he quotes long passages, presumably the ones he feels tell "lots about your own affairs that you didn't know before," including some "exceptionally entertaining" Australian history "whether true or not." Perhaps intending a slam at the earlier reviewers, this one says, "a hasty glance . . . is disappointing. To read it carefully is unalloyed pleasure." The *Sydney Daily Telegraph* reviewer cited Twain passages on Sydney Harbour, losing a day at the International Date Line, the Southern Cross constellation, the break of guage at Albury (and the geographical misplacement of the Blue Mountains), the "working men's holidays," and Ballarat English—the "jewels . . . tucked away behind a mass of solid statistics" (22 Jan., p. 8).

In Wellington, after only "dipping into an advance copy," "Scrutator" expressed disappointment that Twain "dismisses the Empire City in about half a dozen lines" (*New Zealand Mail*, 13 Jan. 1898, p. 23).

He appreciated the "high compliment to Mrs Ross's gardens at the Hutt, but on the whole his references to New Zealand are neither numerous or noticeable." "Scrutator" noted Twain's use of the official handbook and his "working up" of old stories such as the Maungatapu murders in the description of Nelson. He thought Twain's account of the journey from Lyttelton to Wellington in the *Flora* was "calculated to give a very unfair and inaccurate idea of the comforts and conveniences usually to be found in the red-funnel boats" operated by the Union Company. If "Scrutator" had seen the Clemenses' letters to the Kinseys in Christchurch, Twain's journal, and Clara's recollection, he might have been more sympathetic with the account in *More Tramps Abroad*. In fact, if he had read the American edition rather than the English edition, he would have had a diatribe not just of two pages but of four pages, suppressed from the London book.

Like the Australian critics, "Scrutator" quoted Twain's remarks about the Australasian governors always being back in England as soon as they have been inaugurated. Evidently, Twain had hit on a point of some dissatisfaction in the colonies. A month later, "Scrutator" apparently had read the book more carefully, and he added a few comments. Although the book contains "some unmistakable padding," it "has many good things in it" (*New Zealand Mail*, 10 Feb. 1898, p. 23). His "homely aphorisms of the Josh Billings order, but fortunately not in the 'spellin'' which made Josh at times so trying to read" are praised and a few quoted. These are, of course, Pudd'nhead Wilson's sayings that appear at the beginning of each chapter: "The English are mentioned in the Bible: 'Blessed are the meek, for they shall inherit the earth.' "

"It Fooled the Reader"

In April 1899, Twain wrote his long-time friend, novelist William Dean Howells: "I wrote my last travel book in hell .... How I did loathe that journey around the world!—except the sea-part and India."[22] Clara Clemens, many years later recalled her father saying to her mother,

> Do you remember, Livy, the hellish struggle it was to settle on making that lecture trip around the world? How we fought the idea, the horrible idea, the heart-torturing idea. I, almost an old man, with ill health, carbuncles,

---

22. Samuel L. Clemens to William Dean Howells, *Mark Twain–Howells Letters*, ed. Henry Nash Smith and William Gibson (Cambridge: Belknap, 1960), p. 690.

bronchitis and rheumatism ... with patience worn to rags, I was to pack my bag and be jolted around the devil's universe ... to pay debts that were not even of my making.

No doubt racked by grief and even guilt that Susy might have died because he had not been with her, Twain said to Livy, "And you were worried at the thought of facing such hardships of travel, and SHE was unhappy to be left alone. But once the idea of that infernal trip struck us we couldn't shake it."[23]

Twain's *Autobiography*, dictated to A. B. Paine in 1906, sheds light on the "hell" he had experienced. It was not really the trip itself that he loathed, but the surrounding circumstances of his previous bankruptcy, that put him in such a frame of mind. At the end of the dictation, he exclaimed, "There—Thanks be! A hundred times I have tried to tell this intolerable story with a pen but I never could do it. It always made me sick before I got halfway to the middle of it. But this time I have held my grip and walked the floor and emptied it all out of my system, and I hope to never hear of it again."[24] Besides the bitter recollection of the relationship with his nephew in the failed publishing business and the dashed hopes for the Paige typesetting machine that forced his trip around the world, there were also other unpleasant aspects of the trip, including illness and fatigue, disappointment in South Africa, and the death of his daughter Susy.

While Twain was still encumbered with Webster and Company's debts,[25] reviews of *More Tramps Abroad* began to trickle in from Europe, and his friend Rogers wrote from America that he had liked the book. Twain's response reveals the agony the humorist was still suffering over his financial and familial losses: "I am very glad you like the book. The London papers and the Vienna papers like it, and so do my personal friends in England .... I like the book myself. All this shows — what? That the common notion that a book infallibly reveals the

---

23. *My Father, Mark Twain*, p. 179; other evidence contradicts Twain's belief stated here that Susy was unhappy to stay in America.

24. *Autobiography*, ed. Neider, p. 288.

25. "I throw up the sponge. I pull down the flag. Let us begin on those debts. I cannot bear the weight any longer. It totally unfits me for work. I have lost three entire monthys, now. In that time I have begun twenty magazine articles and books — and flung every one of them aside in turn. The debts interfered every time, and took the spirit out of the work," Twain wrote to Rogers in November 1897 (*Correspondence with Rogers*, ed. Leary, p. 303.)

man and his condition, is a mistake. This book has not exposed me. It pretends to an interest in its subject — which was mostly not the case ....I would rather be hanged, drawn and quartered than write it again. All the heart I had was in Susy's grave and the Webster debts. And so, behold a miracle! — a book which does not give its writer away."[26]

But other evidence mitigates such a harsh description of the trip itself. The notebooks, the surviving family letters, and the newspaper accounts all conspire to give the impression that, while he was actually undergoing the journey, especially the Antipodean portion, he enjoyed nearly the whole experience. Certainly, the trip must be classified as a success in that it fulfilled its purpose. In two and a half years—not the four years projected for repaying his and Webster & Company's creditors—his business manager Henry Huttleston Rogers wired him that "all [have] been paid a hundred cents on the dollar. There is eighteen thousand five hundred dollars left."[27] Twain told Howells, "I let on, the best I could, that it was an excursion through heaven. Some day I will read [the book], & if its lying cheerfulness fools me, then I shall believe it fooled the reader."[28]

---

26. Ibid., p. 309.

27. Ibid., pp. 287–288.

28. Samuel L. Clemens to Howells, *Mark Twain-Howells Letters*, ed. Smith and Gibson, p. 690.

WORKS CITED

Blair, Walter. *Mark Twain & Huck Finn*. Berkeley, University of California Press, 1960.

Branch, Edgar M. "'The Babes in the Wood': Artemus Ward's 'Double Health' to Mark Twain." *PMLA* 93 (1978), pp. 955–972.

Budd, Louis. "A Listing of and Selection from the Newspaper and Magazine Interviews with Samuel L. Clemens." *American Literary Realism* 10 (1977), 1–100.

————. "Mark Twain Talks Mostly about Humor and Humorists." *Studies in American Humor* 1 (April, 1974), 1–22.

————. *Our Mark Twain*. Philadelphia, University of Pennsylvania Press, 1983.

Cannon, Michael. *The Land Boomers*. Melbourne, Melbourne University Press, 1966.

Cardwell, Guy A. *Twins of Genius*. East Lansing, Michigan State College Press, 1953.

Carnegie, Andrew. *Autobiography of Andrew Carnegie*. Boston. Houghton Mifflin, 1920.

Collins, R. D. J. "Sketch Recalls Mark Twain's Visit to Dunedin In 1895." *Otago Daily Times*, 4 November, 1977.

Doyle, Paul A. "Henry Harper's Telling of a Mark Twain Anecdote." *Mark Twain Journal* 15 (Summer, 1970), 13.

Duckett, Margaret. *Mark Twain and Bret Harte*. Norman, University of Oklahoma Press, 1964.

Fatout, Paul. *Mark Twain on the Lecture Circuit*. Bloomington, Indiana University Press, 1960.

FitzHenry, W. E. Unpublished history of the *Bulletin*. Australian National Library, Canberra.

Frear, Walter F. *Mark Twain and Hawaii*. Chicago, Priv. Print., 1947.

Gabrilowitsch, Clara Clemens. *My Father, Mark Twain*. New York, Harper, 1931.

Gribben, Alan. "Mark Twain, Business Man: The Margins of Profit." *Studies in American Humor* n. s. 1 (June, 1982), 24–43.

————. *Mark Twain's Library*. 2 Vols. Boston, G. K. Hall & Co., 1980.

Harnsberger, Caroline. *Mark Twain, Family Man*. New York, Citadel Press, 1960.

Hill, Lucy. Bendigo Branch of the Royal Historical Society, *News Letter*, May, 1974.

Hogan, J. F. *Some Melbourne Notabilities*. London, Eyre & Spottiswoode, 1896.

Hopkins, Dorothy June. *Hop of the "Bulletin."* Sydney, Angus and Robertson, 1929.

Kaplan, Justin. *Mr. Clemens and Mark Twain*. New York, Simon and Schuster, 1966.

Krause, Sydney J. *Mark Twain as Critic*. Baltimore, Johns Hopkins Press, 1967.

Little, William. *Ballarat the Beautiful*. 1907.

Lorch, Fred W. "Mark Twain's Lecture Tour of 1868–1869: The American Vandal Abroad." *American Literature* 26 (January, 1955), 515–527.

————. "Mark Twain's 'Morals' Lecture During the American Phase of His World Tour in 1895–1896." *American Literature* 26 (March, 1954), 52–66.

————. "Mark Twain's Public Lectures in England in 1873." *American Literature* 29 (November, 1957), 297–304.

————. "Mark Twain's 'Sandwich Islands' Lecture and the Failure at James-town, New York." *American Literature* 25 (November, 1953), 314–325.

————. *The Trouble Begins at Eight*. Ames, Iowa State University Press, 1968.

Luckie, D. M. *The Maungatapu Mountain Murders*. Preface by A. A. Grace. Nelson NZ, R. W. Stiles, 1924.

Martin, A. W. *Henry Parkes*. Melbourne, Oxford University Press, 1964.

McKay, George. *Annals of Bendigo*. Bendigo, 1891.

Nesbit, Edward Planta. *Christ, Christians, and Christianity*. Book *I*. London, Simpkin, Marshall, & Co., 1895.

————. *Occasional Poems*. Adelaide, J. T. Shawyer, 1858.

Paine, Albert Bigelow. *Mark Twain: A Biography*. 4 Vols. New York, Harper & Brothers, 1912.

Palmer, Vance. *The Legend of the Nineties*. Melbourne, Melbourne University Press, 1954. Reprinted 1980.

Parkes, Sir Henry. *Sonnets and Other Verse*. London, Kegan Paul, Trench, Trubner, & Co., 1895.

Parsons, Coleman O. "Mark Twain in Adelaide." *Mark Twain Journal* 21 (Spring, 1983), 51–55.

————. "Mark Twain in Australia." *The Antioch Review* 21 (Winter, 1961–1962), 455–468.

————. "Mark Twain in Melbourne." *Mark Twain Journal* 22 (Spring, 1984), 41–42.

————. "Mark Twain in New Zealand." *South Atlantic Quarterly* 61 (1962), 51–76.

Potts, E. Daniel, and Annette Potts. "The Mark Twain Family in Australia." *Overland* 70 (1978), 46–50.

Sadler, James. *Lyrics and Rhymes*. Adelaide, 1890.

Searight, Sarah. "Mark Twain in New Zealand." *New Zealand Heritage* 13 (1972), 1703–1705.

Shillingsburg, Miriam J. "American Humour in an Inter-Cultural Context: 'Distinctively Her Own.'" *Australasian Journal of American Studies* 6 (July, 1987), 35–45.

————. "From Ballarat to Bendigo with Mark Twain." *Australian Literary Studies* 12 (May, 1985), 116–119.

Smythe, Carlyle G. "The Real 'Mark Twain,'" *Pall Mall Magazine* 16 (September, 1898), 35.

Twain, Mark. *Autobiography of Mark Twain*. Edited by Charles Neider. London, Chatto and Windus, 1969.

————. *A Connecticut Yankee in King Arthur's Court*. Edited by Bernard L. Stein. Berkeley, University of California Press, 1984.

————. *Following the Equator*. Hartford, American Publishing Company, 1897.

————. "How to Tell a Story," *Tom Sawyer Detective*. London: Chatto and Windus, 1909, pp. 161–171.

————. *Mark Twain's Correspondence with Henry Huttleston Rogers*. Edited by Lewis Leary. Berkeley, University of California Press, 1969.

————. *Mark Twain in Eruption*. Edited by Bernard DeVoto. New York, Harper & Brothers, 1940.

————. *Mark Twain's Letters to His Publishers*. Edited by Hamlin Hill. Berkeley, University of California Press, 1967.

————. *Mark Twain's Letters*. Edited by Albert Bigelow Paine. New York, Harper and Brothers, 1917.

————. *Mark Twain's Notebook*. Edited by Albert Bigelow Paine. New York, Harper & Brothers, 1935. Reprinted Scholarly Press, 1971.

————. *Mark Twain's Notebooks and Journals, III, 1883-1891*. Edited by R. P. Browning, M. B. Frank and L. Salamo. Berkeley, University of California Press, 1979.

————. *Mark Twain Speaking*. Edited by Paul Fatout. Iowa City, University of Iowa Press, 1976.

————. *Mark Twain–Howells Letters*. Edited by Henry Nash Smith and William Gibson. Cambridge, Belknap Press, 1960.

————. *More Tramps Abroad*. London, Chatto and Windus, 1897.

————. Unpublished Notebooks 34, 35, 36. Mark Twain Papers. Bancroft Library, University of California, Berkeley.

————. "What Paul Bourget Thinks of Us." *Tom Sawyer Detective*. London, Chatto and Windus, 1909, pp. 191–221.

Welland, Dennis. *Mark Twain and England*. London, Chatto and Windus, 1979.

INDEX

www.ingramcontent.com/pod-product-compliance
Lightning Source LLC
Chambersburg PA
CBHW030302060726
47498CB00002BB/463